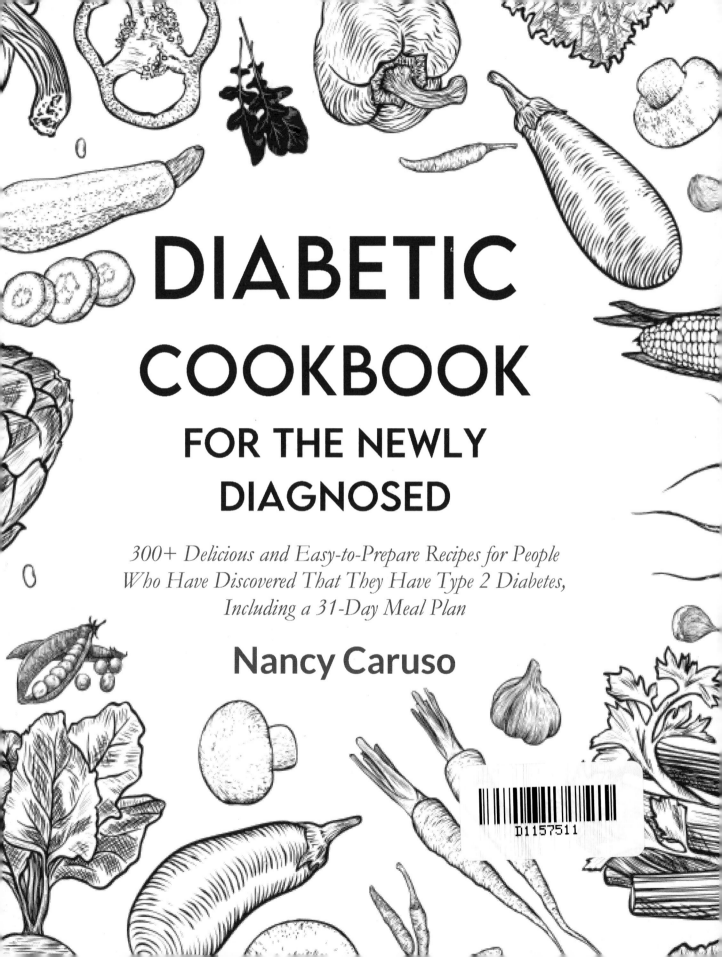

DIABETIC COOKBOOK

FOR THE NEWLY DIAGNOSED

300+ Delicious and Easy-to-Prepare Recipes for People Who Have Discovered That They Have Type 2 Diabetes, Including a 31-Day Meal Plan

Nancy Caruso

Table of Contents

About the Author

Nancy Caruso was born in Palermo, Italy, in 1981. Her love for food is imprinted in her DNA; she is a descendant of a famous family of Sicilian restaurant owners.

She grew up in her parents' restaurant, where she learned the traditional techniques that have been passed down four generations through verbal teachings and recipe books not accessible to people outside the family.

However, Nancy's passion for food also has a negative side. Since adolescence, she has been bullied because she was overweight.

At the age of 14, her business was booming, and she moved to New York, where her parents opened a new restaurant.

Nancy kept studying and graduated in Nutritional Sciences.

Thanks to her studies, she finally managed to regain her healthy weight by applying a specific program, the same program that she now shares with her patients and readers.

The author's mission is to teach as many people as possible the principles of a healthy Mediterranean diet, how to maintain a healthy weight, and continue to enjoy delicious dishes.

Introduction

Diabetes is a long-term condition that impairs your body's ability to produce and use insulin. Heart disease, stroke, blindness, and limb amputation are all possible outcomes. This book, "Diabetic Diet Cookbook" has recipes for type 1 and type 2 diabetes patients to maintain a healthy lifestyle.

Diabetes is considered to be caused by too much sugar in the body. The blood glucose level increases due to insulin resistance, impaired pancreatic beta-cell function, or both. The rising blood glucose level causes many complications for diabetics, including heart diseases, nerve damage, and amputation. Acute complications include stroke, heart failure, and limb loss. Other chronic complications include kidney disease and leg ulcers. Fortunately, there are ways to lower these complications by following a diet that mimics the effects of insulin in the body. Type 1 diabetes is diagnosed when the body doesn't make enough insulin or can't use insulin properly to regulate blood glucose levels. It is a chronic condition that causes a person's blood glucose level to become too high.

In type 2 diabetes, the body either does not produce enough insulin, or the cells are resistant to insulin, preventing the body from properly using insulin. It is a chronic condition characterized by high blood glucose levels because the body cannot correctly use sugars from digested food for energy. In this case, a food plan geared towards managing blood glucose levels can help a person with diabetes live a healthy life. The goal of any successful diet plan is a healthier lifestyle and improved quality of life for people with diabetes.

Diabetic diet cookbook has recipes for low-carb, whole wheat, vegetarian, vegan, and gluten-free diabetes patients. It also includes nutritional information to help people understand how to substitute simple ingredients in their cooking.

People with diabetes who want to reduce weight should stick to a diet plan that is tailored to their specific circumstances. Slimming down can reduce blood pressure, LDL cholesterol levels, and death risk in obese diabetics by 50%. The greatest approach to reduce weight is to eat a well-balanced diet and exercise regularly. This book shows you how to make delicious meals with healthier ingredients while following a diabetic way of eating.

With the rising number of diabetics, there is a demand for a cookbook that would assist diabetics in leading a healthy lifestyle.

Diabetes is a chronic illness, and it has no treatment. However, there is now an effective way to prevent and control the complications of diabetes at the same time with diet and physical activity. By following a balanced and healthy lifestyle, people with diabetes can enjoy an everyday life without complications.

The diabetic diet cookbook also includes tips for planning menus, recipes for traditional meals, and more. This cookbook is perfect for people with diabetes who want to follow a healthier way of eating that is low-carbogenic, high protein, and whole-grain based diets that can help reduce high blood glucose levels in type 1 and type 2 diabetics patients with insulin resistance. These recipes are also great for any person with diabetes who wants to keep their blood sugar levels down without feeling deprived.

CHAPTER 1:

Best Diet for People with Diabetes

For people battling diabetes, there are three fundamental goals in any diabetic health plan. After being diagnosed with diabetes, your doctor will most likely put you on medication and discuss exercise and diet for diabetic patients. Diet is perhaps one of the most significant changes you will need to make in your lifestyle, and you must take the time to learn more about why diet is so important. Many people with diabetes, especially type 2 diabetics, do not take their condition seriously. They place themselves at significant risk because they are constantly disobeying the diabetes guidelines outlined by their doctors.

The ideal diabetic diet should include the following ingredients:

- Fresh roots
- Vegetables
- Lean cuts of meat
- Fruits
- Whole wheat

In addition, diabetic patients must avoid or reduce taking the following things:

- Alcohol consumption (especially full-strength beer)
- Foods with processed sugars
- Highly fatty foods

The fact is that, on an appropriate diet, your doctor is not asking you to give up alcohol consumption completely but to consume alcohol moderately and responsibly. The same applies to many of the sweet things often excluded from a diet for diabetic patient management. Many people with diabetes enjoy high-sugar foods, such as cream cakes, chocolate, and ice cream. What many doctors are suggesting is not that you completely cut these out of your diet. For diabetic patients, willpower is often not strong enough to do this, but you must moderate and control what you can eat.

What Is the Composition of Food to Be Consumed Per Day?

With a proper diet, you can optimize your nutrition to control diabetes. Good nutrition for diabetes includes a well-rounded diet. If you have diabetes, you need to eat healthy foods and be concerned about overeating. People with diabetes should eat whole grains, fruits, beans, non-fat dairy products, lean meats, fish, and poultry.

For most people who have diabetes, a healthy diet consists of 40% to 60% of calories from carbohydrates, 20% from protein, and 30% or less from fat. It should be low in cholesterol, low in salt, and low in added sugar.

To optimize your nutrition, eat a daily diet made from all the different food groups. Make sure you choose foods that are rich in nutrients, fiber, and vitamins. This means that you need to concentrate on a lot of fresh fruits and vegetables, and you should limit your starches.

If your diet is well thought out, it can include your favorite foods, just in moderation. Individuals who have diabetes must plan their daily meals to eat the proper diet for their needs and get the most out of them for good nutrition. Good meal plans will lead to controlling your blood pressure, cholesterol, and blood sugar, as well as leading to you losing weight.

Healthy and nutritious meals can fit into your schedule if you plan them right. Good nutrition is essential for maintaining anyone's health, but it is even more so if one has diabetes. Optimized nutrition will also help you lose weight because your body will get all the nutrients it needs. Hunger signals will be limited, and you will not feel the need to binge on certain foods that are bad for you, like ice cream or candy.

CHAPTER 2:

Foods to Prefer

When you are listing down groceries you need to buy for a type 2 diabetic person, and you need to ensure that the ingredients are rich in nutrients and healthy. Some good ingredients for a type 2 diabetic include:

Vegetables

If it is not already clear, vegetables are the first ingredients that form the basis of a healthy diet. Fiber, minerals, and vitamins are all abundant in them. Most vegetables also consist of complex carbohydrates and fiber, which helps the body feel satisfied and full after eating; this deters over-eating, which eventually leads to blood sugar issues and weight gain. Some great veggies you can put on your shopping list includes:

- Onions
- Peppers (yellow, orange, green, red, etc.)
- Brussels sprouts
- Asparagus
- Green beans
- Cauliflower
- Broccoli
- Salad greens

Fruits

As you might have guessed, fruits are the #2 entry in this list. Whether frozen or fresh, fruits contain high sugar content and are one of the best sources of minerals, vitamins, and fiber. Due to their low glycemic load (GL) and glycemic index (GI), they are a great addition to a diet for type 2 diabetes individuals. Some options include:

- Cherries
- Apricots
- Apples
- Tomatoes
- Peaches
- Oranges
- Berries
- Plums

Dairy Products

Dairy products contain protein, calcium, and other essential nutrients. Some studies even suggest that dairy products can have a positive effect on controlling the secretion of insulin in people suffering from type 2 diabetes. Some great dairy products that you can use in a meal include:

- Plain yogurt
- Skimmed milk
- Cottage, ricotta, or parmesan cheese

Meat Products

Here are the following products for people with type 2 diabetes:

Poultry

Chicken, turkey, duck, and quail are all rich in proteins. They contain certain fats that are good for the heart and other organs; besides, they nourish the brain. They are also high in vitamin B, zinc, and iron—all of which assist in decreasing blood sugar and raise insulin levels while lowering blood pressure. Besides, it is also rich in omega-3 fatty acids, which help in reducing triglycerides as well as bad cholesterol levels.

Red Meats

Pork, beef, and lamb are all rich in proteins, which are very essential for the body's growth and development. They help in building lean muscles while boosting metabolism at the same time.

Fish

Fish is rich in proteins and low in fat and sodium, which makes it one of the best-healthiest types of meats out there. It is also rich in omega-3 fatty acids, which help in reducing triglycerides as well as bad cholesterol levels. It is an excellent source of vitamin D, selenium, and zinc. These nutrients are all essential to help control insulin levels at a normal level while boosting metabolism.

Other kinds of Meat Like Turkey or Duck

These fatty meats contain healthy fats that are great for the heart and other organs while promoting healthy skin conditions too.

Other products for people with type 2 diabetes:

- Legumes and beans
- Whole grains
- Nuts and seeds
- Dairy products like yogurt and milk
- Fruits, veggies, and juices
- Low-fat diet foods
- Fish high in omega-3 fatty acids
- Lean red meats
- Poultry like chicken and turkey
- Nuts, egg whites, fish, yogurt, and other non-fat dairy products

CHAPTER 3:

Smart Ideas and Advice

The diabetic menu should aspire to achieve a balance of carbohydrates and nutrients, such as proteins and healthy fats. This is essential for proper diabetes management and also to ensure that the meals are satisfying.

About half of your meal should be non-starchy vegetables. One portion should be proteins, while the remaining portion should be grains or starch.

Remember the Following

20% to 25% of the calories should be from protein. Remember, lean meats like beef and chicken are better.

25% to 30% of the calories must be from fat. Stay away or limit the intake of saturated and trans fats.

50% to 60% of the calories must be from carbohydrates. You must eat plenty of orange and green vegetables every day, such as broccoli and carrots. Opt for brown rice, which is vitamin-rich, or sweet potatoes, while avoiding regular potatoes or white rice.

Maintain a food diary for the first few days so that you know what you like and dislike. Keep it detailed. You can then modify your food menu accordingly while maintaining the basic diabetes food principles.

But remember, some modifications might be necessary, especially if you have other goals, like, for instance, to lose weight. Calorie counting will then also be needed. Again, if you want to build muscles, then you will have to take lower fat and increase the percentage of carbohydrates.

The "Correct" Amount

How many carbohydrates should you eat? There is no right amount. The suggested carb amount is always different for each person. It's critical to figure out what works best for you. The daily food diary will once again help you here.

Also, pay attention to the salt (sodium) content on the food labels. Taking a lot of salt can cause hypertension or high blood pressure. Many patients with diabetes also have high blood pressure. They might have to keep their sodium intake under control so that they can lower their risk of some related health problems. It is always best to avoid sodium as much as possible so that the risk of hypertension is reduced.

Remember to watch out for fat and its type. Cholesterol, trans fats, and saturated fats can cause heart issues. Always remember that diabetics are at a higher risk of developing heart disease, especially if their blood lipid levels are abnormal.

Finding Your Calorie Requirement

All of us have different calorie requirements. How many calories you will need will depend on your fitness level, size, gender, everyday activity, and some other factors. While creating a healthy diabetic meal plan, the first step must be to find out your "calorie equilibrium," which means the number of calories daily you need to maintain the present weight.

Here is a simple way to find the equilibrium:

- **Step #1**: Now your body weight in kilograms (those from the US should divide the weight in pounds by 2.2 to get it in kilograms).
- **Step #2**: Men must multiply the weight by 1 and women by 0.9.
- **Step #3:** Now multiply by 24.
- **Step #4**: Multiply by your "lean factor." What you will get is your BMR or "Basal Metabolic Rate," which is the number of calories you burn every day if you just stay on the couch throughout the day, doing nothing. Now multiply by your "activity monitor" to find out the number of calories you actually burn in a day.
- **Step #5:** Finally, multiply by your activity monitor.

Activity Level Multiplier (Daily)

- **1.3 (Very Light):** Mostly sedentary work like studying, sitting with little walking during the day.
- **1.55 (Light):** Jobs where you mostly walk very little or stand like shop/lab work and teaching involving little walking during the day.
- **1.65 (Moderate):** Work that requires physical activity, such as cleaning, landscaping, maintenance work, biking, or jogging for 2 hours a day.
- **1.80 (Heavy):** Work involving manual labor including dancing, construction, athletics, or hard physical activities for 4 hours a day minimum.
- **2.00 (Very Heavy):** Hard to moderate physical activity for 8 hours a day, minimum.

So, the first step is to find out your calorie equilibrium. Having done so, you can now adjust the daily calories you need so that your goals can be met. For example, if you are also trying to reduce weight, you should consume 500 calories less than what your equilibrium will be for the day. This way, you can have a healthy diet while still achieving your weight loss goal.

On the other hand, if you are trying to gain muscle, then add 300 to 500 calories daily to your equilibrium. Reduce the calorie intake if you are getting too much fat until you achieve the perfect balance.

Meal Prep Principles

Here are the most popular meal preparation principles:

- **Make-Ahead Meals:** These are pre-cooked full meals that can be kept in the refrigerator and then reheated during mealtime. This is very useful, especially for dinner-time meals.
- **Batch Cooking:** This involves cooking a particular recipe in large batches and then dividing it into small individual portions. You can then freeze and eat them over time. This is a good option for warm lunches and dinners.
- **Individually Portioned Meals:** Make fresh meals and then portion them individually. Refrigerate and have small portions over several days. You will find this very handy for a quick lunch.
- **Ready-To-Cook Ingredients:** Arrange and prepare the ingredients you need for specific meals in advance. This will help you reduce the cooking time.

CHAPTER 4:

Breakfast

1. Zucchini Noodles with Creamy Avocado Pesto

Preparation Time: 10 minutes
Cooking Time: 20 minutes
Servings: 2
Ingredients:

- 6 cups spiralized zucchini
- 1 tbsp. olive oil
- 6 oz. avocado
- 1 basil leaf
- 3 garlic cloves
- 1/3 oz. pine nuts
- ½ tsp. salt
- ¼ tsp. black pepper
- Parmesan cheese, to taste

Directions:

1. Spiralize the courgettis and set them aside on paper towels to absorb the surplus water.
2. In a kitchen appliance, put the avocados, juice basil leaves, garlic, pine nuts, and sea salt. Then pulse until chopped. Put the vegetable oil in a slow stream till emulsified and creamy. Drizzle the vegetable oil in a skillet over medium-high heat, and then add the zucchini noodles, cooking for about 2 minutes, or until tender. Put the zucchini noodles into a large bowl and toss them with the avocado pesto. Season with black pepper and a little of Parmesan, then serve.

Nutrition: Calories: 115, Protein: 30 g, Fats: 0 g, Carbs: 3 g, Sugars: 19.27 g

2. Avocado-Chicken Salad

Preparation Time: 5 minutes
Cooking Time: 10 minutes
Servings: 2
Ingredients:

- 10 oz. cooked chicken, diced
- ½ cup 2% plain Greek yogurt
- 3 oz. avocado, chopped
- 12 tsp. garlic powder
- ¼ tsp. salt
- 1/8 tsp. pepper
- 1 tbsp. + 1 tsp. lime juice
- ¼ cup fresh cilantro, chopped

Directions:

1. Combine all the ingredients in a medium-sized bowl. Refrigerate until able to serve.
2. Cut the salad in half, and serve it together with your favorite greens.

Nutrition: Calories: 265, Protein: 35 g, Fats: 13 g, Carbs: 5 g, Sugars: 1.89 g

3.   Pancakes with Berries

Preparation Time: 5 minutes
Cooking Time: 20 minutes
Servings: 2
Ingredients:
For the Pancake:

- 1 egg
- 50 g spelled flour
- 50 g almond flour
- 15 g coconut flour
- 150 ml salted water

Other Ingredients:

- ¼ cup Granulated sugar
- 150 g Berries
- 1/2 cup Chocolate
- 1/8 cup Yogurt

Directions:

1. Put the flour, egg, and a few salts in a blender jar. Add 150 ml of water.
2. Mix everything with a whisk.
3. Mix everything into a batter.
4. Heat a coated pan.
5. Put in half of the batter.
6. Once the pancake is firm, turn it over.
7. Remove the pancake, add the last half of the batter to the pan, and repeat.
8. Melt the chocolate over a water bath.
9. Let the pancakes cool.
10. Brush the pancakes with the yogurt.
11. Wash the berries and let them drain.
12. Put the berries on the yogurt.
13. Roll up the pancakes.
14. Sprinkle them with granulated sugar.
15. Decorate the entire thing with the melted chocolate.

Nutrition: Calories: 298, Carbs: 26 g, Protein: 21 g, Fats: 9 g, Sugars: 2.96 g

4.   Omelette à la Margherita

Preparation Time: 10 minutes
Cooking Time: 20 minutes
Servings: 2
Ingredients:

- 3 eggs
- 50 g Parmesan cheese
- 2 tbsp. heavy cream
- 1 tbsp. olive oil
- 1 tsp. oregano
- 1 tsp. nutmeg
- Salt, to taste
- Pepper, to taste

For the Covering:

- 3–4 basil leaves
- 1 tomato
- 100 g grated mozzarella

Directions:

1. Mix the cream and eggs in a medium bowl.
2. Add the grated parmesan, nutmeg, oregano, pepper, and salt. Stir everything.
3. Heat the oil to a pan.
4. Add half of the egg and cream to the pan.
5. Let the omelet set over medium heat, turn it, and then remove it.
6. Repeat with the last half of the egg mixture.
7. Cut the tomatoes into slices and place them on top of the omelets.
8. Scatter the mozzarella over the tomatoes.
9. Place the omelets on a baking sheet.
10. Cook at 180ºF for 5 to 10 minutes.
11. Then take the omelets out and decorate them with the basil leaves.

Nutrition: Calories: 402, Carbs: 7 g, Protein: 21 g, Fats: 34 g, Sugars: 9.88 g

5.   Omelet with Tomatoes and Spring Onions

Preparation Time: 5 minutes
Cooking Time: 20 minutes
Servings: 2
Ingredients:

- 6 eggs
- 2 tomatoes
- 2 spring onions

- 1 shallot
- 2 tbsp. butter
- 1 tbsp. olive oil
- A pinch nutmeg
- Salt, to taste
- Pepper, to taste

Directions:

1. Whisk the eggs in a bowl.
2. Mix them and season them with salt and pepper.
3. Peel the shallot and chop it up.
4. Clean the onions and cut them into rings.
5. Wash the tomatoes and cut them into pieces.
6. Heat the butter and oil in a pan.
7. Braise half the shallots in it.
8. Add half of the egg mixture.
9. Let everything set over medium heat.
10. Scatter a couple of tomatoes and onion rings on top.
11. Repeat with the last half of the egg mixture.
12. At the top, spread the grated nutmeg over the entire thing.

Nutrition: Calories: 263, Carbs: 8 g, Protein: 20.3 g, Fats: 24 g, Sugars: 6.68 g

6. Coconut Chia Pudding with Berries

Preparation Time: 20 minutes
Cooking Time: 30 minutes
Servings: 2
Ingredients:

- 150 g raspberries and blueberries
- 60 g chia seeds
- 500 ml coconut milk
- 1 tsp. agave syrup
- ½ tsp. ground bourbon vanilla

Directions:

1. Put the chia seeds, agave syrup, and vanilla in a bowl.
2. Pour in the coconut milk.
3. Mix thoroughly and let it soak for ½ hour.
4. Meanwhile, wash the berries and allow them to drain well.
5. Divide the coconut chia pudding between 2 glasses.
6. Put the berries on top.

Nutrition: Calories: 662, Carbs: 18 g, Protein: 8 g, Fats: 55 g, Sugars: 17.82 g

7. Eel on Scrambled Eggs and Bread

Preparation Time: 5 minutes
Cooking Time: 10 minutes
Servings: 2
Ingredients:

- 4 eggs
- 1 shallot
- 4 low-carb bread slices
- 2 dill sticks
- 200 g smoked eel
- 1 tbsp. salt
- White pepper, to taste

Directions:

1. Mix the eggs in a bowl and season with salt and pepper.
2. Peel the shallot and cut it into fine cubes.
3. Chop the dill.
4. Remove the skin from the eel and cut it into pieces.
5. Heat the oil in a pan and steam the shallot in it.
6. Add the eggs in and allow them to set.
7. Use the spatula to show the eggs several times.
8. Reduce the warmth and add the dill.
9. Stir everything.
10. Spread the scrambled eggs over 4 slices of bread. Put the eel pieces on top.
11. Add some fresh dill and serve everything.

Nutrition: Calories: 830, Carbs: 8 g, Protein: 45 g, Fats: 64 g, Sugars: 2.88 g

8. Chia Seed Gel with Pomegranate and Nuts

Preparation Time: 5 minutes
Cooking Time: 10 minutes
Servings: 2
Ingredients:

- 20 g hazelnuts
- 20 g walnuts
- 120 ml almond milk
- 4 tbsp. chia seeds
- 4 tbsp. pomegranate seeds
- 1 tsp. agave syrup

Directions:

1. Chop the nuts finely.
2. Mix the almond milk with the chia seeds.
3. Let everything soak for 10 to 20 minutes.
4. Occasionally, stir the mixture with the chia seeds.
5. Stir in the agave syrup.
6. Pour 2 tablespoons of the mixture into a dessert glass. Layer the chopped nuts on top. Cover the nuts with 1 tablespoon of the chia mixture.
7. Sprinkle the pomegranate seeds on top and serve everything.

Nutrition: Calories: 248, Carbs: 7 g, Protein: 1 g, Fats: 19 g, Sugars: 80.51 g

9. Lavender, Blueberry, and Chia Seed Pudding

Preparation Time: 1 hour and 10 minutes
Cooking Time: 0 minutes
Servings: 2
Ingredients:

- 100 g blueberries
- 70 g organic quark
- 50 g soy yogurt
- 30 g hazelnuts
- 200 ml almond milk
- 2 tbsp. chia seeds
- 2 tsp. agave syrup
- 2 tsp. lavender

Directions:

1. Bring the almond milk to a boil alongside the lavender.
2. Let the mixture simmer for 10 minutes at a reduced temperature.
3. Allow them to cool down afterwards.
4. If the milk is cold, add the blueberries and purée everything.
5. Mix the entire thing with the chia seeds and agave syrup.
6. Let everything soak in the refrigerator for 1 hour.
7. Mix the yogurt and curd cheese.
8. Add both to the mixture.
9. Divide the pudding into glasses.
10. Chop the hazelnuts finely and sprinkle them on top.

Nutrition: Calories: 252, Carbs: 12 g, Protein: 1 g, Fats: 11 g, Sugars: 8 g

10. Yogurt with Granola and Persimmon

Preparation Time: 5 minutes
Cooking Time: 5 minutes
Servings: 1
Ingredients:

- 150 g Greek-style yogurt
- 20 g oatmeal
- 60 g fresh persimmons
- 30 ml tap water

Directions:

1. Put the nonfat oatmeal in the pan.
2. Toast them, continually stirring, until golden brown.
3. Then put them on a plate and allow them to cool down briefly.
4. Peel the persimmons and put them in a bowl with the water. Mix the entire thing into a fine purée.
5. Add in the yogurt and the toasted oatmeal, and then purée in layers in a glass. Serve.

Nutrition: Calories: 286, Carbs: 29 g, Protein: 1 g Fats: 11 g, Fiber: 1.3 g

11. Smoothie Bowl with Spinach, Mango, and Muesli

Preparation Time: 10 minutes
Cooking Time: 0 minutes
Servings: 1
Ingredients:

- 150 g yogurt
- 30 g apple
- 30 g mango
- 30 g low-carb muesli
- 10 g spinach
- 10 g chia seeds

Directions:

1. Soak the spinach leaves and allow them to drain.
2. Peel the mango and cut it into strips.
3. Remove the apple core and cut it into pieces.
4. In a blender, put everything except the mango alongside the yogurt, and make a fine purée out of it.
5. Put the spinach smoothie in a bowl.
6. Add the muesli, chia seeds, and mango.
7. Serve the entire thing.

Nutrition: Calories: 362, Carbs: 21 g, Protein: 12 g, Fats: 21 g, Sugars: 12.53 g

12. Fried Eggs with Bacon

Preparation Time: 5 minutes
Cooking Time: 10 minutes
Servings: 1
Ingredients:

- 2 eggs
- 30 g bacon
- 2 tbsp. olive oil
- Salt, to taste
- Pepper, to taste

Directions:

1. Heat the oil in the pan and fry the bacon.
2. Reduce the heat and beat the eggs in the pan. Cook the eggs and season with salt and pepper.
3. Serve the fried eggs hot with the bacon.

Nutrition: Calories: 405, Carbs: 1 g, Protein: 19 g, Fats: 38 g, Sugars: 3.6 g

13. Smoothie Bowl with Berries, Poppy Seeds, Nuts, and Seeds

Preparation Time: 15 minutes
Cooking Time: 0 minutes
Servings: 2
Ingredients:

- 5 almonds, chopped
- 2 walnuts, chopped
- 1 apple
- ¼ banana
- 300 g yogurt
- 60 g raspberries
- 20 g blueberries
- 20 g rolled oats, roasted in a pan
- 10 g poppy seeds
- 1 tsp. pumpkin seeds Agave syrup

Directions:

1. Clean the fruit and let it drain.
2. Take some berries and set them aside.
3. Place the remaining berries in a tall mixing vessel.
4. Cut the banana into slices. Put a couple of slices aside.
5. Add the remainder of the banana to the berries. Remove the core of the apple and cut it into quarters.
6. Cut the quarters into thin wedges and set a couple of them aside.

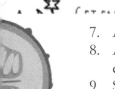

7. Add the remaining wedges to the berries.
8. Add the yogurt to the fruits and blend everything into a purée.
9. Sweeten the smoothie with the agave syrup. Divide it into 2 bowls.
10. Serve it with the remaining fruit, poppy seeds, oatmeal, nuts, and seeds.

Nutrition: Calories: 284, Carbs: 21 g, Protein: 11 g, Fats: 19 g, Sugars: 21.05 g

14. Porridge with Walnuts

Preparation Time: 5 minutes
Cooking Time: 10 minutes
Servings: 1
Ingredients:

- 50 g raspberries
- 50 g blueberries
- 25 g ground walnuts
- 20 g crushed flaxseed
- 10 g oatmeal - 200 ml nut drink
- ½ tsp. cinnamon salt

Directions:

1. Warm the nut drink in a saucepan.
2. Add the walnuts, flaxseed, and oatmeal, stirring constantly.
3. Stir in the cinnamon and salt.
4. Simmer for 8 minutes.
5. Keep stirring everything.
6. Sweeten the entire thing.
7. Put the porridge in a bowl.
8. Wash the berries and allow them to drain. Add them to the porridge and serve everything.

Nutrition: Calories: 378, Carbs: 11 g, Protein: 18 g, Fats: 27 g, Sugars: 21.72 g

15. Alkaline Blueberry Spelt Pancakes

Preparation Time: 6 minutes
Cooking Time: 20 minutes
Servings: 2
Ingredients:

- 2 cups spelt flour
- 1 cup coconut milk

- 1/2 cup alkaline water
- 2 tbsp. grape seed oil
- 1/2 cup agave
- 1/2 cup blueberries
- 1/4 tsp. sea moss

Directions:

1. Mix the spelt flour, agave, grape seed oil, hemp seeds, and sea moss in a bowl.
2. Add 1 cup of hemp milk and alkaline water to the mixture until you get the consistent mix you wish.
3. Crimp the blueberries into the batter.
4. Heat the skillet to moderate heat, then lightly coat it with the grape seed oil.
5. Pour the batter into the skillet, then allow it to cook for about 5 minutes on every side.
6. Serve and enjoy.

Nutrition: Calories: 203, Fats: 1.4 g, Carbs: 41.6 g, Protein: 4.8 g, Sugars: 20.29 g

16. Alkaline Blueberry Muffins

Preparation Time: 5 minutes
Cooking Time: 20 minutes
Servings: 2
Ingredients:

- 1 cup coconut milk
- 3/4 cup spelt flour
- 3/4 teff flour
- 1/2 cup blueberries
- 1/3 cup agave
- 1/4 cup sea moss gel
- 1/2 tsp. sea salt
- Grapeseed oil, as needed

Directions:

1. Adjust the temperature of the oven to 365°F.
2. Grease 6 regular-size muffin cups with muffin liners.
3. In a bowl, mix the sea salt, sea moss, agave, coconut milk, and flours until appropriately blended. Then crimp in the blueberries.

4. Coat the muffin pan lightly with the grapeseed oil.
5. Pour in the muffin batter.
6. Bake for at least ½ hour, or until it turns golden brown. Serve.

Nutrition: Calories: 160, Fats: 5 g, Carbs: 25 g, Protein: 2 g, Sugars: 14.37 g

17. Coconut Pancakes

Preparation Time: 5 minutes
Cooking Time: 15 minutes
Servings: 2
Ingredients:

- 1 cup coconut flour
- 2 tbsp. arrowroot powder
- 1 tsp. baking powder
- 1 cup coconut milk
- 3 tbsp. coconut oil

Directions:

1. In a medium container, mix the dry ingredients all together.
2. Add the coconut milk and a couple of tablespoons of the copra oil, then mix properly.
3. In a skillet, melt 1 teaspoon of copra oil.
4. Pour a ladle of the batter into the skillet, then swirl the pan to spread the batter evenly into a smooth pancake.
5. Cook it for like 3 minutes on medium heat until it becomes firm.
6. Turn the pancake to the other side, then cook it for an additional 2 minutes, or until it turns golden brown.
7. Cook the remaining pancakes in the same process. Serve.

Nutrition: Calories: 377, Fats: 14.9 g, Carbs: 60.7 g, Protein: 6.4 g, Sugars: 4.65 g

18. Quinoa Porridge

Preparation Time: 5 minutes
Cooking Time: 25 minutes
Servings: 2
Ingredients:

- 2 cups coconut milk

- 1 cup rinsed quinoa
- 1/8 tsp. ground cinnamon
- 1 cup fresh blueberries

Directions:

1. In a saucepan, boil the coconut milk over high heat.
2. Add the quinoa to the milk, then allow the mixture to boil.
3. You then let it simmer for ¼ hour on medium heat, or until the milk is reduced.
4. Add the cinnamon, then mix it properly in the saucepan.
5. Cover the saucepan and cook for at least 8 minutes, or until the milk is absorbed.
6. Add in the blueberries, then cook for 30 more seconds.
7. Serve.

Nutrition: Calories: 271, Fats: 3.7 g, Carbs: 54 g, Protein: 6.5 g, Sugars: 34.21 g

19. Amaranth Porridge

Preparation Time: 5 minutes
Cooking Time: 30 minutes
Servings: 2
Ingredients:

- 2 cups coconut milk
- 2 cups alkaline water
- 1 cup amaranth
- 2 tbsp. copra oil
- 1 tbsp. ground cinnamon

Directions:

1. In a saucepan, mix the milk with water, and then boil the mixture.
2. You stir in the amaranth, then reduce the heat to medium.
3. Cook on medium heat, then simmer for at least ½ hour as you stir it occasionally.
4. Close up the heat.
5. Add in the cinnamon and copra oil, then stir.
6. Serve.

Nutrition: Calories: 434, Fats: 35 g, Carbs: 27 g, Protein: 6.7 g, Sugars: 8.1 g

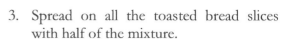

20. Banana Barley Porridge

Preparation Time: 15 minutes
Cooking Time: 5 minutes
Servings: 2
Ingredients:

- 1 cup unsweetened coconut milk, divided
- 1 small banana, peeled and sliced
- 1/2 cup barley
- 3 drops liquid Stevia
- 1/4 cup coconut, chopped

Directions:

1. In a bowl, properly mix the barley with half the coconut milk and Stevia.
2. Cover the blending bowl, then refrigerate for about 6 hours.
3. In a saucepan, mix the barley mixture with coconut milk.
4. Cook over moderate heat for about 5 minutes. Then top it with the chopped coconut and the banana slices.
5. Serve.

Nutrition: Calories: 159 Fats: 8.4 g, Carbs: 19.8 g, Protein: 4.6 g, Sugars: 11.37 g

21. Healthy Avocado Toast

Preparation Time: 5 minutes
Cooking Time: 13 minutes
Servings: 2
Ingredients:

- 1 avocado, peeled and seeded
- 2 tbsp. chopped cilantro
- ½ lime, juiced
- ½ tbsp. red pepper flakes (optional)
- Salt and pepper, to taste
- 1 whole grain bread slice, or bread of your choice
- 2 eggs fried, scrambled (optional)

Directions:

1. Toast 2 whole grain slices in the oven until they are crispy and golden.
2. Mix and crush the avocado, lime, cilantro, salt, and pepper in a shallow bowl.
3. Spread on all the toasted bread slices with half of the mixture.
4. Top with fried poached or scrambled egg if you wish.

Nutrition: Calories: 501, Fats: 28 g, Protein: 16 g, Sugars: 1.99 g, Carbs: 9.81 g

22. Whole Egg Baked Sweet Potatoes

Preparation Time: 30 minutes
Cooking Time: 60 minutes
Servings: 2
Ingredients:
For the Potatoes:

- 4 medium sweet potatoes
- 2 garlic heads
- 2 tsp. extra-virgin olive oil
- ½ tbsp. taco seasoning
- ¼ cup fresh cilantro, plus additional for garnish
- Salt and pepper, to taste
- 4 eggs

For the Sauce:

- ½ cup avocado, about 1 medium avocado
- Salt and pepper, to taste
- 1 tomatoes, sliced

Directions:

1. Preheat the oven to 395°F, cover with a baking sheet and tin foil and then place the potatoes on it.
2. Rip off the garlic tips, keep the head intact, and softly rub in the olive oil on top of the uncovered cloves. Create 2 layers of tinfoil in a small packet and wrap the garlic in it, then put it in the pan.
3. Bake the garlic for about 40 minutes, or until tender. Remove it from the pan and proceed to cook the potatoes for an additional 25–35 minutes, or until fork-tender and soft.
4. When the potatoes are tender, set them aside for about 10 minutes, or until they're cool enough to treat. In addition,

decrease the temperature of the oven to375°F.

5. Break the potatoes down the middle and softly peel the skin back, leaving the skin intact on the sides. In a wide cup, carefully scoop out the skin, leaving a little amount on the sides of the potato to help maintain its form.

6. Mash the flesh of the sweet potato and then cut half of it from the bowl (you will not use this flesh, so use it at a later date in another meal!) Add in the taco seasoning and cilantro and season with salt and pepper to taste into the mashed flesh. Finally, from the roasted heads, squeeze in all the fluffy garlic. Blend well.

7. Divide the flesh between the 4 sweet potatoes, spreading it softly to fill the meat and leaving a large hole in the middle of each potato.

8. Back on the baking sheet, put the sweet potatoes and crack an egg into each hole, and then spray it with pepper and salt. Bake to your taste, or until the egg is well fried. (For a good runny yolk, it normally takes about 10–15 minutes.) Blend until smooth.

9. Then, with the food processor running, pour in the water and combine until well mixed. Sprinkle with salt and pepper to taste. Break the avocado sauce between them until the potatoes are cooked, spreading it out on top.

10. Garnish with sliced tomatoes and cilantro in addition. Enjoy!

Nutrition: Calories: 399, Fats: 32 g, Protein: 18 g, Sugars: 12.02 g, Carbs: 49.34 g

23. Black Bean Tacos Breakfast

Preparation Time: 9 minutes
Cooking Time: 13 minutes
Servings: 2
Ingredients:
- ½ cup red onion, diced
- 8 – 10 86-inch white soft corn tortillas, warmed
- 1 garlic clove, minced
- 1 tsp. avocado oil
- ¼ cup fresh cilantro, chopped
- 4 eggs
- 1 (15-oz.) can black beans, rinsed and drained
- 1 small avocado, diced
- ½ cup fresh jarred salsa or your favorite

Directions:
1. Scramble the eggs. You know how it can be done. Make them as you would usually make them. Here's a guide if you need a reminder, maybe!
2. Sauté the beans. Heat the avocado oil in a large skillet over moderate heat. Sauté the onion for about 3 minutes, or until tender.
3. Add the garlic and beans, and heat until fully cooked, about 2–5 minutes.
4. Blister the tortillas or heat them in a dry skillet over an open fire on the range. Put aside, wrapped to keep them warm, in a cloth napkin.
5. Layer the beans, then slice each tortilla with the eggs. Use only ¼ cup of beans per taco. (You may be tempted, but try not to overstuff the tortillas.) Top up as needed with salsa, avocado, and cilantro.

Nutrition: Calories: 349, Protein: 11.5 g, Fats: 15 g, Carbs: 9.11 g, Sugars: 2.89 g

24. Strawberry-Coconut Bake

Preparation Time: 11 minutes
Cooking Time: 40 minutes
Servings: 2
Ingredients:
- ½ cup chopped walnuts
- 2 cups unsweetened coconut flakes
- 1 tsp. cinnamon
- ¼ cup chia seeds
- 2 cups diced strawberries
- 1 ripe banana, mashed

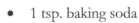

- 1 tsp. baking soda
- 4 large eggs
- ¼ tsp. salt
- 1 cup unsweetened nut milk
- 2 tbsp. melted coconut oil

Directions:

1. Preheat your oven to 375°F. Grease a square 8-inch pan and set it aside.
2. Combine the dried ingredients in a big bowl (walnuts, chia seeds, cinnamon, salt, and baking soda).
3. Whisk the eggs and milk together in a smaller dish. Now add the mashed banana and coconut oil to the mixture. To dry, add the wet ingredients and blend properly.
4. Fold the strawberries in.
5. Bake for about 40 minutes, or until the top is golden and solid.
6. Serve hot!

Nutrition: Calories: 395, Fats: 40 g, Protein: 7.5 g, Carbs: 76.48 g, Sugars: 8.68 g

25. Paleo Breakfast Hash

Preparation Time: 7 minutes
Cooking Time: 35 minutes
Servings: 2
Ingredients:

- 8 oz. white mushroom, quartered
- 1 lb. Brussels sprouts, quartered
- 1 ½ tsp. bagel seasoning
- 1 tbsp. olive oil or avocado oil
- 3 garlic cloves, minced
- 1 small onion, diced
- Crushed red pepper, optional
- 8 slices nitrate-free bacon sugar-free, for whole 30, cut into pieces
- Sea salt and pepper, to taste
- 6 large eggs

Directions:

1. Preheat to 425°F in your oven. Arrange the mushrooms and Brussels sprouts in a single layer on a sheet tray, drizzle with the olive oil, and add salt and pepper. Sprinkle the onions on the end and place the strips of bacon equally over the vegetables.
2. Roast for 15 minutes in the preheated oven, then sprinkle with the garlic and stir gently. Roast for 10 minutes, or until the bacon and vegetables are crisp and fluffy. Extract from the oven.
3. For each egg, make tiny gaps in the hash, and gently smash one at a time into a space, careful not to "split" the yolk. Sprinkle all the bagel seasoning and crushed red pepper over the bacon, eggs, and vegetables as you wish.
4. Return the baking tray to the oven and bake for another 5–10 minutes, or until the eggs are ideally fried. (For me, for solid whites and light yolks, it was 7 minutes.) Remove from the oven and serve quickly. Enjoy!

Nutrition: Calories: 250, Protein: 14 g, Fats: 18 g, Carbs: 22.32 g, Sugars: 5.03 g

26. Omelet with Chickpea Flour

Preparation Time: 10 minutes
Cooking Time: 20 minutes
Servings: 1
Ingredients:

- ½ tsp. onion powder
- ¼ tsp. black pepper
- 1 cup chickpea flour
- ½ tsp. garlic powder
- ½ tsp. baking soda
- ¼ tsp. white pepper
- 1/3 cup nutritional yeast
- 3 green onions, finely chopped
- 4 oz. sautéed mushrooms
- 1 cup water
- Spinach, tomatoes, hot sauce, and salsa, for serving

Directions:

1. Combine the onion powder, chickpea flour, garlic powder, black and white pepper, baking soda, and nutritional yeast.
2. Add 1 cup of water and create a smooth batter. Put a frying pan over medium heat, and add the batter just like the way you would cook pancakes.
3. Sprinkle some green onion and mushrooms into the batter. Flip the omelet and cook evenly on both sides. Once both sides are cooked, serve the omelet with spinach, tomatoes, hot sauce, and salsa.

Nutrition: Calories: 150, Fats: 1.9 g, Carbs: 24.4 g, Protein: 10.2 g, Sugars: 7.07 g

27. White Sandwich Bread

Preparation Time: 10 minutes
Cooking Time: 40–50 minutes
Servings: 2
Ingredients:

- 1 cup warm water
- 1 tbsp. active dry yeast
- 4 tbsp. oil
- 2 ½ tsp. salt
- 2 tbsp. raw sugar or 4 tbsp. maple syrup/agave nectar
- 1 cup warm almond milk or any other non-dairy milk of your choice
- 6 cups all-purpose flour

Directions:

1. Add warm water, yeast, and sugar into a bowl, and stir. Set aside for 5 minutes, or until lots of tiny bubbles are formed, sort of frothy.
2. Add the flour and salt into a mixing bowl, and stir. Add the oil, yeast mix, and milk to the dough. If the dough is too hard, add a little water, a tbsp. at a time, and mix well each time. If the dough is too sticky, add more flour, a tbsp. at a time. Knead the dough until

soft and supple. Use your hands or the hook attachment of a stand mixer.

3. Now spray some water on top of the dough. Keep the bowl covered with a towel. Let it rest until it doubles in size.
4. Remove the dough from the bowl and place it on your countertop. Punch the dough.
5. Line a loaf pan with parchment paper. You can also grease with some oil if you prefer.
6. Place the dough in the loaf pan. Now spray some more water on top of the dough. Keep the loaf pan covered with a towel. Let it rest until the dough doubles in size.
7. Bake in a preheated oven at 370°F for about 40–50 minutes.
8. Let it cool to room temperature. Cut it into 16 equal slices, and use them as required. Store them in a breadbox at room temperature.

Nutrition: Calories: 209, Fats: 4 g, Carbs: 35 g, Protein: 1 g, Sugars: 2.39 g

28. Sprouted Toast with Creamy Avocado and Sprouts

Preparation Time: 10 minutes
Cooking Time: 0 minutes
Servings: 2
Ingredients:

- 1 small bread sprouts
- 1 cup tomatoes, finely cut
- 2 medium avocados - 1 small cup alfalfa
- Pure sea salt, to taste
- Bell pepper, to taste

Directions:

1. Add the avocado, alfalfa, and tomatoes to the bread. Season to taste with pure sea salt and pepper.
2. Have a sumptuous breakfast with any freshly extracted juice of your choice.

Nutrition: Calories: 82, Fiber: 15 g, Protein: 30 g, Sugar: 7 g, Carbs: 40.78 g

29. Scrambled Turmeric Tofu

Preparation Time: 5 minutes
Cooking Time: 0 minutes
Servings: 2
Ingredients:

- 1 serving of tofu, crumbled
- 1 cup onions, finely chopped
- 1 tsp. fresh parsley
- 1 tsp. coconut oil
- 1 cup soft spinach
- 1 tsp. turmeric
- 1 avocado
- 75 g tomatoes
- 1 tsp. roasted paprika

Directions:

1. Make the tofu crumbs with your hands and keep them separately. Sauté the diced onions in oil.
2. Add the tofu, tomatoes, and other seasonings. Then mix until the tofu is well prepared. Add the veggies and stir. Serve in a bowl alongside some avocado.

Nutrition: Calories: 91, Fiber: 12 g, Protein: 30 g, Sugar: 8 g, Carbs: 9.81 g

30. Breakfast Salad

Preparation Time: 5 minutes
Cooking Time: 0 minutes
Servings: 2
Ingredients:

- 1 cup kale, finely diced
- 1 cup cabbage, red and Chinese
- 2 tbsp. coconut oil
- 2 cups spinach
- 1.2 kg medium avocados
- 1 chickpeas sprout
- 1 tbsp. sunflower seed sprouts
- Pure sea salt (seasoning)
- Bell pepper (seasoning)
- Lemon juice (seasoning)

Directions:

1. Add the spinach, cabbage, kale, and coconut oil to a container.

2. Add seasoning to taste, and mix evenly.
3. Add the other ingredients and mix.

Nutrition: Calories: 112, Protein: 28 g, Fiber: 10 g, Sugar: 1 g, Carbs: 13.35 g

31. Green Goddess Bowl with Avocado Cumin Dressing

Preparation Time: 10 minutes
Cooking Time: 4 minutes
Servings: 2
Ingredients:

- 1 cup kale, finely sliced
- 1 cup diced broccoli florets
- ½ cup spiralized zucchini noodles
- ½ cup soaked kelp noodles
- 3 cups tomatoes
- 2 tbsp. hemp seeds

For the Tahini Dressing:

- 1 small cup sesame butter
- 1 cup alkaline water
- 1 cup lemon, freshly extracted
- 1 garlic clove, finely chopped
- ¾ tbsp. pure sea salt
- 1 tbsp. olive oil - Bell pepper

For the Avocado Dressing:

- 1 large avocado
- Freshly extracted lime
- 1 cup alkaline water
- 1 tbsp. olive oil - Bell pepper
- 1 tbsp. powdered cumin

Directions:

1. Simmer the veggies, kale, and broccoli for about 4 minutes.
2. Combine the noodles with the avocado and the cumin dressing. Toss for a while. Add the tomatoes and combine well.
3. Put the cooked kale and broccoli on a plate, add the tahini dressing, and then add the noodles and tomatoes. Add a couple of hemp seeds to the whole dish and enjoy it.

Nutrition: Calories: 109, Protein: 25 g, Fiber: 17 g, Sugar: 8 g, Carbs: 45.57 g

32. Quinoa Burrito

Preparation Time: 15 minutes
Cooking Time: 15 minutes
Servings: 1
Ingredients:

- 1 cup quinoa
- 1 cup black beans
- 4 green onions, finely chopped
- 4 garlic, finely chopped
- 2 limes, freshly cut
- 1 tbsp. cumin
- 2 avocados, diced
- 1 small cup cilantro, diced

Directions:

1. Boil the quinoa. During this process, put the beans over low heat.
2. Add the other ingredients to the bean pot and let it mix well for about 15 minutes. Serve the quinoa and add the prepared beans.

Nutrition: Calories: 117, Protein: 27 g, Fiber: 10 g, Carbs: 274.99 g, Sugars: 8.53 g

33. Baked Banana-Nut Oatmeal Cups

Preparation Time: 17 minutes
Cooking Time: 30 minutes
Servings: 2
Ingredients:

- 3 cups rolled oats
- 1 ½ cups low-fat milk
- 2 ripe bananas
- ¼ cup packed brown sugar
- 2 large eggs, lightly beaten
- 1 tsp. leaven
- 1 tsp. ground cinnamon
- 1 tsp. vanilla extract
- ½ tsp. salt
- ½ cup toasted pecans, chopped

Directions:

1. Preheat the cooking appliance to 375°F. Coat a gem tin with cooking spray.
2. Combine the oats, milk, bananas, refined sugar, eggs, leaven, cinnamon, vanilla, and salt in a large bowl. Fold in the pecans. Divide the mixture among the gem cups (about 1/3 cup each). Bake till a pick inserted in the center comes out clean, about 25 minutes.
3. Let it cool in the pan for 10 minutes, then place it onto a wire rack.
4. Serve.

Nutrition: Calories: 178, Protein: 5.3 g, Fats: 6.3 g, Carbs: 74.7, Sugars: 2.17 g

34. Veggie Breakfast Wrap

Preparation Time: 12 minutes
Cooking Time: 13 minutes
Servings: 2
Ingredients:

- 1 tsp. olive oil
- 1 cup sliced mushrooms
- 2 eggs
- ½ cup egg white or egg replacement
- 1 cup firmly packed spinach or other greens
- 2 tbsp. sliced scallions
- Cooking nonstick spray
- 2 Whole wheat and low-carb battercakes
- 2 tbsp. salsa
- Avocado slices, for topping
- Bell pepper, for topping
- Tomato, for topping

Directions:

1. Add the oil to a frying pan over medium heat. Add the mushrooms and sauté till nicely brown on the edges (about 3 minutes), then set aside.
2. Beat the eggs whites or egg substitute in a medium-sized bowl, using a mixer or by hand, till emulsified. Stir in the spinach and scallions. You could also add dried herbs like basil or parsley for more flavor.
3. Begin heating a medium/large frying pan over medium-low heat. Coat a pan with

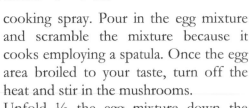

cooking spray. Pour in the egg mixture and scramble the mixture because it cooks employing a spatula. Once the egg area broiled to your taste, turn off the heat and stir in the mushrooms.

4. Unfold ½ the egg mixture down the middle of every battercake. Top every battercake with 1 tablespoon of fresh condiment or an alternative sauce of your preference. Garnish with further toppings like avocado slices, bell pepper, or tomato if desired, then roll it up to form a wrap.

Nutrition: Calories: 220, Fats: 11 g, Protein: 19 g, Carbs: 3.37 g, Sugars: 1.18 g

35. Breakfast Egg and Ham Burrito

Preparation Time: 21 minutes
Cooking Time: 13 minutes
Servings: 2
Ingredients:

- 4 eggs
- 4 Egg whites
- A dash hot pepper sauce
- ¼ tsp. black pepper
- 2 tbsp. cheddar cheese
- 2 tbsp. margarine
- ¼ cup sliced onion
- ¼ cup diced green pepper
- 4 batter cakes
- 1/2 tsp. Hot sauce poivrade
- 6 slices of Ham

Directions:

1. Using a medium bowl, whisk the eggs, egg whites, hot Poivrade, black pepper, and cheese. Heat the mixture in a medium non-stick pan over medium heat. Add the ham and sauté for 2–3 minutes. Remove the ham from the pan.

2. Add the onions and fresh peppers to the recent pan, and cook for 5 minutes. Add the ham back to the pan.

3. Reduce the heat to low and add the eggs to the pan. Gently stir the eggs with a spoon or spatula, and continue to gently stir it over low heat till the eggs are broiled and set.

4. Equally, divide the egg mixture into 4 servings. Spoon every portion of the egg mixture into a battercake and top each one with 1 teaspoon of sauce. Fold the battercake.

Nutrition: Calories: 210, Fats: 9 g, Carbs: 16 g, Protein: 45.23 g, Sugars: 4.41 g

36. Breakfast Cups for Meat Lover

Preparation Time: 12 minutes
Cooking Time: 13 minutes
Servings: 6
Ingredients:

- 1 tbsp light sour cream
- 2 precooked turkey breakfast sausage patties (thawed and diced)
- 1 clove garlic (minced)
- 2 tbsp Onion (s) (finely chopped)
- 1 1/4 cup frozen hash browns (thawed)
- 1 tsp canola oil
- 1/4 tsp salt
- 1/8 tsp black pepper
- 1 cup egg substitute
- 2 tbsp turkey bacon
- 2 tbsp Monterey jack cheese

Directions:

1. Preheat the oven to 400 F. Coat a six-cup muffin tin with nonstick cooking spray. Evenly divide the hash browns among the muffin cups and press firmly into the bottom and up the sides of each cup.

2. In a large skillet, heat the oil over medium heat. Sauté the onion until tender. Add the garlic and sausage; cook for 1 minute more. Remove the skillet from the heat; stir in the sour cream.

3. In a medium bowl, beat the egg substitute with the salt and black pepper, then pour it evenly into the potato-lined muffin cups. Top each cup with some of the sausage mixture, bacon, and cheese.

4. Bake 15 to 18 minutes, or until the eggs are set. Serve immediately, or freeze for later.

Nutrition: Calories: 120, Fats: 4 g, Carbs: 10 g, Protein: 6.87 g, Sugars: 1.84 g

37. Breakfast Quesadilla

Preparation Time: 13 minutes
Cooking Time: 16 minutes
Servings: 2
Ingredients:

- Cooking spray, as needed
- ¼ cup canned green chiles
- 4 beaten eggs
- ¼ tsp. black pepper
- 4-6 10-inch whole wheat flour tortillas
- 1 ½ reduced-fat cup cheddar cheese
- 4 turkey bacon slices, cooked, crisp, and crumbled

Directions:

1. Lightly brush a small skillet with cooking oil.
2. Sauté the green chilies over medium-low heat for 1–2 minutes. Add the beaten eggs and cook until scrambled and set, stirring. Season with some pepper.
3. Lightly brush a second large skillet with cooking oil. Place 1 tortilla in the skillet and cook over medium heat for about 1 minute, or until air bubbles begin to form. Flip the tortilla and cook for another 1 minute (don't let the tortilla get crispy).
4. Layer half of the cheese thinly over the tortilla, protecting the corners.
5. Reduce the heat to low. Arrange half of the fried bacon and half of the egg mixture over the cheese easily. Cook

until the cheese begins to melt, about 1 minute.

6. To make a half-moon shape, fold the tortilla in half. Flip the folded tortilla over and cook for 1–2 minutes, or until lightly toasted and the cheese filling is fully melted.

Nutrition: Calories: 160, Fats: 19 g, Carbs: 8 g, Protein: 11.99 g, Sugars: 0.73 g

38. Toasts with Egg and Avocado

Preparation Time: 17 minutes
Cooking Time: 0 minutes
Servings: 2
Ingredients:

- 4 eggs
- 4 hearty whole grain bread slices
- 1 avocado, mashed
- ½ tsp. salt (optional)
- ¼ tsp. black pepper
- ¼ cup non-fat Greek yogurt
- 1/2–1 cup water

Directions:

1. To poach each egg, fill ½ cup of water or 1 cup of water using a microwaveable bowl or teacup. Crack an egg into the water softly, making sure it's fully submerged.
2. Cove it and place it over high heat for about 1 minute (you could also use a saucer and a microwave), or before the white is set and the yolk starts to set but still fluffy (not runny).
3. Toast the bread and use ¼ of the mashed avocado to scatter each slice.
4. Sprinkle the salt with avocado (optional) and pepper. Top with a poached egg on each piece. Top the egg with 1 tablespoon of Greek yogurt.

Nutrition: Calories: 230, Fats: 13 g, Carbs: 26 g, Protein: 11.76 g, Sugars: 2.12 g

39. Turkey Sausages and Egg Casserole

Preparation Time: 13 minutes
Cooking Time: 60 minutes
Servings: 2
Ingredients:

- ½ cup green onions, chopped
- 2 cups non-fat milk
- Non-stick cooking spray, as needed
- ½ tsp. mustard powder
- ¼ tsp. salt - ¼ tsp. black pepper
- 2 Egg substitute
- 4 whole wheat bread slices, cut into ½–inch cubes
- 3 turkey breakfast sausage patties, precooked and diced
- ¼ cup reduced-fat cheddar cheese, shredded

Directions:

1. Preheat the oven to 350°F. Coat a 9x13 baking dish with cooking spray.
2. In a medium bowl, whisk the non-fat milk, green onions, dry mustard, salt (optional), pepper, and egg substitute.
3. Place the bread cubes and sausage on the bottom of the baking dish, and then pour the egg mixture evenly over the bread and sausage. Top with cheddar cheese.
4. Cover the pan with aluminum foil and bake for 20 minutes. Remove the foil and bake for an additional 40 minutes.

Nutrition: Calories: 120, Fats: 3 g, Carbs: 9 g, Protein: 4.52 g, Sugars: 6.51 g

40. Apple-Walnut French Toast

Preparation Time: 12 minutes
Cooking Time: 14 minutes
Servings: 2
Ingredients:

- 4 multigrain Italian bread slices, about 6 oz. - 1 cup egg substitute
- 4 tsp. pure maple syrup
- 1 cup diced apple walnuts (chopped)
- 1 apples sliced
- Cooking spray, as needed

Directions:

1. Preheat the oven to 450°F. Meanwhile, put the bread in a baking pan of 13 to 9 inches, pour over all the egg substitutes, and turn several times until the bread slices are thoroughly coated and the egg mixture is used. Put the bread slices coated with cooking spray on the baking sheet.
2. Bake for 6 minutes, turn, and bake for 5 minutes, or until the bottom is golden. Serve with similar proportions of syrup, apples, and nuts in the mixture.

Nutrition: Calories: 276, Fats: 12 g, Carbs: 33.56 g, Protein: 11.56 g, Sugars: 7.29 g

41. Summer Smoothie Fruit

Preparation Time: 12 minutes
Cooking Time: 0 minutes
Servings: 2
Ingredients:

- 1 cup fresh blueberries
- 1 cup fresh strawberries, chopped
- 3 Peaches, peeled, seeded, and chopped
- ¼ cup Peach-flavored, Greek-style non-fat yogurt
- 1 cup unsweetened almond milk
- 2 tbsp. ground flax seed - ½ cup ice

Directions:

1. Combine all the ingredients in a blender and purée until creamy.

Nutrition: Calories: 130, Fats: 4 g, Carbs: 23 g, Protein: 2.89 g, Sugars: 12.15 g

42. Chicken and Egg Salad

Preparation Time: 5 minutes
Cooking Time: 25 minutes
Servings: 2
Ingredients:

- 2 cooked chicken breasts

- 3 hard-boiled eggs
- 1 tbsp. curry powder
- Chives or basil (optional)
- Salt (optional)
- Toasts or muffins, for serving
- ½ cup Cream cheese

Directions:
1. Bake the chicken in the oven at around 360°F for maybe 15 minutes (confirming with just a knife to know if the meat is cooked all the way through).
2. Cook the eggs for 8 minutes. Cut the eggs and chicken into a small-sized piece.
3. Combine the cream cheese with the curry powder
4. In a large bowl, combine everything and mix.
5. Allow a minimum of 10 minutes to chill in the refrigerator (it gets even better if you leave it overnight in the refrigerator).
6. Serve with chives on toasts or muffins and a bit of salt on top.

Nutrition: Calories: 139, Fats: 9 g, Carbs: 23 g, Protein: 63.61 g, Sugars: 1.68 g

43. Niçoise Salad Tuna

Preparation Time: 12 minutes
Cooking Time: 5 minutes
Servings: 1
Ingredients:
- 4 oz. ahi tuna steak

- 1 whole egg
- 2 cups baby spinach, about 3 oz.
- 2 oz. green beans
- 1 ½ oz. broccoli
- ½ red bell peppers
- 1 radish
- 3 large black olives
- A handful parsley
- 1 tsp. olive oil
- 1 tsp. balsamic vinegar
- ½ tsp. Dijon mustard
- ½ tsp. pepper
- ½ cup Grapefruit
- Water, as needed

Directions:
1. Cook the egg and place it aside to cool.
2. Steam the beans and broccoli, then set aside for 2–3 minutes in a little of water in the microwave or 3 minutes in a hot kettle.
3. In a tub, heat a bit of oil over high heat.
4. On all sides, season the seafood using pepper, then place it there over the heat and stir on each edge for about 2 minutes.
5. Add the spinach to a salad bowl or pan.
6. Chop the red pepper, grapefruit, and egg into bite-sized pieces. Add the spinach on top.
7. Cut the radish into slices and mix the broccoli, beans, and olives together. Add the spinach salad on top.
8. Break the tuna into strips and add it to the salad.
9. Toss the olive oil, balsamic vinegar, mustard, salt, and pepper together.
10. Chop the parsley and add it to the vinaigrette.
11. Use a spoon for drizzling the vinaigrette over the salad.

Nutrition: Calories: 149, Fats: 6 g, Carbs: 21 g, Protein: 44.45 g, Sugars: 5.39 g

44. Rolls with Spinach

Preparation Time: 15 minutes
Cooking Time: 50 minutes
Servings: 2
Ingredients:

- 16 oz. frozen spinach leaves
- 3 eggs
- 2 ½ oz. onion
- 2 oz. carrot
- 1 oz. low-fat mozzarella cheese
- 4 oz. fat-free cottage cheese
- ½ cup parsley
- 1 tsp. curry powder
- ¼ tsp. chili flakes Salt
- 1 tsp. pepper
- Cooking spray, as needed
- 1 ½ cup Water

Directions:

1. Preheat the oven to 400°F.
2. Thaw the spinach and squeeze the water out (you can use a strainer). In order to accelerate the thawing process, you can microwave the spinach for a few minutes.
3. Mix the spinach, 2 eggs, mozzarella, ginger, half the salt, and pepper together in a baking bowl.
4. Place parchment paper on a baking sheet and coat it with cooking spray. Move the spinach mixture to the sheet, about half an inch thick and about 10 to 12 inches in height, and press it down.
5. Bake for 15 minutes and then set aside to cool on a rack. Don't turn the oven off.
6. Finely chop the onion and parsley. Grate the carrots.
7. In a pan with a bit of cooking oil, fry the onions for about a minute. Add the carrots and parsley to the pan and let the mixture cook for about 2 minutes.
8. Add the cottage cheese, curry, chili, salt, and pepper to the other half. Briefly mix.
9. Remove the fire from the pan, add an egg, and mix it all together.
10. Spread the filling over the spinach that has been cooled. Do not stretch it all the way to the corners or, as you fold it out, it will fall out.
11. Roll the spinach mat carefully and fill it, then bake for 25 minutes.
12. Take out the roll once the time is up, and let it cool for 5–10 minutes before cutting it into slices and serving.

Nutrition: Calories: 149, Fats: 11 g, Carbs: 26 g, Protein: 18.13 g, Sugars: 4.87 g

45. Curried Chicken with Apples

Preparation Time: 12 minutes
Cooking Time: 0 minutes
Servings: 2
Ingredients:

- 1 lb. cooked chicken breast, diced
- 1 Granny Smith apple, diced
- 1 Celery stalks, diced
- 2 green onions, diced
- ½ cup sliced cashew
- 1 cup plain Greek yogurt
- 1 tbsp. tahini
- 4 tsp. curry powder
- 1 tsp. ground cinnamon
- Papaya, for serving (optional)
- 3 ½ cup Milk

Directions:

1. In a big mixing cup, add the milk, tahini, curry powder, and cinnamon.
2. Add the chicken, apple, celery, cashews, and green onions. Stir to blend.
3. To offer it something of a tropical feel, this salad can be eaten on its own, as a snack, or in a plucked-out papaya.

Nutrition: Calories: 139, Fats: 8 g, Carbs: 19 g, Protein: 31.44 g, Sugars: 5.41 g

46. Homemade Chicken Nuggets

Preparation Time: 15 minutes
Cooking Time: 23 minutes
Servings: 2
Ingredients:

- ½ cup almond flour
- 1 tbsp. Italian seasoning
- 1 tbsp. extra-virgin olive oil
- ½ tsp. salt
- ½ tsp. pepper
- 1 lb. Chicken breasts

Directions:

1. Preheat the oven to 400°F. Using parchment paper to arrange a large baking dish.
2. Whisk the Italian seasoning, almond flour, pepper, and salt together in a dish.
3. Start cutting and remove any fat from the chicken breasts, after which slice it into 1-inch-thick bits.
4. Sprinkle the extra-virgin olive oil to the chicken.
5. Place each chicken piece in the flour bowl and toss until thoroughly covered, then move the chicken to the baking sheet that has been prepared.
6. Roast for 20 minutes.
7. To get them crispy, toggle the broiler on and put the chicken nuggets underneath the broiler for 3–4 minutes.

Nutrition: Calories: 149, Fats: 9 g, Carbs: 29 g, Protein: 0.51 g, Sugars: 1.05 g

47. Beef Fajitas

Preparation Time: 6 minutes
Cooking Time: 19 minutes
Servings: 2
Ingredients:

- 1 lb. beef stir-fry strips
- 1 medium red onion
- 1 red bell pepper
- 1 yellow bell pepper
- ½ tsp. cumin
- ½ tsp. chili powder
- A splash oil
- Salt, to taste
- Pepper, to taste
- ½ lemon, juiced
- 1 tbsp. Freshly chopped cilantro (also called coriander)
- 1 avocado, chopped

Directions:

1. Steam a cast-iron pan over medium heat.
2. Clean the bell peppers and cut them into long strips of 0.5 cm thick and then set them aside.
3. Clean the red onion and cut it into strips. Set it aside.
4. Add a little bit of oil once the skillet is heated. Add 2–3 packets of stir-fry strips while the oil is hot. Please ensure the strips don't hit each other.
5. Inside the pan, stir-fry each beef batch thoroughly with salt and pepper. Cook on each side for around 1 minute, and then set aside on a plate covered to stay warm. Introduce the chopped onion as well as the ringer peppers to the residual meat juice when all the beef is finished cooking and set aside. Sweetened with the chili powder and cumin, then simmer-fry till the preferred consistency is achieved. Transfer the stir-fry vegetable strips and beef to just a plate and eat with the chopped avocado, a sprinkling of lemon juice, and as pray of fresh cilantro. Serve.

Nutrition: Calories: 151, Fats: 6 g, Carbs: 27 g, Protein: 21.93 g, Sugars: 6.52 g

48. Keto Salad

Preparation Time: 11 minutes
Cooking Time: 0 minutes
Servings: 2
Ingredients:

- 4 cherry tomatoes

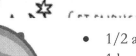    

- 1/2 avocado
- 1 hard-boiled egg
- 1 cup mixed salad greens
- 2 oz. chicken breast, shredded
- 1 oz. feta cheese, crumbled
- ¼ cup cooked bacon, crumbled

Directions:

1. Slice the avocado and tomatoes. Slice the egg that is hard-boiled.
2. On a large plate, put the mixed greens.
3. Quantify the pulverized chicken breast, crushed bacon, and feta cheese.
4. Position the tomatoes, egg, chicken, avocado, feta, and bacon on top of the greens in horizontal rows.

Nutrition: Calories: 152, Fats: 9 g, Carbs: 24 g, Protein: 17.51 g, Sugars: 1.8 g

49. Instant Pot Chicken Chili

Preparation Time: 6 minutes
Cooking Time: 21 minutes
Servings: 2
Ingredients:

- 1 tbsp. vegetable oil
- 1 yellow onion, diced
- 4 garlic cloves, minced
- 1 tsp. ground cumin
- 1 tsp. oregano
- ½ lb. chicken breasts, boneless and skinless
- 16 oz. salsa verde

For the Toppings:

- 2 packages fresh cheese, crumbled, or sour cream
- 2 avocados, diced
- Finely chopped radishes
- 8 cilantro springs (optional)

Directions:

1. Set the instant pot to a medium sauté setting.
2. Add the oil to the vegetables.

3. Add the onion and simmer for 3 minutes, or until the onion starts to melt, stirring regularly.
4. Add the garlic, then stir for a minute.
5. Add the oregano and cumin, and simmer for the next minute.
6. Add ½ of the salsa verde to the pot. Finish only with the chicken breasts and pour the leftover salsa Verde over the chicken.
7. Position the cover on the instant pot, switch the nozzle to "Seal," choose "Manual," and set the timer to 10 minutes. Then let the pressure release naturally when the time is up.
8. Lift the cover, transfer the chicken to a small bowl just after the pressure has dropped, and slice it with a fork.
9. To mix with the remaining ingredients, transfer the meat to the pot and stir.

Nutrition: Calories: 144, Fats: 7 g, Carbs: 20 g, Protein: 15.93 g, Sugars: 6.8 g

50. Smoked Cheese Wraps with Salmon and Cream

Preparation Time: 12 minutes
Cooking Time: 15 minutes
Servings: 2
Ingredients:

- 1 (8-inch) low-carb flour tortilla
- 2 oz. smoked salmon
- 1 ¾ tsp. low-fat cream cheese
- 1 ½ oz. red onion
- A handful arugulas
- ½ tsp. fresh or dried basil
- A pinch pepper

Directions:

1. In the oven or microwave, warm the tortilla (pro tip: to prevent it from drying out, warm it between 2 pieces of moist paper towel).
2. The cream cheese, basil, and pepper are mixed together and then scattered over the tortilla.

3. With the salmon, arugula, and finely sliced onion, finish it off. Roll it up and enjoy the wrap!

Nutrition: Calories: 138, Fats: 6 g, Carbs: 19 g, Protein: 6.77 g, Sugars: 2.2 g

51. Cheese Yogurt

Preparation Time: 12 minutes
Cooking Time: 15 minutes
Servings: 2
Ingredients:

- 1 thick and creamy Yogurt, or store-bought yogurt
- ½ tsp. kosher salt

Directions:

1. Line a strainer of twice the normal thickness with cheesecloth.
2. Place the strainer on top of a bowl and apply the yogurt.
3. Cover and refrigerate for 2 hours. Stir in the salt and continue to drip for another 2 hours, or until the yogurt cheese is ready to spread.

Nutrition: Calories: 83, Protein: 5 g, Fats: 5.4 g, Carbs: 5.3 g, Sugars: 2.1 g

52. Shrimp Frittata

Preparation Time: 10 minutes
Cooking Time: 15 minutes
Servings: 2
Ingredients:

- 4 eggs
- ½ tsp. basil, dried
- Cooking spray, as needed
- Salt and black pepper, to taste
- ½ cup cooked rice
- ½ cup shrimp, cooked, peeled, deveined, and chopped
- ½ cup baby spinach, chopped
- ½ cup Monterey jack cheese, grated

Directions:

1. In a bowl, mix the eggs with salt, pepper, and basil. Then whisk. Grease your air fryer's pan with cooking spray, and add the rice, shrimp, and spinach. Add the egg mixture, sprinkle cheese all over, and cook in your air fryer at 350ºF for 10 minutes.
2. Divide among plates and serve for breakfast. Enjoy!

Nutrition: Calories: 162, Fats: 6 g, Fiber: 5 g, Carbs: 8 g, Protein: 4 g

53. Zucchini Fritters

Preparation Time: 15 minutes
Cooking Time: 7 minutes
Servings: 2
Ingredients:

- 10 ½ oz. zucchini, grated and squeezed
- 7 oz. halloumi cheese
- ¼ cup all-purpose flour
- 2 eggs
- 1 tsp. fresh dill, minced
- Salt and ground black pepper, as required

Directions:

1. In a large bowl, mix all the ingredients.
2. Make a small-sized fritter from the mixture.
3. Press the "Power" button of the Air Fry Oven and turn the dial to select the "Air Fry" mode.
4. Press the "Time" button and again turn the dial to set the cooking time to 7 minutes.
5. Now push the "Temp" button and rotate the dial to set the temperature to 355ºF.
6. Press the "Start/Pause" button to start.
7. Open the lid when the unit beeps to show that it is preheated.
8. Arrange the fritters into a greased "Sheet Pan," and insert it in the oven.
9. Serve warm.

Nutrition: Calories: 253 Fats: 17.2 g, Carbs: 10 g, Fiber: 1.1 g, Sugar: 2.7 g, Protein: 15.2 g

54. Chicken Omelet

Preparation Time: 10 minutes
Cooking Time: 12 minutes
Servings: 2
Ingredients:

- 1 tsp. butter
- 1 small yellow onion, chopped
- ½ jalapeño pepper, seeded and chopped
- 3 eggs
- Salt and ground black pepper, as required
- ¼ cup cooked chicken, shredded

Directions:

1. In a frying pan, melt the butter over medium heat and cook the onion for about 4–5 minutes. Add the jalapeño pepper and cook for about 1 minute.
2. Remove from the heat and set aside to cool slightly. Meanwhile, in a bowl, add the eggs, salt, and black pepper. Beat well.
3. Add the onion mixture and chicken, and stir to combine. Place the chicken mixture into a small baking pan.
4. Press the "Power" button of the Air Fry Oven and turn the dial to select the "Air Fry" mode.
5. Press the "Time" button and again turn the dial to set the cooking time to 6 minutes.
6. Now push the "Temp" button and rotate the dial to set the temperature to 355°F.
7. Press the "Start/Pause" button to start.
8. Open the lid when the unit beeps to show that it is preheated.
9. Arrange the pan over the "Wire Rack" and insert it in the oven.
10. Cut the omelet into 2 portions and serve them hot.

Nutrition: Calories: 153, Fats: 9.1 g, Carbs: 4 g, Fiber: 0.9 g, Sugar: 2.1 g, Protein: 13.8 g

55. Scrambled Eggs

Preparation Time: 5 minutes
Cooking Time: 20 minutes
Servings: 2
Ingredients:

- 4 large eggs
- ½ cup sharp Cheddar cheese, shredded
- 2 tbsp. unsalted butter; melted

Directions:

1. Crack the eggs into a 2-cup round baking dish, and whisk.
2. Place the dish into the air fryer basket.
3. Adjust the temperature to 400°F and set the timer to 10 minutes. After 5 minutes, stir the eggs and add the butter and cheese. Let cook for 3 more minutes and stir again. Allow the eggs to finish cooking for an additional 2 minutes, or remove them if they are to your liking.
4. Use a fork to fluff. Serve warm.

Nutrition: Calories: 359, Protein: 19.5 g, Fiber: 0.0 g, Fats: 27.6 g, Carbs: 1.1 g

56. Almond Crust Chicken

Preparation Time: 10 minutes
Cooking Time: 25 minutes
Servings: 2
Ingredients:

- 2 chicken breasts, skinless and boneless
- 1 tbsp. Dijon mustard
- 2 tbsp. mayonnaise - ¼ cup almonds

Directions:

1. Add the almonds into the food processor, and process until finely ground. Transfer the almonds to a plate, and set them aside.
2. Mix the mustard with the mayonnaise, and the mixture spread over chicken.
3. Coat the chicken with the almonds, place the mixture into the air fryer basket, and cook at 350°F for 25 minutes. Serve and enjoy.

Nutrition: Calories: 409, Fats: 22 g, Carbs: 6 g, Sugar: 1.5 g, Protein: 45 g

CHAPTER 5

First Courses

57. Butternut Fritters

Preparation Time: 10 minutes
Cooking Time: 8 minutes
Servings: 2
Ingredients:

- 5 cups butternut squash, grated
- 2 large eggs
- 1 tbsp. fresh sage, finely diced
- 2/3 cup flour
- 2 tbsp. olive oil
- Salt and pepper, to taste
- Dipping sauce, for serving

Directions:

1. Heat the oil in a large skillet over medium-high heat.
2. In a large bowl, combine the squash, eggs, sage, salt, and pepper to taste. Fold in the flour.
3. Drop ¼ cup of the mixture into the skillet, keeping fritters at least 1-inch apart. Cook till golden brown on both sides, about 2 minutes per side.
4. Transfer to paper towel-lined plate. Repeat. Serve immediately with your favorite dipping sauce.

Nutrition: Calories: 164, Carbs: 24 g, Net Carbs: 21 g, Protein: 4 g, Fats: 6 g, Sugar: 3 g, Fiber: 3 g

58. Cauliflower in Vegan Alfredo Sauce

Preparation Time: 10 minutes
Cooking Time: 10 minutes
Servings: 1
Ingredients:

- 1 tbsp. olive oil
- 2 garlic cloves
- 1 cup vegetable broth
- ½ tsp. sea salt
- Pepper, to taste
- 1 tsp. chili flakes
- 1 medium onion, diced
- 4 cups cauliflower florets, chopped
- 1 tsp. lemon juice, freshly squeezed
- 1 tbsp. nutritional yeast
- 2 tbsp. vegan butter
- Zucchini noodles, for serving

Directions:

1. Begin by positioning a cooking pot over low heat. Stream in the oil and allow it to heat through.
2. Immediately, you're done, so toss in the chopped onion and cook for about 4 minutes. The onion should be translucent.
3. Put in the garlic and prepare for about 30 seconds. Stir continuously to prevent them from sticking.
4. Put in the vegetable broth and the shredded cauliflower florets. Ensure you mix well, and cover the stockpot with a lid. Allow the cauliflower to cook for 5 minutes, and then remove it from the heat.
5. Get a blender and move the cooked cauliflower into it. Pulse until the purée is smooth and creamy in texture. (Add 1 tablespoon of broth if required.)
6. Add the salt, lemon juice, nutritional yeast, butter, chili flakes, and pepper to the blender. Mix until all the ingredients are fully combined to form a smooth purée.
7. Place the zucchini noodles over a dishing platter and stream the prepared cauliflower Alfredo sauce over the noodles.

Nutrition: Fats: 9.1 g, Protein: 3.9 g, Carbs: 10 g

59. Creamed Spinach

Preparation Time: 10 minutes
Cooking Time: 20 minutes
Servings: 2
Ingredients:

- 1/2 cup white onion, chopped
- 10 oz. frozen spinach, thawed
- 1 tsp. salt
- 1 tsp. ground black pepper
- 2 tsp. minced garlic
- 1/2 tsp. ground nutmeg

- 4 oz. reduced-fat cream cheese, diced
- 1/4 cup reduced-fat Parmesan cheese, shredded
- Olive oil, as needed

Directions:

1. Switch on the air fryer, insert the fryer basket, grease it with olive oil, shut with its lid, set the fryer at 350°F, and preheat for 5 minutes.
2. Meanwhile, take a 6-inch baking pan and grease it with oil, then set it aside.
3. Place the spinach in a bowl, add remaining ingredients except for Parmesan cheese, stir until well mixed, and then add the mixture into the prepared baking pan.
4. Open the fryer, insert the pan in it, close with its lid, and cook for 10 minutes, or until cooked and cheese has melted, stirring halfway through.
5. Then sprinkle the Parmesan cheese on top of the spinach and continue to air-fry at 400°F for 5 minutes., or until the top is nicely golden and the cheese has melted. Serve straight away.

Nutrition: Calories: 273, Carbs: 8 g, Fats: 23 g, Protein: 8 g, Fiber: 2 g

60. Eggplant Parmesan

Preparation Time: 20 minutes
Cooking Time: 15 minutes
Servings: 2
Ingredients:

- 1/2 cup + 3 tbsp. almond flour, divided
- 1 ¼ lb. eggplant, ½-inch sliced
- 1 tbsp. chopped parsley
- 1 tsp. Italian seasoning
- 2 tsp. salt
- 1 cup marinara sauce
- 1 egg, pastured - 1 tbsp. water
- 3 tbsp. reduced-fat Parmesan cheese, grated
- 1/4 cup reduced-fat mozzarella cheese, grated

Directions:

1. Slice the eggplant into ½-inch pieces, place them in a colander, sprinkle with 1 ½ tsp. salt on both sides, and let it rest for 15 minutes.
2. Meanwhile, place ½ cup of flour in a bowl, add the egg and water, and whisk until blended.
3. Place the remaining flour in a shallow dish, and add remaining salt, Italian seasoning, and parmesan cheese. Stir until mixed.
4. Switch on the air fryer, insert the fryer basket, grease it with olive oil, shut it with its lid, set the fryer at 360°F, and preheat for 5 minutes.
5. Meanwhile, drain the eggplant pieces, pat them dry, and then dip each slice into the egg mixture and coat with flour mixture.
6. Open the fryer, add the coated eggplant slices it in a single layer, close it with its lid, and cook for 8 minutes, or until nicely golden and cooked, flipping the eggplant slices halfway through the frying. Then top each eggplant slice with a tablespoon of marinara sauce and some of the mozzarella cheese, and continue air-frying for 1 to 2 minutes, or until the cheese has melted.
7. When the air fryer beeps, open its lid, transfer the eggplants onto a serving plate, and keep them warm.
8. Cook the remaining eggplant slices in the same manner, and serve.

Nutrition: Calories: 193, Carbs: 27 g, Fats: 5.5 g, Protein: 10 g, Fiber: 6 g

61. Lime Asparagus with Cashews

Preparation Time: 10 minutes
Cooking Time: 20 minutes
Servings: 2
Ingredients:

- 2 lb. asparagus, woody ends trimmed
- 1 tbsp. extra-virgin olive oil
- Sea salt and freshly ground black pepper, to taste
- ½ cup chopped cashews
- 1 lime, zested and juiced

Directions:

1. Preheat the oven to 400°F. Line a baking sheet with aluminum foil.
2. Toss the asparagus with the olive oil in a medium bowl. Sprinkle the salt and pepper to season.
3. Arrange the asparagus on the baking sheet and bake for 15 to 20 minutes, or until lightly browned and tender.
4. Remove the asparagus from the oven onto a serving bowl. Add the cashews and lime zest and juice, and toss to coat well. Serve immediately.

Nutrition: Calories: 173, Fats: 11.8 g, Protein: 8.0 g, Carbs: 43.7 g, Fiber: 4.9 g, Sugar: 5.0 g, Sodium: 65 mg

62. Cabbage Wedges

Preparation Time: 10 minutes
Cooking Time: 30 minutes
Servings: 2
Ingredients:

- 1 small green cabbage head
- 6 bacon strips, thickly cut and pastured
- 1 tsp. onion powder
- ½ tsp. ground black pepper
- 1 tsp. garlic powder
- ¾ tsp. salt
- 1/4 tsp. red chili flakes
- 1/2 tsp. fennel seeds
- 3 tbsp. olive oil

Directions:

1. Switch on the air fryer, insert the fryer basket, grease it with olive oil, then shut it with its lid, set the fryer at 350°F, and preheat for 5 minutes.
2. Open the fryer, add the bacon strips in it, close it with its lid, and cook for 10 minutes, or until nicely golden and

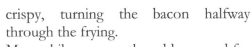

crispy, turning the bacon halfway through the frying.

3. Meanwhile, prepare the cabbage, and for this, remove the outer leaves of the cabbage, and then cut it into eight wedges, keeping the core intact.

4. Prepare the spice mix, and for this, place the onion powder in a bowl, add the black pepper, garlic powder, salt, red chili, and fennel. Then stir until mixed.

5. Drizzle the cabbage wedges with oil and then sprinkle with spice mix until well coated.

6. When air fryer beeps, open its lid, transfer the bacon strips to a cutting board, and let them rest.

7. Add the seasoned cabbage wedges into the fryer basket, close with its lid, and cook at 400°F for 8 minutes. Flip the cabbage, spray with oil, and continue air-frying for 6 minutes, or until nicely golden and cooked.

8. When done, transfer the cabbage wedges onto a plate.

9. Chop the bacon, sprinkle it over the cabbage, and serve.

Nutrition: Calories: 123, Carbs: 2 g, Fats: 11 g, Protein: 4 g, Fiber: 0 g

63. Broccoli and Bacon Salad

Preparation Time: 10 minutes
Cooking Time: 0 minutes
Servings: 2
Ingredients:

- 2 cups broccoli, separated into florets
- 4 bacon slices, chopped and cooked until crisp
- ½ cup cheddar cheese, cubed
- ¼ cup low-fat Greek yogurt
- 1/8 cup red onion, finely diced
- 1/8 cup almonds, sliced
- ¼ cup reduced-fat mayonnaise
- 1 tbsp. lemon juice
- 1 tbsp. apple cider vinegar

- 1 tbsp. granulated sugar substitute
- ¼ tsp. salt
- ¼ tsp. pepper

Directions:

1. In a large bowl, combine the broccoli, onion, cheese, bacon, and almonds.

2. In a small bowl, whisk the remaining ingredients together till combined.

3. Pour the dressing over the broccoli mixture and stir. Cover and chill at least 1 hour before serving.

Nutrition: Calories: 217, Carbs: 12 g, Net Carbs: 10 g, Protein: 11 g, Fats: 14 g, Sugar: 6 g, Fiber: 2 g

64. Black Pepper and Garlic Tofu

Preparation Time: 10 minutes
Cooking Time: 20 minutes
Servings: 2
Ingredients:

- 1 (14-oz.) pkg. extra-firm tofu
- 1 lb. asparagus, trim & cut in 1-inch pieces
- 8 oz. kale, stems removed and leaves sliced
- 3 oz. Shiitake mushrooms, sliced
- 1 onion, halved and sliced into thin wedges
- 1 green bell pepper, sliced
- ½ cup low-sodium vegetable broth
- 8 garlic cloves, pressed, divided
- 2 ½ tbsp. light soy sauce, divided
- 2–4 tbsp. water
- 2 tsp. cornstarch
- 2 tsp. black pepper, freshly ground, divided
- 1 tsp. rice vinegar
- 1 tsp. sriracha
- ½ liters Water or as needed

Directions:

1. Heat the oven to 400°F. Line a baking sheet with parchment paper.

2. Cut the tofu into ½-inch slices, and then press them between paper towels to remove excess moisture. Cut each slice into smaller rectangles.
3. In a Ziploc® bag, combine 1 tablespoon of soy sauce, water, 2 tablespoons of garlic, rice vinegar, and 1 teaspoon of pepper. Add the tofu and turn it to coat. Let it marinate for 15 minutes.
4. Place the tofu on the prepared pan and bake for 15 minutes. Flip over and bake for 15 minutes more. Remove from the oven.
5. Place a large non-stick skillet over medium-high heat. Add the onion and cook until translucent, stirring frequently. Add the bell pepper and cook for 1 minute more.
6. Add the garlic and mushrooms, and cook for 2 minutes. Add a little water if the vegetables start to stick.
7. Stir in the kale and 2 tablespoons of water, and cover. Let cook for 1 minute, and then stir and add more water if needed. Cover and cook for another minute before adding asparagus, stirring until the asparagus is tender-crisp.
8. In a small bowl, stir together the remaining soy sauce, broth, sriracha, cornstarch, and pepper. Pour over the vegetables and cook until heated through.
9. To serve, plate the vegetables and place the tofu on top.

Nutrition: Calories: 176, Carbs: 33 g, Net Carbs: 27 g, Protein: 16 g, Fats: 4 g, Sugar: 12 g, Fiber: 6 g

65. Broccoli & Mushroom Salad

Preparation Time: 10 minutes
Cooking Time: 0 minutes
Servings: 2
Ingredients:

- 4 sun-dried tomatoes, cut in half
- 3 cups torn leaf lettuce
- 1 ½ cups broccoli florets
- 1 cup mushrooms, sliced
- 1/3 cup radishes, sliced
- 2 tbsp. boiling water
- 1 tbsp. balsamic vinegar
- 1 tsp. vegetable oil
- ¼ tsp. chicken bouillon granules
- ¼ tsp. parsley
- ¼ tsp. dry mustard
- 1/8 tsp. cayenne pepper

Directions:
1. Place the tomatoes in a small bowl and pour the boiling water over, just enough to cover. Let stand for 5 minutes, then drain. Chop the tomatoes and place them in a large bowl. Add the lettuce, broccoli, mushrooms, and radishes.
2. In a jar with a tight-fitting lid, add the remaining ingredients, and shake well. Pour over the salad and toss to coat. Serve.

Nutrition: Calories: 54, Carbs: 9 g, Net Carbs: 7 g, Protein: 3 g, Fats: 2 g, Sugar: 2 g, Fiber: 2 g

66. Homemade Vegetable Chili

Preparation Time: 10 minutes
Cooking Time: 30 minutes
Servings: 2
Ingredients:

- 2 tbsp. extra-virgin olive oil
- 1 onion, finely chopped
- 1 green bell pepper, deseeded and chopped
- 1 (14-oz.) can kidney beans, drained and rinsed
- 2 (14-oz.) cans crushed tomatoes
- 2 cups veggie crumbles
- 1 tsp. garlic powder
- 1 tbsp. chili powder
- ½ tsp. sea salt

Directions:

1. Heat the olive oil in a large skillet over medium-high heat until shimmering.
2. Add the onion and bell pepper and sauté for 5 minutes, stirring occasionally.
3. Fold in the beans, tomatoes, veggie crumbles, garlic powder, chili powder, and salt. Stir to incorporate and bring them to a simmer.
4. Reduce the heat and cook for an additional 5 minutes, stirring occasionally, or until the mixture is heated through.
5. Allow the mixture to cool for 5 minutes, and serve warm.

Nutrition: Calories: 282, Fats: 10.1 g, Protein: 16.7 g, Carbs: 38.2 g, Fiber: 12.9 g, Sugar: 7.2 g, Sodium: 1128 mg

67. Collard Greens with Tomato

Preparation Time: 10 minutes
Cooking Time: 30 minutes
Servings: 2
Ingredients:

- 1 cup low-sodium vegetable broth, divided
- ½ onion, thinly sliced
- 2 garlic cloves, thinly sliced
- 1 medium tomato, chopped
- 1 large bunch collard greens including stems, roughly chopped
- 1 tsp. ground cumin
- ½ tsp. freshly ground black pepper

Directions:

1. Add ½ cup of vegetable broth to a Dutch oven over medium heat and bring it to a simmer.
2. Stir in the onion and garlic and cook for about 4 minutes, or until tender.

3. Add the remaining broth, tomato, greens, cumin, and pepper. Stir gently to combine.
4. Reduce the heat to low and simmer uncovered for 15 minutes. Serve warm.

Nutrition: Calories: 68, Fats: 2.1 g, Protein: 4.8 g, Carbs: 13.8 g, Fiber: 7.1 g, Sugar: 2.0 g, Sodium: 67 mg

68. Okra

Preparation Time: 10 minutes
Cooking Time: 10 minutes
Servings: 2
Ingredients:

- 1 cup almond flour
- 8 oz. fresh okra
- 1/2 tsp. sea salt
- 1 cup reduced-fat milk
- 1 egg, pastured

Directions:

1. Crack the egg into a bowl, pour in the milk, and whisk until blended.
2. Cut the stem from each okra, and cut it into ½-inch pieces, add them into the egg, and stir until well coated.
3. Mix the flour and salt, and put this mixture into a large plastic bag.
4. Working on one okra piece at a time, drain the okra well by letting excess egg drip off. Add it to the flour mixture, seal the bag, and shake well until okra is well coated.
5. Place the coated okra on a grease air fryer basket, coat the remaining okra pieces in the same manner, and place them into the basket.
6. Switch on the air fryer, insert the fryer basket, spray the okra with oil, shut it with its lid, set the fryer at 390°F, and cook for 10 minutes, or until nicely golden and cooked, stirring the okra halfway through the frying.

Nutrition: Calories: 250, Carbs: 2 g, Fats: 11 g, Protein: 4 g, Fiber: 2 g

69. Harvest Salad

Preparation Time: 15–20 minutes
Cooking Time: 25 minutes
Servings: 2
Ingredients:

- 10 oz. kale, deboned and chopped
- 1 ½ cups blackberries
- ½ butternut squash, cubed
- ¼ cup goat cheese, crumbled
- Maple Mustard Salad Dressing (chapter 16)
- 1 cup raw pecans
- 1/3 cup raw pumpkin seeds
- ¼ cup dried cranberries
- 3 1/2 tbsp. olive oil
- 1 ½ tbsp. sugar free maple syrup
- 3/8 tsp. salt, divided
- Pepper, to taste
- Nonstick cooking spray

Directions:

1. Heat the oven to 400°F. Spray a baking sheet with cooking spray.
2. Spread the squash on the prepared pan, and add in 1 ½ tablespoons of oil, 1/8 teaspoon of salt, and pepper. Stir to coat the squash evenly. Bake for 20–25 minutes. Place the kale in a large bowl. Add 2 tablespoons of oil and ½ teaspoon of salt. Then massage it into the kale with your hands for 3–4 minutes. Spray a clean baking sheet with cooking spray. In a medium bowl, stir together the pecans, pumpkin seeds, and maple syrup until the nuts are coated. Pour the mixture onto the prepared pan and bake for 8–10 minutes (these can be baked at the same time as the squash).
3. To assemble the salad: place all of the ingredients in a large bowl. Pour dressing over and toss to coat. Serve.

Nutrition: Calories: 436, Carbs: 24 g, Net Carbs: 17 g, Protein: 9 g, Fats: 37 g, Sugar: 5 g, Fiber: 7 g

70. Spicy Potatoes

Preparation Time: 10 minutes
Cooking Time: 35 minutes
Servings: 2
Ingredients:

- 400 g potatoes
- 2 tbsp. spicy paprika
- 1 tbsp. olive oil
- Salt, to taste

Directions:

1. Wash the potatoes with a brush. Unpeeled, cut them vertically in a crescent shape, about 1 finger-thick. Place the potatoes in a bowl and cover with water. Let stand for about half an hour.
2. Preheat the air fryer. Set the timer to 5 minutes and the temperature to 200°C.
3. Drain the water from the potatoes and dry them with paper towels or a clean cloth. Put them back in the bowl and pour the oil, salt, and paprika over them. Mix well with your hands so that all of them are covered evenly with the spice mixture. Pour the spiced potatoes into the basket of the air fryer. Set the timer to 30 minutes and press the power button. Stir the potatoes in half the time.
4. Remove the potatoes from the air fryer, and transfer them onto a plate.

Nutrition: Calories: 153, Carbs: 2 g, Fats: 11 g, Protein: 4 g, Fiber: 0 g

71. Buffalo Cauliflower Wings

Preparation Time: 15 minutes
Cooking Time: 30 minutes
Servings: 2
Ingredients:

- 1 tbsp. almond flour
- 1 medium cauliflower head
- 1 ½ tsp. salt
- 4 tbsp. hot sauce
- 1 tbsp. olive oil

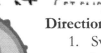

Directions:

1. Switch on the air fryer, insert the fryer basket, grease it with olive oil, shut it with its lid, set the fryer to 400°F, and preheat for 5 minutes.
2. Meanwhile, cut the cauliflower into bite-size florets, and set them aside.
3. Place the flour in a large bowl, and then whisk in the salt, oil, and hot sauce until combined. Add the cauliflower florets and toss until combined.
4. Open the fryer, add the cauliflower florets in it in a single layer, close with its lid, and cook for 15 minutes, or until nicely golden and crispy, shaking halfway through the frying.
5. When air fryer beeps, open its lid, transfer cauliflower florets onto a serving plate, and keep them warm.
6. Cook the remaining cauliflower florets in the same manner, and serve.

Nutrition: Calories: 48, Carbs: 2 g, Fats: 11 g, Protein: 4 g, Fiber: 0.3 g

72. Asian Noodle Salad

Preparation Time: 20 minutes
Cooking Time: 10 minutes
Servings: 2
Ingredients:

- 2 carrots, thinly sliced
- 2 radishes, thinly sliced
- 1 English cucumber, thinly sliced
- 1 mango, julienned
- 1 bell pepper, julienned
- 1 small serrano pepper, seeded and thinly sliced
- 1 bag Tofu Shirataki Fettuccini® noodles
- ¼ cup lime juice
- ¼ cup fresh basil, chopped
- ¼ cup fresh cilantro, chopped
- 2 tbsp. fresh mint, chopped
- 2 tbsp. rice vinegar
- 2 tbsp. sweet chili sauce

- 2 tbsp. roasted peanuts, finely chopped
- 1 tbsp. Splenda®
- ½ tsp. sesame oil

Directions:

1. Pickle the vegetables. In a large bowl, place the radish, cucumbers, and carrots. Add the vinegar, coconut sugar, and lime juice. Stir to coat the vegetables. Cover and chill for 15–20 minutes.
2. Prep the noodles by removing the noodles from the package and rinsing them under cold water. Cut them into smaller pieces. Pat them dry with paper towels.
3. To assemble the salad. Remove the vegetables from the marinade, reserving the marinade, and place the vegetables in a large mixing bowl. Add the noodles, mango, bell pepper, chili, and herbs.
4. In a small bowl, combine 2 tablespoons of marinade with the chili sauce and sesame oil. Pour over the salad and toss to coat. Top with the peanuts, and serve.

Nutrition: Calories: 158, Carbs: 30 g, Net Carbs: 24 g, Protein: 4 g, Fats: 4 g, Sugar: 19 g, Fiber: 6 g

73. Cheesy Mushroom and Pesto Flatbreads

Preparation Time: 10 minutes
Cooking Time: 13–17 minutes
Servings: 2
Ingredients:

- 1 tsp. extra-virgin olive oil
- ½ red onion, sliced
- ½ cup mushrooms, sliced
- Salt and freshly ground black pepper, to taste
- ¼ cup store-bought pesto sauce
- 2 whole wheat flatbreads
- ¼ cup mozzarella cheese, shredded

Directions:

1. Preheat the oven to 350°F (180°C).

2. Heat the olive oil in a small skillet over medium heat. Add the onion slices and mushrooms to the skillet, and sauté for 3 to 5 minutes, stirring occasionally, or until they start to soften. Season with salt and pepper.
3. Meanwhile, spoon 2 tablespoons of pesto sauce onto each flatbread and spread it all over. Divide the mushroom mixture evenly between 2 flatbreads, then scatter each top with 2 tablespoons of shredded cheese.
4. Transfer the flatbreads to a baking sheet and bake until the cheese melts and bubbles, about 10 to 12 minutes.
5. Let the flatbreads cool for 5 minutes, and serve warm.

Nutrition: Calories: 346, Fats: 22.8 g, Protein: 14.2 g, Carbs: 27.6 g, Fiber: 7.3 g, Sugar: 4.0 g, Sodium: 790 mg

74. Honey Roasted Carrots

Preparation Time: 15 minutes
Cooking Time: 12 minutes
Servings: 2–4
Ingredients:

- 454 g rainbow carrots, peeled and washed
- 15 ml olive oil
- 30 ml honey
- 2 fresh thyme sprigs
- Salt and pepper, to taste

Directions:

1. Wash the carrots and dry them with a paper towel. Leave aside.
2. Preheat the air fryer to 180°C for a few minutes.
3. Place the carrots in a bowl with olive oil, honey, thyme, salt, and pepper. Place the carrots in the air fryer at 180°C for 12 minutes. Be sure to shake the baskets in the middle of the cooking.

Nutrition: Calories: 123, Fats: 42 g, Carbs: 9 g, Protein: 1 g

75. Mushrooms Stuffed with Tomato

Preparation Time: 35 minutes
Cooking Time: 10 minutes
Servings: 2
Ingredients:

- 4 large tomatoes
- Dash salt
- 1 pound sliced fresh mushrooms
- 1/4 cup butter
- 2 tablespoons all-purpose flour
- 1 cup half-and-half cream
- 2 tablespoons soft bread crumbs
- 3/4 cup minced fresh parsley
- 2/3 cup shredded cheddar cheese, divided

Directions:

1. Cut tomatoes in half; scoop out and discard pulp, leaving a thin shell. Sprinkle lightly with salt; invert on paper towels to drain for 15 minutes.
2. In a large skillet, saute mushrooms in butter until most of the liquid has evaporated, about 5 minutes. Sprinkle with flour; stir in cream. Bring to a boil; cook and stir until thickened, about 2 minutes. Remove from the heat. Stir in the bread crumbs, parsley and 1/3 cup of cheese. Spoon into tomato cups; sprinkle with remaining cheese.
3. Place in a greased 13x9-in. baking dish. Bake, uncovered, at 400° until cheese is melted, about 10 minutes.

Nutrition: 165 calories, 12g fat 40mg cholesterol, 145mg sodium, 9g carbohydrate

76. Sweet Potato with Salt and Pepper

Preparation Time: 3 minutes
Cooking Time: 30 minutes
Servings: 2
Ingredients:

- 1 large sweet potato

 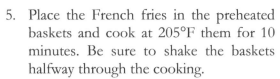

- 1/4 cup Extra-virgin olive oil, as needed
- Salt, to taste
- Ground pepper, to taste

Directions:

1. Peel the sweet potato and cut it into thin strips; if you have a mandolin, it will be easier for you.
2. Wash well and add salt.
3. Add a little oil to impregnate the sweet potato strips, and then place them in the air fryer basket.
4. Select 180ºC and 30 minutes, or so. From time to time, shake the basket so that the sweet potato moves.
5. Transfer to a tray or plate and sprinkle with fine salt and ground pepper.

Nutrition: Calories: 107, Fats: 0.6 g, Carbs: 24.19 g, Protein: 1.61 g, Sugar: 5.95 g, Cholesterol: 0 mg

77. **Sweet Potato Chips**

Preparation Time: 10 minutes
Cooking Time: 10 minutes
Servings: 2
Ingredients:

- 2 large sweet potatoes, cut into 2-mm-thick strips
- 15 ml oil
- 10 g salt
- 2 g black pepper
- 2 g paprika
- 2 g garlic powder
- 2 g onion powder

Directions:

1. Cut the sweet potatoes into strips 25 mm thick.
2. Preheat the air fryer for a few minutes.
3. Add the cut sweet potatoes to a large bowl, and mix them with the oil until the potatoes are all evenly coated.
4. Sprinkle with salt, black pepper, paprika, garlic powder, and onion powder. Mix well.

5. Place the French fries in the preheated baskets and cook at 205°F them for 10 minutes. Be sure to shake the baskets halfway through the cooking.

Nutrition: Calories: 123, Carbs: 2 g, Fats: 11 g, Protein: 4 g, Fiber: 0 g

78. **Cauliflower Rice**

Preparation Time: 10 minutes
Cooking Time: 27 minutes
Servings: 2
Ingredients:

- 1 cup diced carrot
- 6 oz. extra-firm tofu, drained
- 1/2 cup diced white onion
- 2 tbsp. soy sauce
- 1 tsp. turmeric

For the Cauliflower:

- 1/2 cup chopped broccoli
- 3 cups cauliflower rice
- 1 tbsp. minced garlic
- 1/2 cup frozen peas
- 1 tbsp. minced ginger
- 2 tbsp. soy sauce
- 1 tbsp. apple cider vinegar
- 1 1/2 tsp. toasted sesame oil

Directions:

1. Switch on the air fryer, insert the fryer pan, grease it with olive oil, shut with its lid, set the fryer at 370°F, and preheat for 5 minutes.
2. Meanwhile, place the tofu in a bowl and crumble it. Add the remaining ingredients and stir until mixed.
3. Open the fryer, add the tofu mixture, spray with oil, close it with its lid, and cook for 10 minutes, or until nicely golden and crispy, stirring halfway through the frying.
4. Meanwhile, place all the ingredients for the cauliflower in a bowl, and toss until mixed.
5. When the air fryer beeps, open its lid, add cauliflower mixture, shake the pan

gently to mix, and continue cooking for 12 minutes, shaking halfway through the frying.

Nutrition: Calories: 258, Carbs: 2 g, Fats: 11 g, Protein: 4 g, Fiber: 7 g

79. Pizza-Stuffed Portobello Mushrooms

Preparation Time: 20 minutes
Cooking Time: 10 minutes
Servings: 2
Ingredients:

- 8 Portobello mushrooms, stems removed
- 1 cup mozzarella cheese, grated
- 1 cup cherry tomatoes, sliced
- ½ cup crushed tomatoes
- ½ cup fresh basil, chopped
- 2 tbsp. balsamic vinegar
- 1 tbsp. olive oil
- 1 tbsp. oregano
- 1 tbsp. red pepper flakes
- ½ tbsp. garlic powder
- ¼ tsp. pepper
- A pinch salt
- 1 tbsp. Parsley, as needed

Directions:

1. Heat the oven to broil. Line a baking sheet with foil.
2. Place the mushrooms stem-side down on the foil, and drizzle with oil. Sprinkle with garlic powder, salt and pepper. Broil for 5 minutes.
3. Flip the mushrooms over, and top with the crushed tomatoes, oregano, parsley, pepper flakes, cheese, and sliced tomatoes. Broil for another 5 minutes.
4. Top with the basil and drizzle with the balsamic vinegar. Serve.

Nutrition: Calories: 113, Carbs: 11 g, Net Carbs: 7 g, Protein: 9 g, Fats: 5 g, Sugar: 3 g, Fiber: 4 g

80. Cajun-Style French Fries

Preparation Time: 10 minutes
Cooking Time: 28 minutes
Servings: 2
Ingredients:

- 2 reddish potatoes, peeled, and cut into strips of 76x25 mm
- 1 l cold water
- 15 ml oil
- 7 g Cajun seasoning
- 1 g cayenne pepper
- Tomato sauce or ranch sauce, for serving
- Salt and pepper, to taste

Directions:

1. Cut the potatoes into 76x25-mm strips and soak them in water for 15 minutes.
2. Drain the potatoes, rinse them with cold water, and pat them dry with paper towels.
3. Preheat the air fryer to 195°F.
4. Add the oil and spices to the potatoes until they are completely covered.
5. Add the potatoes to the preheated air fryer and set the timer to 28 minutes.
6. Be sure to shake the baskets in the middle of the cooking.
7. Remove the baskets from the air fryer when you have finished cooking, and season the fries with salt and pepper.

Nutrition: Calories: 158, Carbs: 2 g, Fats: 11 g, Protein: 4 g, Fiber: 0 g

81. Avocado and Citrus Shrimp Salad

Preparation Time: 10 minutes
Cooking Time: 5 minutes
Servings: 2
Ingredients:

- 1 lb. medium shrimp, peeled and deveined, tails removed
- 8 cup salad greens
- 1 lemon

- 1 avocado, diced
- 1 shallot, finely diced
- ½ cup almonds, sliced and toasted
- 1 tbsp. olive oil
- Salt and freshly ground black pepper, to taste

Directions:

1. Cut the lemon in half and squeeze the juice from both halves into a small bowl, then set it aside. Slice the lemon into thin wedges.
2. Heat the oil in a skillet over medium heat. Add the lemon wedges and let cook for about 1 minute to infuse the oil with the lemons.
3. Add the shrimp and cook, stirring frequently, until the shrimp turns pink. Discard the lemon wedges and let cool.
4. Place the salad greens in a large bowl. Add the shrimp, with the juices from the pan, and toss to coat. Add the remaining ingredients and toss to combine. Serve.

Nutrition: Calories: 425, Carbs: 17 g, Net Carbs 8 g, Protein: 35 g, Fats: 26 g, Sugar: 2 g, Fiber: 9

82. **Florentine Pizza**

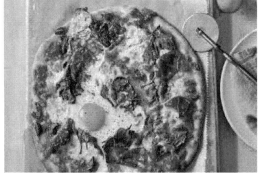

Preparation Time: 45 minutes
Cooking Time: 20 minutes
Servings: 2
Ingredients:

- 1 3/4 cups grated mozzarella cheese
- ½ cup frozen spinach, thawed
- 1 egg
- 2 tbsp. reduced-fat Parmesan cheese, grated

- 2 tbsp. soft cream cheese
- ¾ cup almond flour
- ¼ cup light Alfredo sauce
- ½ tsp. Italian seasoning
- ¼ tsp. red pepper flakes
- A pinch salt

Directions:

1. Heat the oven to 400°F.
2. Squeeze all the excess water out of the spinach.
3. In a glass bowl, combine the mozzarella and almond flour. Stir in the cream cheese. Microwave for 1 minute on high, then stir. If the mixture is not melted, microwave for another 30 seconds.
4. Stir in the egg, seasoning, and salt. Mix well. Place the dough on a piece of parchment paper and press it into a 10-inch circle.
5. Place it directly on the oven rack and bake for 8–10 minutes, or until lightly browned.
6. Remove the crust and spread with the Alfredo sauce, then add the spinach, Parmesan, and red pepper flakes evenly over the top. Bake for another 8–10 minutes. Slice and serve.

Nutrition: Calories: 441, Carbs: 14 g, Net Carbs: 9 g, Protein: 24 g, Fats: 35 g, Sugar: 4 g, Fiber: 5 g

83. **Vegetables in Air Fryer**

Preparation Time: 10–15 minutes
Cooking Time: 30 minutes
Servings: 2
Ingredients:

- 2 potatoes
- 1 zucchini
- 1 onion
- 1 red pepper
- 1 green pepper
- Salt, to taste
- Ground pepper, to taste
- Extra-virgin olive oil, as needed

Directions:

1. Cut the potatoes into slices.
2. Cut the onion into rings.
3. Cut the zucchini into slices.
4. Cut the peppers into strips.
5. Put all the ingredients in a bowl and add a little of salt, ground pepper, and some extra-virgin olive oil. Mix well.
6. Transfer the mixture to the basket of the air fryer.
7. Select 160°C and 30 minutes.
8. Check that the vegetables are cooked to your liking.

Nutrition: Calories: 135, Carbs: 2 g, Fats: 11 g, Protein: 4 g, Fiber: 5 g

84. Fried Peppers with Sriracha Mayo

Preparation Time: 20 minutes
Cooking Time: 12–14 minutes
Servings: 2
Ingredients:

- 4 bell peppers, seeded and sliced into 1-inch pieces
- 1 onion, sliced into 1-inch pieces
- 1 tbsp. olive oil
- 1/2 tsp. dried rosemary
- 1/2 tsp. dried basil
- Kosher salt, to taste
- 1/4 tsp. ground black pepper
- 1/3 cup mayonnaise
- 1/3 tsp. sriracha

Directions:

1. Toss the bell peppers and onions with olive oil, rosemary, basil, salt, and black pepper.
2. Place the peppers and onions on an even layer in the cooking basket. Cook at 400°F for 12 to 14 minutes.
3. Meanwhile, make the sauce by whisking the mayonnaise and sriracha. Serve immediately.

Nutrition: Calories: 346, Fats: 34.1 g, Carbs: 9.5 g, Protein: 2.3 g, Sugars: 4.9 g

85. Classic Fried Pickles

Preparation Time: 20 minutes
Cooking Time: 10 minutes
Servings: 2
Ingredients:

- 1 egg, whisked
- 2 tbsp. buttermilk
- 1/2 cup fresh breadcrumbs
- 1/4 cup Romano cheese, grated
- 1/2 tsp. onion powder
- 1/2 tsp. garlic powder
- 1 ½ cups dill pickle chips, pressed dry with kitchen towels

For the Mayo Sauce:

- 1/4 cup mayonnaise
- 1/2 tbsp. mustard
- 1/2 tsp. molasses
- 1 tbsp. ketchup
- 1/4 tsp. ground black pepper

Directions:

1. In a narrow bowl, whisk the egg with the buttermilk.
2. In another bowl, mix the breadcrumbs, cheese, onion powder, and garlic powder. Dredge the pickle chips in the egg mixture, and then in the breadcrumb-cheese mixture.
3. Cook in the preheated air fryer at 400°F for 5 minutes; shake the basket and cook for 5 minutes more.
4. Meanwhile, mix all the sauce ingredients until well combined. Serve the fried pickles with the mayo sauce for dipping.

Nutrition: Calories: 342, Fats: 28.5 g, Carbs: 12.5 g, Protein: 9.1 g, Sugars: 4.9 g

86. Fried Green Beans with Pecorino Romano

Preparation Time: 15 minutes
Cooking Time: 7 minutes
Servings: 2
Ingredients:

- 2 tbsp. buttermilk

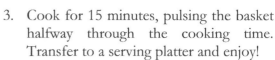

- 1 egg
- 4 tbsp. cornmeal
- 4 tbsp. tortilla chips, crushed
- 4 tbsp. Pecorino Romano cheese, finely grated
- Coarse salt and crushed black pepper, to taste
- 1 tsp. smoked paprika
- 12 oz. green beans, trimmed

Directions:

1. In a small bowl, whisk together the buttermilk and egg.
2. In a separate bowl, combine the cornmeal, tortilla chips, Pecorino Romano cheese, salt, black pepper, and paprika.
3. Dip the green beans into the egg mixture, and then into the cornmeal-cheese mixture. Place the green beans in the lightly greased cooking basket.
4. Cook in the preheated air fryer at 390°F for 4 minutes. Shake the basket and cook for a further 3 minutes.
5. Taste, adjust the seasonings and serve with the dipping sauce if desired. Bon appétit!

Nutrition: Calories: 340, Fats: 9.7 g, Carbs: 50.9 g, Protein: 12.8 g, Sugars: 4.7 g

87. Spicy Glazed Carrots

Preparation Time: 20 minutes
Cooking Time: 15 minutes
Servings: 2
Ingredients:

- 1 lb. carrots, cut into matchsticks
- 2 tbsp. peanut oil
- 1 tbsp. agave syrup
- 1 jalapeño, seeded and minced
- 1/4 tsp. dill - 1/2 tsp. basil
- Salt and white pepper, to taste

Directions:

1. Start by heating your air fryer to 380°F.
2. Toss all the ingredients together and place them in the air fryer basket.

3. Cook for 15 minutes, pulsing the basket halfway through the cooking time. Transfer to a serving platter and enjoy!

Nutrition: Calories: 162, Fats: 9.3 g, Carbs: 20.1 g, Protein: 1.4 g, Sugars: 12.8 g

88. Corn on the Cob with Herb Butter

Preparation Time: 15 minutes
Cooking Time: 8 minutes
Servings: 2
Ingredients:

- 2 fresh corn ears, shucked and cut into halves
- 2 tbsp. butter, at room temperature
- 1 tsp. granulated garlic
- 1/2 tsp. fresh ginger, grated
- Sea salt and pepper, to taste
- 1 tbsp. fresh rosemary, chopped
- 1 tbsp. fresh basil, chopped
- Cooking spray, as needed

Directions:

1. Spritz the corn with cooking spray. Cook at 395°F for 6 minutes, turning them over halfway through the cooking time.
2. Meanwhile, mix the butter with granulated garlic, ginger, salt, black pepper, rosemary, and basil.
3. Spread the butter mixture all over the corn on the cob. Cook in the preheated air fryer for an additional 2 minutes. Bon appétit!

Nutrition: Calories: 239, Fats: 13.3 g, Carbs: 30.2 g, Protein: 5.4 g, Sugars: 5.8 g

89. Rainbow Vegetable Fritters

Preparation Time: 20 minutes
Cooking Time: 12 minutes
Servings: 2
Ingredients:

- 1 zucchini, grated and squeezed

- 1 cup corn kernels
- 1/2 cup canned green peas
- 4 tbsp. all-purpose flour
- 2 tbsp. fresh shallots, minced
- 1 tsp. fresh garlic, minced
- 1 tbsp. peanut oil
- Sea salt and pepper, to taste
- 1 tsp. cayenne pepper
- Cooking spray, as needed

Directions:
1. In a mixing bowl, thoroughly combine all the ingredients until everything is well incorporated.
2. Shape the mixture into patties. Spritz the Air Fryer carrier with cooking spray.
3. Cook in the preheated air fryer at 365°F for 6 minutes. Fit them over and cook for a further 6 minutes
4. Serve immediately and enjoy!

Nutrition: Calories: 215, Fats: 8.4 g, Carbs: 31.6 g, Protein: 6 g, Sugars: 4.1 g

90. Mediterranean Vegetable Skewers

Preparation Time: 30 minutes
Cooking Time: 13 minutes
Servings: 2
Ingredients:

- 2 medium-sized zucchinis, cut into 1-inch pieces
- 2 red bell peppers, cut into 1-inch pieces
- 1 green bell pepper, cut into 1-inch pieces
- 1 red onion, cut into 1-inch pieces
- 2 tbsp. olive oil - Sea salt, to taste
- 1/2 tsp. black pepper, preferably freshly cracked - 1/2 tsp. red pepper flakes
- Water, as needed

Directions:
1. Soak the wooden skewers in water for 15 minutes.

2. Thread the vegetables on skewers, drizzle olive oil all over the vegetable skewers, and sprinkle with spices.
3. Cook in the preheated air fryer at 400°F for 13 minutes. Serve warm and enjoy!

Nutrition: Calories: 138, Fats: 10.2 g, Carbs: 10.2 g, Protein: 2.2 g, Sugars: 6.6 g

91. Roasted Veggies with Yogurt-Tahini Sauce

Preparation Time: 20 minutes
Cooking Time: 10 minutes
Servings: 2
Ingredients:

- 1 lb. Brussels sprouts
- 1 lb. button mushrooms
- 2 tbsp. olive oil - 1/2 tsp. white pepper
- 1/2 tsp. dried dill weed
- 1/2 tsp. cayenne pepper
- 1/2 tsp. celery seeds
- 1/2 tsp. mustard seeds
- Salt, to taste

For the Yogurt Tahini Sauce:

- 1 cup plain yogurt
- 2 tbsp. tahini paste
- 1 tbsp. lemon juice
- 1 tbsp. extra-virgin olive oil
- 1/2 tsp. Aleppo pepper, minced

Directions:
1. Toss the Brussels sprouts and mushrooms with olive oil and spices. Preheat your air fryer to 380°F.
2. Add the Brussels sprouts to the cooking basket and cook for 10 minutes.
3. Add the mushrooms, turn the temperature to 390°F and cook for 6 minutes more.
4. While the vegetables are cooking, make the sauce by whisking all the ingredients. Serve the warm vegetables with the sauce on the side. Bon appétit!

Nutrition: Calories: 254, Fats: 17.2 g, Carbs: 19.6 g, Protein: 11.1 g, Sugars: 8.1 g

92. Swiss Cheese and Vegetable Casserole

Preparation Time: 50 minutes
Cooking Time: 48 minutes
Servings: 2
Ingredients:

- 1 lb. potatoes, peeled and sliced into 1/4-inch pieces - 2 tbsp. olive oil
- 1/2 tsp. red pepper flakes, crushed
- 1/2 tsp. freshly ground black pepper
- Salt, to taste -3 bell peppers, thinly sliced
- 1 serrano pepper, thinly sliced
- 2 medium-sized tomatoes, sliced
- 1 leek, thinly sliced
- 2 garlic cloves, minced
- 1 cup Swiss cheese, shredded

Directions:

1. Start by warming your air fryer to 350°F. Spritz a casserole dish with cooking oil.
2. Place the potatoes in the casserole dish in an even layer, and drizzle 1 tablespoon of olive oil over the top. Then add the red pepper, black pepper, and salt. Add 2 bell peppers and 1/2 of the leeks. Add the tomatoes and the remaining 1 tablespoon of olive oil.
3. Add the remaining peppers, leeks, and minced garlic. Top with the cheese.
4. Cover the casserole with foil and bake for 32 minutes. Remove the foil, increase the temperature to 400°F, and bake for an additional 16 minutes. Bon appétit!

Nutrition: Calories: 328, Fats: 16.5 g, Carbs: 33.1 g, Protein: 13.1 g, Sugars: 7.6 g

93. American-Style Brussels Sprout Salad

Preparation Time: 35 minutes
Cooking Time: 15 minutes
Servings: 2
Ingredients:

- 1 lb. Brussels sprouts
- 1 apple, cored and diced
- 1/2 cup mozzarella cheese, crumbled
- 1/2 cup pomegranate seeds
- 1 small-sized red onion, chopped
- 4 eggs, hardboiled and sliced

For the Dressing:

- 1/4 cup olive oil
- 2 tbsp. champagne vinegar
- 1 tsp. Dijon mustard
- 1 tsp. honey
- Sea salt and ground black pepper, to taste

Directions:

1. Start by preheating your air fryer to 380°F.
2. Add the Brussels sprouts to the cooking basket. Spritz with cooking spray and cook for 15 minutes. Let it cool to room temperature, about 15 minutes.
3. Toss the Brussels sprouts with apple, cheese, pomegranate seeds, and red onion.
4. Mix all ingredients for the dressing and toss to combine well. Serve topped with hard-boiled eggs. Bon appétit!

Nutrition: Calories: 319, Fats: 18.5 g, Carbs: 27 g, Protein: 14.7 g, Sugars: 14.6 g

94. The Best Cauliflower Tater Tots

Preparation Time: 25 minutes
Cooking Time: 20 minutes
Servings: 2
Ingredients:

- 1 lb. cauliflower florets
- 2 eggs
- 1 tbsp. olive oil
- 2 tbsp. scallions, chopped
- 1 garlic clove, minced
- 1 cup Colby cheese, shredded
- 1/2 cup breadcrumbs
- Sea salt and ground black pepper, to taste

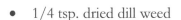

- 1/4 tsp. dried dill weed
- 1 tsp. paprika
- Dipping sauce, for serving
- Cooking spray, as needed

Directions:

1. Blanch the cauliflower in salted boiling water about 3 to 4 minutes, or until al dente. Drain well and pulse in a food processor.
2. Add the remaining ingredients, and mix to combine well. Shape the cauliflower mixture into bite-sized tots.
3. Spritz the air fryer basket with cooking spray.
4. Cook in the preheated air fryer at 375°F for 16 minutes, shaking halfway through the cooking time. Serve with your favorite sauce for dipping. Bon appétit!

Nutrition: Calories: 267, Fats: 19.2 g, Carbs: 9.6 g, Protein: 14.9 g, Sugars: 2.9 g

95. Three-Cheese-Stuffed Mushrooms

Preparation Time: 15 minutes
Cooking Time: 7 minutes
Servings: 2
Ingredients:

- 9 large button mushrooms, stems removed
- 1 tbsp. olive oil
- Salt and ground black pepper, to taste
- 1/2 tsp. dried rosemary
- 6 tbsp. Swiss cheese, shredded
- 6 tbsp. Romano cheese, shredded
- 6 tbsp. cream cheese
- 1 tsp. soy sauce
- 1 tsp. garlic, minced
- 3 tbsp. green onion, minced

Directions:

1. Brush the mushroom caps with olive oil, and sprinkle with salt, pepper, and rosemary.

2. In a mixing bowl, thoroughly combine the remaining ingredients, combine them well, and divide the filling mixture among the mushroom caps.
3. Cook in the preheated air fryer at 390°F for 7 minutes.
4. Let the mushrooms cool slightly before serving. Bon appétit!

Nutrition: Calories: 345, Fats: 28 g, Carbs: 11.2 g, Protein: 14.4 g, Sugars: 8.1 g

96. Sweet Corn Fritters with Avocado

Preparation Time: 20 minutes
Cooking Time: 15 minutes
Servings: 2
Ingredients:

- 2 cups sweet corn kernels
- 1 small-sized onion, chopped
- 1 garlic clove, minced
- 2 eggs, whisked
- 1 tsp. baking powder
- 2 tbsp. fresh cilantro, chopped
- Sea salt and ground black pepper, to taste
- 1 avocado, peeled, pitted, and diced
- 2 tbsp. sweet chili sauce

Directions:

1. In a mixing bowl, thoroughly combine the corn, onion, garlic, eggs, baking powder, cilantro, salt, and black pepper.
2. Shape the corn mixture into 6 patties and transfer them to the lightly greased air fryer basket.
3. Cook in the preheated air fryer at 370°F for 8 minutes, turn them over and cook for 7 minutes longer.
4. Serve the cakes with avocado and chili sauce.

Nutrition: Calories: 383, Fats: 21.3 g, Carbs: 42.8 g, Protein: 12.7 g, Sugars: 9.2 g

97. Greek-Style Vegetable Bake

Preparation Time: 35 minutes
Cooking Time: 20 minutes
Servings: 2
Ingredients:

- 1 eggplant, peeled and sliced
- 2 bell peppers, seeded and sliced
- 1 red onion, sliced
- 1 tsp. fresh garlic, minced
- 4 tbsp. olive oil
- 1 tsp. mustard
- 1 tsp. dried oregano
- 1 tsp. smoked paprika
- Salt and ground black pepper, to taste
- 1 tomato, sliced
- 6 oz. halloumi cheese, sliced lengthways

Directions:

1. Start by preheating your air fryer to 370°F. Spritz a baking pan with nonstick cooking spray.
2. Place the eggplant, peppers, onion, and garlic on the baking pan's bottom. Add the olive oil, mustard, and spices. Transfer to the cooking basket and cook for 14 minutes.
3. Top with the tomatoes and cheese, increase the temperature to 390°F and cook for 5 minutes more, or until bubbling. Let it sit on a cooling rack for 10 minutes before serving.
4. Bon appétit!

Nutrition: Calories: 296, Fats: 22.9 g, Carbs: 16.1 g, Protein: 9.3 g, Sugars: 9.9 g

98. Japanese Tempura Bowl

Preparation Time: 20 minutes
Cooking Time: 10 minutes
Servings: 2
Ingredients:

- 1 cup all-purpose flour
- Kosher salt and ground black pepper, to taste
- 1/2 tsp. paprika
- 2 eggs
- 3 tbsp. soda water
- 1 cup panko crumbs
- 2 tbsp. olive oil
- 1 cup green beans
- 1 onion, cut into rings
- 1 zucchini, cut into slices
- 2 tbsp. soy sauce
- 1 tbsp. mirin
- 1 tsp. dashi granules

Directions:

1. In a shallow bowl, mix the flour, salt, black pepper, and paprika. In a separate bowl, whisk the eggs and soda water. In a third shallow bowl, combine the panko crumbs with olive oil.
2. Dip the vegetables in the flour mixture, then in the egg mixture, and lastly, roll over the panko mixture to coat evenly.
3. Cook in the preheated air fryer at 400°F for 10 minutes, shaking the basket halfway through the cooking time. Work in batches until the vegetables are crispy and golden brown.
4. Then, make the sauce by whisking the soy sauce, mirin, and dashi granules. Bon appétit!

Nutrition: Calories: 446, Fats: 14.7 g, Carbs: 63.5 g, Protein: 14.6 g, Sugars: 3.8 g

99. Balsamic Root Vegetables

Preparation Time: 25 minutes
Cooking Time: 17 minutes
Servings: 2
Ingredients:

- 2 potatoes, cut into 1 1/2-inch pieces
- 2 carrots, cut into 1 1/2-inch pieces
- 2 parsnips, cut into 1 1/2-inch pieces
- 1 onion, cut into 1 1/2-inch pieces
- Pink Himalayan salt and ground black pepper, to taste
- 1/4 tsp. smoked paprika

- 1 tsp. garlic powder
- 1/2 tsp. dried thyme
- 1/2 tsp. dried marjoram
- 2 tbsp. olive oil
- 2 tbsp. balsamic vinegar
- Fresh herbs, for serving (optional)

Directions:

1. Toss all the ingredients in a large mixing dish.
2. Roast them in the preheated air fryer at 400°F for 10 minutes. Shake the basket and cook for 7 minutes more.
3. Serve with some extra fresh herbs if desired. Bon appétit!

Nutrition: Calories: 405, Fats: 9.7 g, Carbs: 74.7 g, Protein: 7.7 g, Sugars: 15.2 g

100. Winter Vegetable Braise

Preparation Time: 25 minutes
Cooking Time: 20 minutes
Servings: 2
Ingredients:

- 4 potatoes, peeled and cut into 1-inch pieces
- 1 celery root, peeled and cut into 1-inch pieces
- 1 cup winter squash
- 2 tbsp. unsalted butter, melted
- 1/2 cup chicken broth
- 1/4 cup tomato sauce
- 1 tsp. parsley
- 1 tsp. rosemary
- 1 tsp. thyme
- Lemon juice, for serving

Directions:

1. Start by preheating your air fryer to 370°F. Add all ingredients to a lightly greased casserole dish. Stir to combine well.
2. Bake in the preheated air fryer for 10 minutes. Gently stir the vegetables with a large spoon and increase the temperature to 400°F, then cook for 10 minutes more.
3. Serve in individual bowls with a few drizzles of lemon juice. Bon appétit!

Nutrition: Calories: 358, Fats: 12.3 g, Carbs: 55.7 g, Protein: 7.7 g, Sugars: 7.4 g

101. Family Vegetable Gratin

Preparation Time: 35 minutes
Cooking Time: 30 minutes
Servings: 2
Ingredients:

- 1 lb. Chinese cabbage, roughly chopped
- 2 bell peppers, seeded and sliced
- 1 jalapeño pepper, seeded and sliced
- 1 onion, thickly sliced
- 2 garlic cloves, sliced
- 1/2 stick butter
- 4 tbsp. all-purpose flour
- 1 cup milk
- 1 cup cream cheese
- Sea salt and freshly ground black pepper, to taste
- 1/2 tsp. cayenne pepper
- 1 cup Monterey Jack cheese, shredded
- Salted water, as needed

Directions:

1. Heat a pan of salted water and bring it to a boil. Boil the Chinese cabbage for 2 to 3 minutes. Transfer the Chinese cabbage to cold water to stop the cooking process.
2. Place the Chinese cabbage in a lightly greased casserole dish. Add the peppers, onion, and garlic.
3. Next, melt the butter in a saucepan over moderate heat. Gradually add the flour and cook for 2 minutes to form a paste.
4. Slowly pour in the milk, stirring continuously until a thick sauce form. Add the cream cheese.
5. Season with salt, black pepper, and cayenne pepper. Add the mixture to the casserole dish.

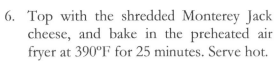

6. Top with the shredded Monterey Jack cheese, and bake in the preheated air fryer at 390°F for 25 minutes. Serve hot.

Nutrition: Calories: 373, Fats: 26.1 g, Carbs: 17.7 g, Protein: 18.7 g, Sugars: 7.7 g

102. Sweet and Sour Mixed Veggies

Preparation Time: 25 minutes
Cooking Time: 22 minutes
Servings: 2
Ingredients:

- ½ lb. sterling asparagus, cut into 1 1/2-inch pieces
- ½ lb. broccoli, cut into 1 1/2-inch pieces
- ½ lb. carrots, cut into 1 1/2-inch pieces
- 2 tbsp. peanut oil
- Salt and white pepper, to taste
- 1/2 cup water
- 4 tbsp. raisins
- 2 tbsp. honey
- 2 tbsp. apple cider vinegar

Directions:

1. Place the vegetables in a single layer in a lightly greased cooking basket. Drizzle the peanut oil over the vegetables.
2. Sprinkle with salt and white pepper.
3. Cook at 380°F for 15 minutes, shaking the basket halfway through the cooking time.
4. Add 1/2 cup of water to a saucepan, bring to a rapid boil, and add the raisins, honey, and vinegar. Cook for 5 to 7 minutes, or until the sauce has reduced by half.
5. Spoon the sauce over the warm vegetables and serve immediately. Bon appétit!

Nutrition: Calories: 153, Fats: 7.1 g, Carbs: 21.6 g, Protein: 3.6 g, Sugars: 14.2 g

103. Carrot and Oat Balls

Preparation Time: 25 minutes
Cooking Time: 15 minutes
Servings: 2
Ingredients:

- 4 carrots, grated
- 1 cup rolled oats, ground
- 1 tbsp. butter, at room temperature
- 1 tbsp. chia seeds
- 1/2 cup scallions, chopped
- 2 cloves garlic, minced
- 2 tbsp. tomato ketchup
- 1 tsp. cayenne pepper
- 1/2 tsp. sea salt
- 1/4 tsp. ground black pepper
- 1/2 tsp. ancho chili powder
- 1/4 cup fresh bread crumbs

Directions:

1. Start by preheating your air fryer to 380°F.
2. In a bowl, mix all the ingredients until everything is well incorporated. Shape the batter into bite-sized balls.
3. Cook the balls for 15 minutes, shaking the basket halfway through the cooking time. Bon appétit!

Nutrition: Calories: 215, Fats: 4.7 g, Carbs: 37.2 g, Protein: 7.5 g, Sugars: 5.6 g

104. Spinach Quiche

Preparation Time: 10 minutes
Cooking Time: 22 minutes
Servings: 2
Ingredients:

- 2 eggs
- 1 cup frozen chopped spinach, softened and drained
- 1 heavy cream
- 1 tbsp. honey mustard
- ½ cup grated Swiss or Havarti cheese
- ½ tsp. dried thyme
- A pinch salt
- Freshly ground black pepper, to taste

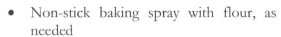

- Non-stick baking spray with flour, as needed

Directions:

1. Beat the eggs until blended in a medium bowl. Mix in the spinach, cream, honey mustard, cheese, thyme, salt, and pepper.
2. Pick a baking pan with non-stick spray and put the egg mixture into the pan.
3. Cook for 18 to 22 minutes, or until the egg mixture is puffed, light golden brown, and set.
4. Leave it to cool for 5 minutes, then chop into wedges.

Nutrition: Calories: 203, Fats: 15 g, Carbs: 6 g, Fiber: 0 g, Protein: 11 g

105. Yellow Squash Fritters

Preparation Time: 15 minutes
Cooking Time: 7–9 minutes
Servings: 2
Ingredients:

- 1 (3-oz.) package cream cheese, softened
- 1 egg, beaten
- ½ tsp. dried oregano
- A pinch salt
- Freshly ground black pepper, to taste
- 1 medium yellow summer squash, grated
- 1 carrot, grated
- 1 cup breadcrumbs
- 1 tbsp. olive oil

Directions:

1. Mix the cream cheese, egg, oregano, salt, and pepper in a medium bowl. Add the squash and carrot, and mix well. Place in the breadcrumbs.
2. Put about 2 tablespoons of this mixture into a patty about ½ inch thick. Repeat with the remaining mixture. Brush the fritters with olive oil.
3. Air-fry until crisp and golden, about 7 to 9 minutes.

Nutrition: Calories: 234, Fats: 17 g, Carbs: 16 g, Fiber: 2 g, Protein: 6 g

106. Pesto Gnocchi

Preparation Time: 5 minutes
Cooking Time: 28 minutes
Servings: 2
Ingredients:

- 1 tbsp. olive oil
- 1 onion, finely chopped
- 2 Garlic cloves, sliced
- 1 (16-oz.) package shelf-stable gnocchi
- 1 (8-oz.) jar pesto
- 1 cup Parmesan cheese, grated

Directions:

1. Mix the oil, onion, garlic, and gnocchi in a 6-by-6-by-2-inch pan, and put it into the air fryer.
2. Cook for 15 minutes, then take out the pan and mix.
3. Put the pan back into the air fryer and cook for 13 minutes.
4. Take out the pan from the air fryer. Place in the pesto and Parmesan cheese, and serve immediately.

Nutrition: Calories: 646, Fats: 32 g, Carbs: 69 g, Fiber: 2 g, Protein: 22 g

107. English Muffin Tuna Sandwiches

Preparation Time: 8 minutes
Cooking Time: 10 minutes
Servings: 2
Ingredients:

- 1 (6-oz.) can chunk light tuna, drained
- ¼ cup mayonnaise
- 1 ¼ tbsp. mustard

 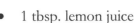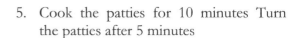
- 1 tbsp. lemon juice
- 1 green onions minced
- 2 English muffins, split with a fork
- 1 tbsp. softened butter
- 1 thin slice provolone or Muenster cheese

Directions:
1. Mix the tuna, mayonnaise, mustard, lemon juice, and green onions in a small bowl.
2. Grease the cut side of the English muffins.
3. Cook them butter-side up in the air fryer for 2 to 4 minutes, or until light golden brown.
4. Take out the muffins from the air fryer basket.
5. Place each muffin with one slice of cheese and go back to the air fryer.
6. Cook for 3 to 6 minutes
7. Take out the muffins from the air fryer, top with the tuna mixture, and serve.

Nutrition: Calories: 389, Fats: 23 g, Carbs: 25 g, Fiber: 3 g, Protein: 21 g

108. Simple Beef Patties

Preparation Time: 10 minutes
Cooking Time: 10 minutes
Servings: 2
Ingredients:

- 1 lb. ground beef
- ½ tsp. garlic powder
- ¼ tsp. onion powder
- Pepper, to taste
- Salt, taste

Directions:
1. Preheat the air fryer oven to 400°F.
2. Add the ground meat, garlic powder, onion powder, pepper, and salt into the mixing bowl. Mix until well combined.
3. Make even-shaped patties from meat mixture and arrange them on the air fryer pan.
4. Place the pan in air fryer oven.

5. Cook the patties for 10 minutes Turn the patties after 5 minutes
6. Serve and enjoy.

Nutrition: Calories: 212, Fats: 7.1 g, Carbs: 0.4 g, Protein: 34.5 g

109. Vegetable Egg Rolls

Preparation Time: 15 minutes
Cooking Time: 10 minutes
Servings: 2
Ingredients:

- ½ cup chopped mushrooms
- ½ cup grated carrots
- ½ cup chopped zucchini
- 1 green onion, chopped
- 1 tbsp. low-sodium soy sauce
- 4 egg roll wrappers
- 1 tbsp. cornstarch
- 1 egg, beaten

Directions:
1. Mix the mushrooms, carrots, zucchini, green onions, and soy sauce, and stir together in a medium bowl.
2. Put the egg roll wrappers on a surface.
3. Place each with about 3 tablespoons of the vegetable mixture.
4. Combine the cornstarch and egg in a small bowl.
5. Roll up the wrappers.
6. Put some of the egg mixtures on the outside of the egg rolls to seal.
7. Air-fry for 8 to 10 minutes, or until the egg rolls are brown and crunchy.

Nutrition: Calories: 112, Fats: 1 g, Carbs: 21 g, Fiber: 1 g, Protein: 4 g

110. Veggies On Toast

Preparation Time: 12 minutes
Cooking Time: 19 minutes
Servings: 2
Ingredients:

- 1 red bell pepper, cut into ½-inch strips
- 1 cup sliced button or cremini mushrooms

- 1 small yellow squash, sliced
- 1 green onion, cut into ½-inch cuts
- Extra-light olive oil, as needed
- 6 French bread pieces, sliced
- 1 tbsp. softened butter
- ½ cup soft goat cheese

Directions:

1. Mix the red pepper, mushrooms, squash, and green onions in the air fryer. Then mist with oil.
2. Cook for 15 minutes, or until the vegetables are tender, shaking the basket once during cooking time.
3. Take out the vegetables from the basket and set them aside.
4. Put the bread with the butter and place it in the air fryer.
5. Heat up for 2 to 4 minutes, or until golden brown.
6. Put the goat cheese on the toasted bread and top with the vegetables. Serve warm.

Nutrition: Calories: 162, Fats: 11 g, Carbs: 9 g, Fiber: 2 g, Protein: 7 g

111. Jumbo Stuffed Mushrooms

Preparation Time: 10 minutes
Cooking Time: 13 minutes
Servings: 2
Ingredients:

- 1 jumbo Portobello mushrooms
- 1 tbsp. olive oil
- ¼ cup ricotta cheese
- 1 tbsp. Parmesan cheese
- 1 cup frozen spinach, chopped, softened, and drained
- 1 cup breadcrumbs
- ¼ tsp. fresh rosemary, minced

Directions:

1. Apply the mushrooms with a damp cloth.

2. Take out the stems and throw them away.
3. With a spoon, lightly scrape out most of the gills.
4. Rub the mushrooms with the olive oil.
5. Place in the air fryer basket, hollow-side up, and bake for 3 minutes.
6. Carefully, take out the mushroom caps, because they will contain liquid. Drain the liquid out of the lids.
7. Mix the ricotta, 3 tablespoons of Parmesan cheese, spinach, bread crumbs, and rosemary. Mix well in a medium bowl.
8. Dash with the remaining 3 tablespoons of Parmesan cheese.
9. Place the mushroom caps back into the basket.
10. Bake for 5 to 10 minutes, or until the filling is hot and the mushroom caps are tender.

Nutrition: Calories: 117, Fats: 7 g, Carbs: 8 g, Fiber: 1 g, Protein: 7 g

112. Mushroom Pita Pizzas

Preparation Time: 10 minutes
Cooking Time: 5–10 minutes
Servings: 2
Ingredients:

- 4 (3-inch) pitas
- 1 tbsp. olive oil
- ¾ cup pizza sauce
- 1 (4-oz.) jar sliced mushrooms, drained
- ½ tsp. dried basil
- 2 green onions, minced
- 1 cup grated mozzarella or provolone cheese
- 1 cup grape tomatoes, sliced

Directions:

1. Put each piece of pita with oil and top them with the pizza sauce.

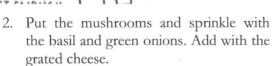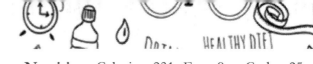

2. Put the mushrooms and sprinkle with the basil and green onions. Add with the grated cheese.

3. Bake for 5 to 10 minutes, or until the cheese is melted and starts to brown. Serve with grape tomatoes.

Nutrition: Calories: 231, Fats: 9 g, Carbs: 25 g, Fiber: 2 g, Protein: 13 g

CHAPTER 6:

Main Courses of Meat

113. Beef Korma Curry

Preparation Time: 10 minutes
Cooking Time: 17–20 minutes
Servings: 2
Ingredients:

- 1 lb. sirloin steak, sliced
- ½ cup yogurt
- 1 tbsp. curry powder
- 1 tbsp. olive oil
- 1 onion, chopped
- 2 garlic cloves, minced
- 1 tomato, diced
- ½ cup frozen baby peas, thawed

Directions:

1. In a medium bowl, combine the steak, yogurt, and curry powder. Stir and set aside.
2. In a metal bowl, combine the olive oil, onion, and garlic. Bake at 350ºF for 3 to 4 minutes, or until crisp and tender.
3. Add the steak along with the yogurt and the diced tomato. Bake for 12 to 13 minutes, or until steak is almost tender.
4. Stir in the peas and bake for 2 to 3 minutes, or until hot.

Nutrition: Calories: 299, Fats: 11 g, Protein: 38 g, Carbs: 9 g, Fiber: 2 g, Sugar: 3 g, Sodium: 100 mg

114. Chicken Fried Steak

Preparation Time: 15 minutes
Cooking Time: 12–16 minutes
Servings: 2

Ingredients:

- 4 (6-oz.) beef cube steaks
- ½ cup buttermilk
- 1 cup flour
- 2 tsp. paprika
- 1 tsp. garlic salt
- 1 egg
- 1 cup soft breadcrumbs
- 2 tbsp. olive oil

Directions:

1. Place the cube steaks on a plate or cutting board, and gently pound until they are slightly thinner. Set aside.
2. In a shallow bowl, combine the buttermilk, flour, paprika, garlic salt, and egg until combined.
3. On a plate, combine the breadcrumbs and olive oil, and mix well.
4. Dip the steaks into the buttermilk batter to coat, and let sit on a plate for 5 minutes.
5. Dredge the steaks in the breadcrumbs. Pat the crumbs onto both sides to coat the steaks thoroughly.
6. Air-fry the steaks at 350ºF for 12 to 16 minutes, or until the meat reaches 160ºF on a meat thermometer and the coating is brown and crisp. You can serve this with heated beef gravy.

Nutrition: Calories: 631, Fats: 21 g, Protein: 61 g, Carbs: 46 g, Fiber: 2 g, Sugar: 3 g, Sodium: 358 mg

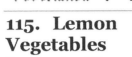

115. Lemon Greek Beef and Vegetables

Preparation Time: 10 minutes
Cooking Time: 9–19 minutes
Servings: 2
Ingredients:

- ½ lb. 96% lean ground beef
- 2 medium tomatoes, chopped
- 1 onion, chopped
- 2 garlic cloves, minced
- 2 cups fresh baby spinach
- 2 tbsp. freshly squeezed lemon juice
- 1/3 cup low-sodium beef broth
- 2 tbsp. low-sodium feta cheese, crumbled

Directions:

1. In a baking pan, crumble the beef. Place in the air fryer basket. Air-fry at 370ºF for 3 to 7 minutes, stirring once during cooking until browned. Drain off any fat or liquid.
2. Swell the tomatoes, onion, and garlic into the pan. Air-fry for 4 to 8 minutes more, or until the onion is tender.
3. Add the spinach, lemon juice, and beef broth.
4. Air-fry for 2 to 4 minutes more, or until the spinach is wilted.
5. Sprinkle with the feta cheese and serve immediately.

Nutrition: Calories: 98, Fats: 1 g, Protein: 15 g, Carbs: 5 g, Fiber: 1 g, Sugar: 2 g, Sodium: 123 mg

116. Country-Style Pork Ribs

Preparation Time: 5 minutes
Cooking Time: 20–25 minutes
Servings: 2
Ingredients:

- 12 country-style pork ribs, trimmed of excess fat
- 2 tbsp. cornstarch
- 2 tbsp. olive oil

- 1 tsp. dry mustard
- ½ tsp. thyme
- ½ tsp. garlic powder
- 1 tsp. dried marjoram
- A pinch salt
- Freshly ground black pepper, to taste

Directions:

1. Place the ribs on a clean work surface.
2. In a small bowl, combine the cornstarch, olive oil, mustard, thyme, garlic powder, marjoram, salt, and pepper. Rub into the ribs.
3. Add the ribs to the air fryer basket and roast them at 400ºF for 10 minutes.
4. Carefully, turn the ribs using tongs, and roast them for 10 to 15 minutes, or until the ribs are crisp and register an internal temperature of at least 150ºF.

Nutrition: Calories: 579, Fats: 44 g, Protein: 40 g, Carbs: 4 g, Fiber: 0 g, Sugar: 0 g, Sodium: 155 mg

117. Lemon and Honey Pork Tenderloin

Preparation Time: 5 minutes
Cooking Time: 10 minutes
Servings: 2
Ingredients:

- 1 (1-lb.) pork tenderloin, cut into ½-inch slices
- 1 tbsp. olive oil
- 1 tbsp. freshly squeezed lemon juice
- 1 tbsp. honey
- ½ tsp. grated lemon zest
- ½ tsp. dried marjoram
- A pinch salt
- Freshly ground black pepper, to taste

Directions:

1. Put the pork tenderloin slices in a medium bowl.
2. In a minor bowl, combine the olive oil, lemon juice, honey, lemon zest, marjoram, salt, and pepper. Mix.

3. Pour this marinade over the tenderloin slices and massage gently with your hand to work it into the pork.

4. Place the pork in the air fryer basket and roast at 400°F for 10 minutes, or until the pork registers at least 145°F using a meat thermometer.

Nutrition: Calories: 208, Fats: 8 g, Protein: 30 g, Carbs: 5 g, Fiber: 0 g, Sugar: 4 g, Sodium: 104 mg

118. Dijon Pork Tenderloin

Preparation Time: 10 minutes
Cooking Time: 12–14 minutes
Servings: 2
Ingredients:

- 1 lb. pork tenderloin, cut into 1-inch slices
- A pinch salt
- Freshly ground black pepper, to taste
- 2 tbsp. Dijon mustard
- 1 garlic clove, minced
- ½ tsp. dried basil
- 1 cup soft breadcrumbs
- 2 tbsp. olive oil

Directions:

1. Slightly pound the pork slices until they are about ¾ inch thick. Sprinkle with salt and pepper on both sides.

2. Coat the pork with the Dijon mustard and sprinkle with the garlic and basil.

3. On a plate, combine the breadcrumbs and olive oil, and mix well. Coat the pork slices with the breadcrumb mixture, patting so the crumbs adhere.

4. Place the pork in the air fryer basket, leaving a little space between each piece. Air-fry at 390°F for 12 to 14 minutes, or until the pork reaches at least 145°F on a meat thermometer and the coating is crisp and brown. Serve immediately.

Nutrition: Calories: 336, Fats: 13 g, Protein: 34 g, Carbs: 20 g, Fiber: 2 g, Sugar: 2 g, Sodium: 390 mg

119. Air Fryer Pork Satay

Preparation Time: 15 minutes
Cooking Time: 9–14 minutes
Servings: 2
Ingredients:

- 1 (1-lb.) pork tenderloin, cut into 1 ½-inch cubes
- ¼ cup minced onion
- 2 garlic cloves, minced
- 1 jalapeño pepper, minced
- 2 tbsp. freshly squeezed lime juice
- 2 tbsp. coconut milk
- 2 tbsp. unsalted peanut butter
- 2 tsp. curry powder

Directions:

1. In a medium bowl, mix the pork, onion, garlic, jalapeño, lime juice, coconut milk, peanut butter, and curry powder until well combined. Let it stand for 10 minutes at room temperature.

2. With a slotted spoon, remove the pork from the marinade. Reserve the marinade.

3. Thread the pork onto about 8 bamboo or metal skewers. Air-fry at 380°F for 9 to 14 minutes, brushing once with the reserved marinade until the pork reaches at least 145°F (63°C) on a meat thermometer. Discard any remaining marinade. Serve immediately.

Nutrition: Calories: 195, Fats: 7 g, Protein: 25 g, Carbs: 7 g, Fiber: 1 g, Sugar: 3 g, Sodium: 65 mg

120. Pork Burgers with Red Cabbage Slaw

Preparation Time: 20 minutes
Cooking Time: 7–9 minutes
Servings: 2
Ingredients:

- ½ cup Greek yogurt
- 2 tbsp. low-sodium mustard, divided
- 1 tbsp. freshly squeezed lemon juice
- ¼ cup sliced red cabbage
- ¼ cup grated carrots
- 1 lb. lean ground pork - ½ tsp. paprika
- 1 cup mixed baby lettuce greens
- 2 small tomatoes, sliced
- 8 small low-sodium whole wheat sandwich buns, cut in half

Directions:

1. In a small bowl, add the yogurt, 1 tablespoon of mustard, lemon juice, cabbage, and carrots. Mix and refrigerate. In a medium bowl, combine the pork, remaining 1 tablespoon of mustard, and paprika. Form the mixture into 8 small patties. Lay the patties into the air fryer basket. Air-fry at 400°F for 7 to 9 minutes, or until the patties register 165°F when tested with a meat thermometer.
2. Assemble the burgers by placing some of the lettuce greens on a bun's bottom. Top with a tomato slice, the patties, and the cabbage mixture. Add the bun's top, and serve immediately.

Nutrition: Calories: 473, Fats: 15 g, Protein: 35 g, Carbs: 51 g, Fiber: 8 g, Sugar: 8 g, Sodium: 138 mg

121. Greek Lamb Pita Pockets

Preparation Time: 15 minutes
Cooking Time: 5–7 minutes
Servings: 2
Ingredients:
For the Dressing:

- 1 cup plain Greek yogurt
- 1 tbsp. lemon juice
- 1 tsp. dried dill weed, crushed
- 1 tsp. ground oregano
- ½ tsp. salt

For the Meatballs:

- ½ lb. ground lamb
- 1 tbsp. diced onion
- 1 tsp. dried parsley
- 1 tsp. dried dill weed, crushed
- ¼ tsp. oregano
- ¼ tsp. coriander
- ¼ tsp. ground cumin
- ¼ tsp. salt
- 4 pita halves

For the Suggested Toppings:

- Red onion, slivered
- Seedless cucumber, thinly sliced
- Crumbled feta cheese
- Sliced black olives
- Fresh peppers, chopped

Directions:

1. Stir the dressing ingredients together and refrigerate them while preparing lamb.
2. Combine all meatball ingredients in a large bowl and stir to distribute seasonings. Shape the meat mixture into 12 small meatballs, rounded or slightly flattened if you prefer. Air-fry at 390°F for 5 to 7 minutes, or until well done. Remove and drain on paper towels.
3. To serve, pile the meatballs and your choice of toppings in the pita pockets, and drizzle with dressing.

Nutrition: Calories: 270, Fats: 14 g, Protein: 18 g, Carbs: 18 g, Fiber: 2 g, Sugar: 2 g, Sodium: 618 mg

122. Rosemary Lamb Chops

Preparation Time: 30 minutes
Cooking Time: 20–22 minutes
Servings: 2–3
Ingredients:

- 2 tsp. oil

- ½ tsp. ground rosemary
- ½ tsp. lemon juice
- 1 lb. lamb chops, approximately 1-inch thick
- Salt and pepper, to taste
- Cooking spray, as needed

Directions:

1. Mix the oil, rosemary, and lemon juice. Rub the mixture into all sides of the lamb chops. Season to taste with salt and pepper.
2. For best flavor, cover the lamb chops and allow them to rest in the fridge for 15 to 20 minutes.
3. Spray the air fryer basket with non-stick spray and place the lamb chops in it.
4. Air-fry at 360°F for approximately 20 minutes. This will cook the chops to medium. The meat will be juicy but have no remaining pink. Air-fry for 1 to 2 minutes longer for well-done chops. For rare chops, stop cooking after about 12 minutes and check for doneness.

Nutrition: Calories: 237, Fats: 13 g, Protein: 30 g, Carbs: 0 g, Fiber: 0 g, Sugar: 0 g, Sodium: 116 mg

123. Delicious Meatballs

Preparation Time: 15 minutes
Cooking Time: 25 minutes
Servings: 2
Ingredients:

- 200 g ground beef
- 200 g ground chicken
- 100 g ground pork
- 30 g minced garlic
- 1 potato
- 1 egg
- 1 tsp. basil
- 1 tsp. cayenne pepper
- 1 tsp. white pepper
- 2 tsp. olive oil

Directions:

1. Combine the ground beef, chicken meat, and pork in the mixing bowl and stir it gently.
2. Sprinkle it with basil, cayenne pepper, and white pepper.
3. Add the minced garlic and egg.
4. Stir the mixture gently. (You should get a fluffy mass.)
5. Peel the potato and grate it.
6. Add the grated potato to the mixture and stir it again.
7. Preheat the air fryer oven to 180°F.
8. Take a tray and spray it with olive oil.
9. Make the balls from the meat mass and put them on the tray.
10. Lay the tray in the oven and cook for 25 minutes.

Nutrition: Calories: 204, Protein: 26.0 g, Fats: 7.6 g Carbs: 7.1 g

124. Low-fat Steak

Preparation Time: 25 minutes
Cooking Time: 10 minutes
Servings: 2
Ingredients:

- 400 g beef steak
- 1 tsp. white pepper
- 1 tsp. turmeric
- 1 tsp. cilantro
- 1 tsp. olive oil
- 3 tsp. lemon juice
- 1 tsp. oregano
- 1 tsp. salt
- 100 g water

Directions:

1. Rub the steaks with white pepper and turmeric, and put them in the big bowl.
2. Sprinkle the meat with salt, oregano, cilantro, and lemon juice.
3. Leave the steaks for 20 minutes.
4. Combine the olive oil with the water and pour the mixture into the bowl with the steaks.

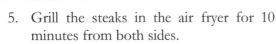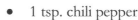

5. Grill the steaks in the air fryer for 10 minutes from both sides.
6. Serve immediately.

Nutrition: Calories: 268, Protein: 40.7 g Fats: 10.1 g, Carbs: 1.4 g

125. Diet Boiled Ribs

Preparation Time: 10 minutes
Cooking Time: 30 minutes
Servings: 2
Ingredients:

- 400 g pork ribs
- 1 tsp. black pepper
- 1 g bay leaf
- 1 tsp. basil
- 1 white onion
- 1 carrot
- 1 tsp. cumin
- 700 ml water

Directions:

1. Cut the ribs on the portions and sprinkle them with black pepper.
2. Take a large saucepan and pour water into it.
3. Add the ribs and bay leaf.
4. Peel the onion and carrot, and add them to the water with the meat.
5. Sprinkle with cumin and basil.
6. Cook it on medium heat in the air fryer for 30 minutes.

Nutrition: Calories: 294, Protein: 27.1 g, Fats: 17.9 g, Carbs: 4.8 g

126. Meatloaf

Preparation Time: 15 minutes
Cooking Time: 30 minutes
Servings: 2
Ingredients:

- 300 g ground beef
- 1 egg
- 1 onion
- 100 g carrot
- 1 tsp. black pepper

- 1 tsp. chili pepper
- 2 tsp. olive oil

Directions:

1. Take the ground beef and put it in a big bowl.
2. Add the egg, black pepper, and chili pepper. Stir the mixture very carefully.
3. Peel the carrot and onion, and chop them.
4. Add the chopped carrot and onion to the bowl with the meat, and stir carefully.
5. Preheat the air fryer oven to 200°F.
6. Meanwhile, take the tray and spray it inside with olive oil. Make the loaf from the meat and put it on the tray.
7. Lay the tray in the oven and cook for 30 minutes.

Nutrition: Calories:198, Protein: 24.7 g, Fats: 8.1 g, Carbs: 5.6 g

127. Beef with Mushrooms

Preparation Time: 15 minutes
Cooking Time: 40 minutes
Servings: 2
Ingredients:

- 300 g beef
- 150 g mushrooms
- 1 onion
- 1 tsp. olive oil
- 100 g vegetable broth
- 1 tsp. basil
- 1 tsp. chili
- 30 g tomato juice

Directions:

1. For this recipe, you should take a solid piece of beef. Take the beef and pierce the meat with a knife.
2. Rub it with olive oil, basil, chili, and lemon juice.
3. Chop the onion and mushrooms, and add them to vegetable broth.
4. Cook the vegetables for 5 minutes.

5. Take a large tray and put the meat in it. Add vegetable broth to the tray too. (It will make the meat juicy.)
6. Preheat the air fryer oven to 180°F and cook for 35 minutes.

Nutrition: Calories: 175, Protein: 24.9 g, Fats: 6.2 g, Carbs: 4.4 g

128. Quick and Juicy Pork Chops

Preparation Time: 10 minutes
Cooking Time: 12 minutes
Servings: 2
Ingredients:
- 4 pork chops
- 1 tsp. olive oil
- 1 tsp. onion powder
- 1 tsp. paprika
- Pepper, to taste - Salt, to taste

Directions:
1. Cover the pork chops with olive oil and season with paprika, onion powder, pepper, and salt.
2. Place the dehydrating tray in a multi-level air fryer basket, and place the basket in the instant pot.
3. Place the pork chops on the dehydrating tray. Seal the pot with the air fryer lid and select the "Air Fry" mode, then set the temperature to 380°F and the timer to 12 minutes. Turn the pork chops over halfway through the cooking.
4. Serve and enjoy.

Nutrition: Calories: 270, Fats: 21.1 g, Carbs: 0.8 g, Sugar: 0.3 g, Protein: 18.1 g, Cholesterol: 69 mg

129. Delicious Lamb

Preparation Time: 10 minutes
Cooking Time: 3 hours
Servings: 2
Ingredients:
- 2 tbsp. olive oil
- 2 red onions, finely sliced
- 3 garlic cloves, crushed
- 1 tbsp. ground ginger
- 1 tbsp. ground cinnamon
- 1 tbsp. ground cumin
- 1 tbsp. sweet paprika
- 1 tbsp. ground turmeric
- 3 lb. British lamb shoulders, diced into 2-cm cubes
- 2 (1-lb.) tins chopped tomatoes
- ½ lb. prunes, stoned and roughly chopped
- 500 ml chicken stock
- 1 tbsp. sugar
- 1 lb. tin chickpeas, drained and rinsed
- ½ lemon, juiced
- Salt, to taste
- Pepper, to taste
- Water, as needed

For the Servings:
- 1 large bunch of fresh parsley
- 1 large bunch of fresh coriander
- 1 cup pistachios, shelled and toasted

Directions:
1. Heat a large amount of oil in a large deep, heat-proof casserole over a medium high heat, and then add in the onions and sauté for about 4 to 5 minutes
2. Add in the garlic and all of your ground spices, and sauté for about 2 additional minutes. Stir with the help of a wooden spoon.
3. Season the lamb meat. Add it to the pot and cook for about 5 minutes, then stir constantly. Add in the chopped tomatoes, the prunes, the stock, and the sugar. Bring to a simmer, and then lower the heat to low.
4. Add in about 100 ml of water and let simmer for about 3 hours.
5. Stir the tagine very often so that it doesn't stick, and if it reduces quickly, add in a splash of water

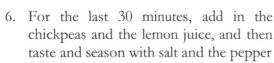 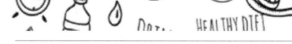
6. For the last 30 minutes, add in the chickpeas and the lemon juice, and then taste and season with salt and the pepper
7. Serve and enjoy with the parsley, coriander, and pistachio.

Nutrition: Calories: 215, Fats: 12 g, Carbs: 10 g, Proteins: 6 g

130. Lamb Curry

Preparation Time: 10 minutes
Cooking Time: 4–8 hours
Servings: 2
Ingredients:

- 1 lb. lamb shoulder, diced into 3-cm cubes
- 2 large onions, roughly chopped
- 2 large eggplants, cut into 3-cm chunks
- 2 tbsp. Rogan Josh curry paste
- 1 tbsp. red wine vinegar
- 1 ½ lb. passata or crushed tomatoes
- ½ lb. natural or Greek yogurt, for serving
- Rice, for serving
- Salt, to taste
- Pepper, to taste
- Olive oil, as needed

Directions:

1. Preheat your slow cooker.
2. Add a dash of olive oil to a large frying pan, and brown the lamb.
3. Add in the lamb, the onion, and the eggplant to the slow cooker.
4. Season with sea salt and cracked pepper.
5. Mix the Rogan Josh paste with the passata, the tomatoes, and the vinegar.
6. Add the mixture to the slow cooker and stir through very well.
7. Cook on low for about 7 to 8 hours or on high for about 4 hours.
8. Serve with rice and a dollop of yogurt.
9. Enjoy your dish!

Nutrition: Calories: 273.6, Fats: 11.4 g, Carbs: 9.9 g, Proteins: 31.3 g

131. Lamb and Veggies

Preparation Time: 20 minutes
Cooking Time: 1 hour
Servings: 2
Ingredients:

- 1 (3-lb.) shoulder of lamb
- 4 small zucchinis
- 4 firm tomatoes
- 4 onions
- 4 garlic cloves
- 1 cup cumin seeds
- 1 cup cilantro seeds
- A bunch mint
- 1 lemon
- Salt, to taste
- Freshly ground pepper, to taste
- ¼ cup Semolina couscous, for serving
- Water, as needed
- Oil, as needed

Directions:

1. Roll and tie a shoulder of lamb.
2. Immerse the tomatoes in boiling water, then place them in a bowl of cold water. Peel them, crush their flesh, and drain them in a colander.
3. Peel and mince the garlic and onion.
4. Rinse the zucchini in cold water, and then quarter them.
5. Heat a little oil in a sauté pan, then brown the roast lamb over high heat so that all sides are nicely browned
6. Set aside and sauté the garlic and onion for 5 minutes, without grilling
7. Add the cumin and cilantro. Season with the salt and pepper to taste; then brown everything over high heat for 2 minutes, stirring.
8. Lower the heat and add the crushed tomatoes. Stir gently and add the shoulder of lamb. Squeeze the lemon and pour its juice into the sauté pan. Cover and cook over low heat for 30 minutes. Add the zucchini and cook for another 30 minutes.

9. Cut out the rolled shoulder of lamb and place the slices in the center of a deep baking tray.
10. Carefully, arrange the vegetables around the meat and cover everything with the sauce Decorate with mint leaves and serve immediately the lamb shoulder rolled into slices with semolina couscous. Enjoy your dish!

Nutrition: Calories: 274, Fats: 19.8 g, Carbs: 5 g, Proteins: 22.3 g

132. Lamb with Okra

Preparation Time: 10 minutes
Cooking Time: 35 minutes
Servings: 2
Ingredients:
- 2 lb. lamb meat
- 1 lb. okra
- 1 small onion, chopped
- 1 cup tomato juice
- 1 tbsp. pepper
- 4 garlic cloves, minced
- A pinch ground cumin
- A pinch black pepper
- ¼ pinch beef spices
- A pinch salt, or to taste
- Vermicelli rice or Muammar rice casserole, for serving
- Water, as needed

Directions:
1. Boil the meat in hot water for about 15 minutes, then put a large saucepan over high heat and melt in 1 tablespoon of butter. Add in the okra and the chopped garlic. Add the tomato juice and purée to the okra and onions, then add the meat, salt, and spices to taste.
2. Let simmer for about 20 minutes.
3. Serve hot with vermicelli rice or Muammar rice casserole. Enjoy your dish!

Nutrition: Calories: 217.1, Fats: 10.7 g, Carbs: 10.1 g, Proteins: 19.9 g

133. Lamb Medallions

Preparation Time: 10 minutes
Cooking Time: 10 minutes
Servings: 2
Ingredients:
- 1 lb. lamb
- 4 oz. sweet potatoes
- 3 garlic cloves, minced
- ¼ cup creamy natural almond butter
- 3 ½ tbsp. warm water
- 3 tbsp. fresh lemon juice
- 2 tbsp. olive oil
- 5 oz. baby arugula
- ¾ tsp. kosher salt
- 1 tsp. black pepper
- 1 mango

Directions:
1. Slice the lambs into medallions.
2. Prick the potatoes with a fork and put them into a microwave-safe baking bowl to tender for about 6 minutes.
3. Quarterly, cut the potato into thick rounds of about ½ inch thickness.
4. Mix the almond butter, the water, and 1 tablespoon of lemon juice into a bowl, then set it aside.
5. Brush the potato slices with a little bit of oil. Heat a wok over medium heat and pour in 1 cup of water with a little bit of salt and olive oil.
6. Toss the slices of meat and cook them for about 4 minutes on each side, or until the water is reduced, then remove the meat and cook the potatoes in batches Add the garlic cloves, lamb portions, arugula, salt, pepper, and the remaining 2 tablespoons of the juice. Peel the mango and cut it into cubes.
7. Serve the lamb portions with the mango and potatoes in a serving dish and drizzle with more almond butter sauce.
8. Enjoy your dish.

Nutrition: Calories: 113, Fats: 4 g, Carbs: 4 g, Proteins: 21 g

134. Beef Dish with Garlic

Preparation Time: 10 minutes
Cooking Time: 10 minutes
Servings: 2
Ingredients:

- ½ lb. sirloin steak, cut into small chunks
- ½ tbsp. olive oil
- 1 tbsp. almond butter or coconut oil
- 1 tsp. minced garlic
- A pinch salt
- A pinch pepper
- ½ tbsp. minced parsley

Directions:

1. Start by heating the olive oil in a large pan over a medium high heat, then season with the salt and pepper to taste.
2. Put the steak in the pan in one single layer, and cook it for about 3 to 4 minutes.
3. Add the almond butter and the garlic to the pan and cook for about 1 to 2 minutes, and stir very well.
4. Sprinkle with parsley, and then serve.
5. Enjoy your dish!

Nutrition: Calories: 272, Fats: 15 g, Carbs: 10 g, Proteins: 31 g

135. Mongolian Beef

Preparation Time: 10 minutes
Cooking Time: 9 minutes
Servings: 2
Ingredients:

- ½ lb. flank steak, sliced into stripes
- 1 tbsp. olive oil, divided
- ½ tbsp. fresh ginger, peeled and grated
- 1 minced garlic clove
- 1 tbsp. coconut aminos
- ¼ cup water
- 1/3 cup So Nourished® erythritol
- ½ tsp. red pepper flakes
- 1 tsp. xanthan gum
- A pinch salt
- A pinch pepper

Directions:

1. In a large saucepan, heat half of the olive oil, and then add the minced garlic and the grated ginger and fry for about 30 seconds.
2. Add the water, the coconut aminos, the erythritol, and the red pepper flakes. Let simmer over high heat for about 3 to 4 minutes.
3. Turn off the heat and set it aside.
4. Add the xanthan gum and the beef strips to a Ziploc® bag and toss very well.
5. In a large frying pan, heat the other half of the olive oil until it becomes hot.
6. Add in the beef strips and stir-fry for several minutes.
7. Heat a pan over medium high heat, then add the sauce and the beef.
8. Add a pinch of salt and 1 pinch of pepper, then cook for about 1 minute.
9. Divide between 2 plates.
10. Serve and enjoy your dish!

Nutrition: Calories: 233, Fats: 13 g, Carbs: 3 g, Proteins: 25 g

136. Stuffed Flank Steak

Preparation Time: 10 minutes
Cooking Time: 35–40 minutes
Servings: 2
Ingredients:

- ½ lb. butterflied flank steak
- 1 cup fresh baby spinach
- 1/3 cup feta cheese, crumbled
- 1/3 cup sun-dried tomatoes, packed in olive oil, drained very well and chopped
- 1 garlic clove, minced
- ¼ tsp. dried basil
- A pinch of fresh ground pepper
- 1 tbsp. pasta tomato, divided
- ½ tbsp. olive oil
- A pinch salt
- A pinch of fresh ground pepper
- Fresh parsley, chopped, for serving

Directions:

1. Preheat the oven to a temperature of 400°F.
2. With a sharp knife, butterfly the beef steak by placing your hand right on top of the meat and then cutting in a horizontal way into the steak, about 1 inch, before cutting the meat into 2 separate pieces.
3. Open up the beef steak and set it aside.
4. In a large mixing bowl, combine the chopped spinach with the cheese, the sun-dried tomatoes, the garlic, the basil, and the fresh ground pepper. Mix very well until your ingredients are very well incorporated.
5. Spread about 1/3 cup of tomato sauce on top of the steak and top with the already prepared mixture of the spinach.
6. Roll up the steak and secure it with kitchen twine.
7. Brush the stuffed flank steak with olive oil and season it with salt and pepper.
8. Spread the rest of the sauce of tomato on top and around the edges.
9. Transfer to a baking dish and bake for about 35 to 40 minutes.
10. Remove from the oven and transfer the steak to a cutting board.
11. Let the stuffed steak rest for about 10 minutes right before removing the kitchen twine.
12. Remove the kitchen twine, then slice the stuffed steak into rounds of about ¼ inch each.
13. Spoon the tomato sauce from the baking dish over the rounds, and top with fresh parsley.
14. Serve and enjoy your dish!

Nutrition: Calories: 349, Fats: 13 g, Carbs: 3 g, Proteins: 25 g

137. Beef Curry

Preparation Time: 10 minutes
Cooking Time: 15 minutes
Servings: 2
Ingredients:

- 1 tbsp. oil
- ½ lb. beef, diced
- 2 tbsp. yellow curry paste
- 2 kaffir lime leaves
- A pinch salt
- 1 tbsp. lime juice
- 1 oz. coconut cream
- 1 tsp. erythritol (optional)
- Cauliflower rice, for serving

Directions:

1. Chop the beef if you have bought rump steak or gravy steak, then place it in a large frying pan over medium high heat with about 1 tablespoon of oil.
2. Sear the beef chunks for about 5 minutes, then add the yellow curry paste, the coconut cream, and the kaffir lime leaves.
3. Add the coconut cream, the yellow curry paste, and the kaffir lime leaves. Cook for about 10 minutes over low heat.

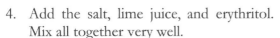 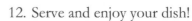

4. Add the salt, lime juice, and erythritol. Mix all together very well.
5. Serve with cauliflower rice.
6. Enjoy your dish!

Nutrition: Calories: 620, Fats: 48 g, Carbs: 14 g, Proteins: 23 g

138. Mediterranean Beef Steak

Preparation Time: 15 minutes
Cooking Time: 40 minutes
Servings: 2–3
Ingredients:

- ½ lb. flank steak
- ¼ lb. bacon, diced
- ½ cup chopped mushrooms
- 2 oz. baby spinach
- A pinch salt
- A pinch fresh black pepper
- 2 tbsp. Coconut oil

Directions:

1. Preheat your oven to a temperature of about 400°F.
2. Arrange the bacon in an oven-proof tray.
3. Drizzle the bacon with a little bit of coconut oil, then place the tray in the oven.
4. Bake the bacon for about 8 to 10 minutes.
5. Remove the tray from the oven; then, in another pan, sauté the mushrooms with the seasonings.
6. Add the spinach into the pan and stir the ingredients.
7. Lay the flank down, then spread the spinach mixture over the steak.
8. Roll the flank steak and the spinach with a twine.
9. Heat up a skillet over medium high heat and pour 1 tablespoon of oil in it.
10. Sear the steak into the skillet for about 25 minutes.
11. Remove the meat from the skillet and set it aside to cool for about 5 minutes.

12. Serve and enjoy your dish!

Nutrition: Calories: 386, Fats: 30 g, Carbs: 3 g, Proteins: 2 g

139. Beef Steak with Green Pepper

Preparation Time: 8 minutes (plus 20 minutes to refrigerate)
Cooking Time: 4 minutes
Servings: 2–3
Ingredients:

- ½ lb. sirloin steak, thinly stripped
- 1 tbsp. olive oil
- 3 mini sweet peppers, thinly sliced
- 1 scallion, diagonally sliced
- 1 tbsp. fresh ginger, minced
- 1 garlic clove, minced

For the Make the Marinade:

- ¼ cup coconut aminos
- 1/3 cup water
- 2 tbsp. white wine vinegar
- 1/4 tsp. fresh coarse ground black pepper

Directions:

1. Combine the ingredients for the marinade into a large bowl.
2. Add the thinly sliced steak to your marinade, then toss the ingredients very well to coat.
3. Refrigerate the marinade for about 15 minutes.
4. Add some coconut oil to a large skillet and place it over medium heat.
5. Add the white parts of the scallions, the bell peppers, the ginger, and the garlic for about 4 minutes.
6. Transfer the ingredients to a plate.
7. Take the steak out of the marinade, and then add it to your skillet and sauté it for about 4 minutes.

Nutrition: Calories: 337.3, Fats: 23.4 g, Carbs: 23.4 g, Proteins: 17.3 g

140. Beef Chili

Preparation Time: 8 minutes
Cooking Time: 35 minutes
Servings: 2
Ingredients:

- 1 lb. beef meat
- ¼ red onion, chopped
- ¼ tsp. minced garlic
- 2 tbsp. tomato sauce
- 1 cup tomatoes, with the juice and roughly diced
- 1 cup beef stock
- ½ cup sliced carrots
- 1 cup sweet potato, peeled and diced
- 1 bay leaf
- ½ tsp. thyme
- A pinch salt
- A pinch black pepper
- ½ cup chili powder
- A pinch oregano
- A pinch of red pepper flakes
- ¼ cup Coconut oil

Directions:

1. In a large and deep saucepan, sauté the beef meat with the onions and the garlic with 1 tablespoon of coconut oil.
2. Drain off any fat from the pan, then add the rest of your ingredients, and mix very well.
3. Let the ingredients boil for about 35 minutes over low heat, or until the vegetables become tender.
4. Remove the bay leaves.
5. Serve and enjoy the chili!

Nutrition: Calories: 367.8, Fats: 26.9 g, Carbs: 5.5 g, Proteins: 24.8 g

141. Ground Beef and Cauliflower Bake

Preparation Time: 15 minutes
Cooking Time: 35 minutes
Servings: 2
Ingredients:

- ½ lb. ground meat
- ½ cup chopped cauliflower
- 1 tsp. steak seasoning
- ¼ cup shredded cheddar cheese
- 2 oz. cream cheese, chopped into cubes
- 1 egg
- ¼ cup heavy cream
- ¼ cup shredded cheddar cheese

Directions:

1. Preheat your oven to a temperature of about 400°F.
2. Microwave the cauliflower for about 5 minutes.
3. In the meantime; add the beef to a large skillet and sprinkle with the steak seasoning on top.
4. Add in the cauliflower, the cream cheese, and the shredded cheddar cheese.
5. Mix the ingredients very well, then pour the mixture into a baking dish.
6. In a medium bowl, beat the eggs and then whisk in the cream and the butter
7. Pour over the beef mixture and top with the remaining quantity of cheese.
8. Bake for about 30 minutes.
9. Serve and enjoy your dish!

Nutrition: Calories: 499.8, Fats: 40.1 g, Carbs: 5.5 g, Protein: 29.2 g

CHAPTER 7:

Main Fish Courses

142. Mustard-Crusted Sole

Preparation Time: 5 minutes
Cooking Time: 8–11 minutes
Servings: 2
Ingredients:

- 5 tsp. low-sodium yellow mustard
- 1 tbsp. freshly squeezed lemon juice
- 4 (3 ½-oz.) sole fillets
- ½ tsp. dried thyme
- ½ tsp. dried marjoram
- 1/8 tsp. freshly ground black pepper
- 1 low-sodium, whole-wheat bread slice, crumbled
- 2 tsp. olive oil

Directions:

1. In a small bowl, blend the mustard and lemon juice. Spread this mixture evenly over the fillets. Place them in the air fryer basket.
2. In another small bowl, mix the thyme, marjoram, pepper, breadcrumbs, and olive oil. Mix until combined.
3. Gently but firmly, press the spice mixture onto each fish fillets top.
4. Bake at 320°F for 8 to 11 minutes, or until the fish reaches an inner temperature of at least 145°F on a meat thermometer and the topping is browned and crisp. Serve immediately.

Nutrition: Calories: 143, Fats: 4 g, Protein: 20 g, Carbs: 5 g, Fiber: 1 g, Sugar: 1 g, Sodium: 140 mg

143. Almond-Crusted Cod with Chips

Preparation Time: 10 minutes
Cooking Time: 21–25 minutes
Servings: 2
Ingredients:

- 2 russet potatoes, peeled, thinly sliced, rinsed, and patted dry
- 1 egg white
- 1 tbsp. freshly squeezed lemon juice
- 1/3 cup ground almonds
- 2 low-sodium, whole-wheat bread slices, finely crumbled
- ½ tsp. dried basil
- 4 (4-oz.) cod fillets

Directions:

1. Preheat the oven.
2. Put the potato slices in the air fryer basket and air-fry at 390°F for 11 to 15 minutes, or until crisp and brown. With tongs, turn the fries twice during cooking.
3. In the meantime, in a deep bowl, beat the egg white and lemon juice until frothy.
4. On a plate, mix the almonds, breadcrumbs, and basil.
5. One at a time, dip the fillets into the egg white mixture and then into the almond-breadcrumb mixture to coat. Place the coated fillets on a wire rack to dry while the fries cook.

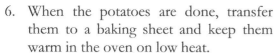

6. When the potatoes are done, transfer them to a baking sheet and keep them warm in the oven on low heat.
7. Air-fry the fish in the air fryer basket for 10 to 14 minutes, or until the fish reaches an internal temperature of at least 140ºF on a meat thermometer and the coating is browned and crisp. Serve immediately with the potatoes.

Nutrition: Calories: 248, Fats: 5 g, Protein: 27 g, Carbs: 25 g, Fiber: 3 g, Sugar: 3 g, Sodium: 131 mg

144. Honey-Lemon Snapper with Fruit

Preparation Time: 15 minutes
Cooking Time: 9–13 minutes
Servings: 2
Ingredients:

- 4 (4-oz.) red snapper fillets
- 2 tsp. olive oil
- 3 nectarines, halved and pitted
- 3 plums, halved and pitted
- 1 cup red grapes
- 1 tbsp. freshly squeezed lemon juice
- 1 tbsp. honey
- ½ tsp. dried thyme

Directions:

1. Put the red snapper in the air fryer basket and drizzle with the olive oil. Air-fry at 390ºF (199ºC) for 4 minutes.
2. Remove the basket and add the nectarines and plums. Scatter the grapes overall.
3. Drizzle with the lemon juice and honey, and sprinkle with the thyme.
4. Return the basket to the air fryer and air-fry for 5 to 9 minutes more, or until the fish flakes when tested with a fork and the fruit is tender. Serve immediately.

Nutrition: Calories: 246, Fats: 4 g, Protein: 25 g, Carbs: 28 g, Fiber: 3 g, Sugar: 24 g, Sodium: 73 mg

145. Easy Tuna Wraps

Preparation Time: 10 minutes
Cooking Time: 4–7 minutes
Servings: 2
Ingredients:

- 1 lb. fresh tuna steak, cut into 1-inch cubes
- 1 tbsp. grated fresh ginger
- 2 garlic cloves, minced
- ½ tsp. toasted sesame oil
- 4 low-sodium, whole-wheat tortillas
- ¼ cup low-fat mayonnaise
- 2 cups shredded romaine lettuce
- 1 red bell pepper, thinly sliced

Directions:

1. In a medium bowl, mix the tuna, ginger, garlic, and sesame oil. Let the mixture stand for 10 minutes, then transfer it to the air fryer basket.
2. Air-fry at 390ºF for 4 to 7 minutes, or until done to your liking and lightly browned.
3. Make wraps with tuna, tortillas, mayonnaise, lettuce, and bell pepper. Serve immediately.

Nutrition: Calories: 289, Fats: 7 g, Protein: 31 g, Carbs: 26 g, Fiber: 1 g, Sugar 1 g, Sodium: 135 mg

146. Asian-Inspired Swordfish Steaks

Preparation Time: 10 minutes
Cooking Time: 6–11 minutes
Servings: 2
Ingredients:

- 4 (4-oz.) swordfish steaks
- ½ tsp. toasted sesame oil
- 1 jalapeño pepper, finely minced
- 2 garlic cloves, grated
- 1 tbsp. grated fresh ginger
- ½ tsp. Chinese five-spice powder
- 1/8 tsp. freshly ground black pepper
- 2 tbsp. freshly squeezed lemon juice

Directions:

1. Place the swordfish steaks on a work surface and drizzle with the sesame oil.
2. In a small bowl, mix the jalapeño, garlic, ginger, five-spice powder, pepper, and lemon juice. Rub this mixture into the fish and let it stand for 10 minutes. Put in the air fryer basket.
3. Roast at 380°F for 6 to 11 minutes, or until the swordfish reaches an inner temperature of at least 140°F on a meat thermometer. Serve immediately.

Nutrition: Calories: 188, Fats: 6 g, Protein: 29 g, Carbs: 2 g, Fiber: 0 g, Sugar 1 g, Sodium: 132 mg

147. Salmon with Fennel and Carrot

Preparation Time: 15 minutes
Cooking Time: 13–14 minutes
Servings: 2
Ingredients:

- 1 fennel bulb, thinly sliced
- 1 large carrot, peeled and sliced
- 1 small onion, thinly sliced
- ¼ cup low-fat sour cream
- ¼ tsp. coarsely ground pepper
- 2 (5-oz.) salmon fillets

Directions:

1. Combine the fennel, carrot, and onion in a bowl. Then toss. Put the vegetable mixture into a baking pan. Cook in the air fryer at 400°F (204°C) for 4 minutes, or until the vegetables are crisp-tender.
2. Remove the pan from the air fryer. Stir in the sour cream and sprinkle the vegetables with the pepper.
3. Top with the salmon fillets.
4. Return the pan to the air fryer. Roast for another 9 to 10 minutes, or until the salmon just barely flakes when tested with a fork.

Nutrition: Calories: 254, Fats: 9 g, Protein: 31 g, Carbs: 12 g, Fiber: 3 g, Sugar 5 g, Sodium: 115 mg

148. Ranch Tilapia fillets

Preparation Time: 7 minutes
Cooking Time: 17 minutes
Servings: 2
Ingredients:

- 2 tbsp. flour
- 1 egg, lightly beaten
- 1 cup crushed cornflakes
- 2 tbsp. ranch seasoning
- 2 tilapia fillets
- Olive oil spray, as needed

Directions:

1. Place a parchment liner in the air fryer basket.
2. Scoop the flour out onto a plate, and set it aside.
3. Put the beaten egg in a medium shallow bowl.
4. Put the cornflakes in a Ziploc® bag and crush them with a rolling pin or another small, blunt object.
5. On another plate, mix the crushed cereal with the ranch seasoning.
6. Dredge the tilapia fillets in the flour, dip in the egg, and press into the cornflake mixture.
7. Place the prepared fillets on the liner in the air fryer in a single layer.
8. Spray lightly with olive oil, and air-fry at 400°F for 8 minutes. Carefully, flip the fillets and spray with more oil. Air-fry for an additional 9 minutes, or until golden and crispy, then serve.

Nutrition: Calories: 395, Fats: 7 g, Protein: 34 g, Carbs: 49 g, Fiber: 3 g, Sugar 4 g, Sodium: 980 mg

149. Chilean Sea Bass with Green Olive Relish

Preparation Time: 10 minutes
Cooking Time: 10 minutes
Servings: 2
Ingredients:

- Olive oil spray, as needed

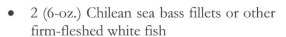

- 2 (6-oz.) Chilean sea bass fillets or other firm-fleshed white fish
- 3 tbsp. extra-virgin olive oil
- ½ tsp. ground cumin
- ½ tsp. kosher salt
- ½ tsp. black pepper
- 1/3 cup pitted green olives, diced
- ¼ cup onion, finely diced
- 1 tsp. chopped capers

Directions:

1. Spray the air fryer basket with olive oil spray. Drizzle the fillets with olive oil and sprinkle with cumin, salt, and pepper. Put the fish in the air fryer basket. Bake at 325°F for 10 minutes, or until the fish flakes easily with a fork.
2. In the meantime, in a smaller bowl, stir together the olives, onion, and capers.
3. Serve the fish topped with the relish.

Nutrition: Calories: 366, Fats: 26 g, Protein: 31 g, Carbs: 2 g, Fiber: 1 g, Sugar: 0 g, Sodium: 895 mg

150. Ginger and Green Onion Fish

Preparation Time: 15 minutes
Cooking Time: 15 minutes
Servings: 2
Ingredients:
For the Bean Sauce:

- 2 tbsp. low-sodium soy sauce
- 1 tbsp. rice wine
- 1 tbsp. doubanjiang (Chinese black bean paste)

- 1 tsp. minced fresh ginger
- 1 garlic clove, minced

For the Vegetables and Fish:

- 1 tbsp. peanut oil
- ¼ cup green onions, julienned
- ¼ cup fresh cilantro, chopped
- 2 tbsp. fresh ginger, julienned
- 2 (6-oz.) white fish fillets, such as tilapia

Directions:

1. For the sauce, combine all the ingredients in a small bowl, and stir until well combined. Set aside.
2. For the vegetables and fish, in a medium bowl, combine the peanut oil, green onions, cilantro, and ginger. Toss to combine.
3. Cut 2 squares of parchment large enough to hold one fillet and half of the vegetables. Place one fillet on each parchment square, top with the vegetables, and pour over the sauce. Bend the parchment paper over and tuck the sides in small, tight folds to hold the fish, vegetables, and sauce securely inside the packet.
4. Put the packets in a single layer in the air fryer basket, and roast at 350°F for 15 minutes.
5. Transfer each packet to a dinner plate. Cut open with scissors just before serving.

Nutrition: Calories: 237, Fats: 9 g, Protein: 36 g, Carbs: 3 g, Fiber: 0 g, Sugar: 0 g, Sodium: 641 mg

151. Asian Sesame Cod

Preparation Time: 5 minutes
Cooking Time: 7–9 minutes
Servings: 1
Ingredients:

- 1 tbsp. reduced-sodium soy sauce
- 2 tsp. honey
- 1 tsp. sesame seeds

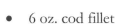

- 6 oz. cod fillet
- Non-stick cooking spray, as needed

Directions:

1. In a small bowl, put the soy sauce and honey.
2. Sprig the air fryer basket with non-stick cooking spray, then place the cod in the basket, brush with the soy mixture, and sprinkle sesame seeds on top. Roast at 360°F for 7 to 9 minutes, or until opaque.
3. Remove the fish from the fryer, and allow it to cool on a wire rack for 5 minutes before serving.

Nutrition: Calories: 141, Fats: 1 g, Protein: 26 g, Carbs: 7 g, Fiber: 1 g, Sugar: 6 g, Sodium: 466 mg

152. Lemon Scallops with Asparagus

Preparation Time: 10 minutes
Cooking Time: 7–10 minutes
Servings: 2
Ingredients:

- ½ lb. asparagus, ends trimmed and cut into 2-inch pieces
- 1 cup sugar snap peas
- 1 lb. sea scallops
- 1 tbsp. lemon juice
- 2 tsp. olive oil
- ½ tsp. dried thyme
- A pinch salt
- Freshly ground black pepper, to taste

Directions:

1. Add the asparagus and sugar snap peas to the air fryer basket. Air-fry at 400°F for 2 to 3 minutes, or until the vegetables are just getting tender.
2. Meanwhile, check the scallops for a small muscle attached to the side, and pull it off and discard.
3. In a medium bowl, toss the scallops with lemon juice, olive oil, thyme, salt, and

pepper. Place it into the air fryer basket on top of the vegetables.

4. Air-fry for 5 to 7 minutes, tossing the basket once during the cooking time until the scallops are just firm when tested with your finger and are opaque in the center and the vegetables are tender. Serve immediately.

Nutrition: Calories: 163, Fats: 4 g, Protein: 22 g, Carbs: 10 g, Fiber: 3 g, Sugar: 3 g, Sodium: 225 mg

153. Fish Tacos

Preparation Time: 15 minutes
Cooking Time: 9–12 minutes
Servings: 2
Ingredients:

- 1 lb. white fish fillets, such as snapper
- 1 tbsp. olive oil
- 3 tbsp. freshly squeezed lemon juice, divided
- 1 ½ cups chopped red cabbage
- ½ cup salsa
- 1/3 cup sour cream
- 6 whole wheat tortillas
- 2 avocados, peeled and chopped

Directions:

1. Spray the fish with olive oil and sprinkle with 1 tablespoon of lemon juice. Place it in the air fryer basket and air-fry at 400°F for 9 to 12 minutes, or until the fish just flakes when tested with a fork.
2. Meanwhile, combine the remaining 2 tablespoons of lemon juice, cabbage, salsa, and sour cream in a medium bowl.
3. As momentarily as the fish is cooked, remove it from the air fryer basket and break it into large pieces.
4. Let everyone assemble their taco, combining the fish, tortillas, cabbage mixture, and avocados.

Nutrition: Calories: 547, Fats: 27 g, Protein: 33 g, Carbs: 43 g, Fiber: 12 g, Sugar: 4 g, Sodium: 679 mg

154. Spicy Cajun Shrimp

Preparation Time: 7 minutes
Cooking Time: 10–13 minutes
Servings: 2 cups
Ingredients:

- ½ lb. shrimp, peeled and deveined
- 1 tbsp. olive oil
- 1 tsp. ground cayenne pepper
- ½ tsp. Old Bay® seasoning
- ½ tsp. paprika
- 1/8 tsp. salt
- ½ lemon, juiced

Directions:

1. In a huge bowl, add the shrimp, olive oil, cayenne pepper, Old Bay Seasoning, paprika, and salt. Toss to combine.
2. Transfer the mixture to the air fryer basket and roast at 390ºF for 10 to 13 minutes, until browned.
3. Sprinkle a bit of lemon juice over the shrimp before serving.

Nutrition: Calories: 159, Fats: 7 g, Protein: 23 g, Carbs: 1 g, Fiber: 0 g, Sugar: 0 g, Sodium: 291 mg

155. Garlic Parmesan Roasted Shrimp

Preparation Time: 7 minutes
Cooking Time: 10–13 minutes
Servings: 2 cups
Ingredients:

- 1 lb. jumbo shrimp, peeled and deveined
- 1/3 cup Parmesan cheese
- 1 tbsp. olive oil
- 1 tsp. onion powder
- 2 tsp. minced garlic
- ½ tsp. ground black pepper
- ¼ tsp. dried basil

Directions:

1. In a large bowl, toss to combine the shrimp, Parmesan cheese, olive oil, onion powder, garlic, pepper, and basil.
2. Transfer to the air fryer basket and roast at 350ºF for 10 to 13 minutes, or until the shrimp are browned, then serve.

Nutrition: Calories: 162, Fats: 6 g, Protein: 25 g, Carbs: 2 g, Fiber: 0 g, Sugar: 0 g, Sodium: 271 mg

156. Quick Shrimp Scampi

Preparation Time: 10 minutes
Cooking Time: 7–8 minutes
Servings: 2
Ingredients:

- 30 (1-lb.) uncooked large shrimp, peeled, deveined, and tails removed
- 2 tsp. olive oil - 1/8 tsp. kosher salt
- 1 garlic clove, thinly sliced
- ½ lemon, juiced and zested
- A pinch red pepper flakes (optional)
- 1 tbsp. fresh parsley, chopped
- Non-stick cooking spray, as needed

Directions:

1. Sprig a baking pan with nonstick cooking spray, and then combine the shrimp, olive oil, sliced garlic, lemon juice and zest, kosher salt, and red pepper flakes (if using) in the pan, tossing to coat. Transfer the mixture to the air fryer basket.
2. Roast at 360ºF for 7 to 8 minutes, or until firm and bright pink.
3. Remove the shrimp from the fryer, place it on a serving plate, and sprinkle the parsley on top. Serve warm.

Nutrition: Calories: 321, Fats: 13 g, Protein: 46 g, Carbs: 5 g, Fiber: 0 g, Sugar: 1 g, Sodium: 383 mg

157. Mustard-Crusted Fish Fillets

Preparation Time: 5 minutes
Cooking Time: 8–11 minutes
Servings: 2
Ingredients:

- 5 tsp. low-sodium yellow mustard

- 1 tbsp. freshly squeezed lemon juice
- 4 (3 ½ oz.) sole fillets
- ½ tsp. dried thyme
- ½ tsp. dried marjoram
- 1/8 tsp. freshly ground black pepper
- 1 low-sodium, whole-wheat bread slice, crumbled
- 2 tsp. olive oil

Directions:

1. In a small bowl, stir the mustard and lemon juice. Spread this evenly over the fillets. Place them in the air fryer basket.
2. In another small bowl, mix the thyme, marjoram, pepper, bread crumbs, and olive oil. Mix until combined.
3. Gently but firmly, press the spice mixture onto each fish fillets top.
4. Bake for 8 to 11 minutes, or until the fish reaches an internal temperature of at least 145°F on a meat thermometer and the topping is browned and crisp. Serve immediately.

Nutrition: Calories: 142, Fats: 4 g, Saturated Fats: 1 g, Protein: 20 g, Carbs: 5 g, Sodium: 140 g, Fiber: 1 g, Sugar: 1 g

158. Fish and Vegetable Tacos

Preparation Time: 15minutes
Cooking Time: 9–12 minutes
Servings: 2
Ingredients:

- 1 lb. white fish fillets, such as sole or cod
- 2 tsp. olive oil
- 3 tbsp. freshly squeezed lemon juice, divided
- 1 ½ cups chopped red cabbage
- 1 large carrot, grated
- ½ cup low-sodium salsa
- 1/3 cup low-fat Greek yogurt

Directions:

1. Scrub the fish with olive oil and drizzle with 1 tablespoon of lemon juice. Fry in the air fryer basket for 9 to 12 minutes,

or until the fish just flakes when tested with a fork.
2. In the meantime, in a medium bowl, stir together the remaining 2 tablespoons of lemon juice, red cabbage, carrot, salsa, and yogurt.
3. As quickly as the fish is cooked, remove it from the air fryer basket and break it up into large pieces.

Nutrition: Calories: 209, Fats: 3 g, Saturated Fats: 0 g, Protein: 18 g, Carbs: 30 g, Sodium: 116 mg, Fiber: 1 g, Sugar: 4 g

159. Lighter Fish and Chips

Preparation Time: 10 minutes
Cooking Time: 11–15 minutes (chips), or 11–15 minutes (cod fillets)
Servings: 2
Ingredients:

- 2 russet potatoes, peeled, thinly sliced, rinsed, and patted dry
- 1 egg white
- 1 tbsp. freshly squeezed lemon juice
- 1/3 cup ground almonds
- 2 low-sodium, whole-wheat bread slices, finely crumbled
- ½ tsp. dried basil
- 4 (4-oz.) cod fillets

Directions:

1. Preheat the oven to warm.
2. Put the potato slices in the air fryer basket and air-fry for 11 to 15 minutes, or until crisp and brown. With tongs, turn the fries twice during cooking.
3. In the meantime, in a shallow bowl, beat the egg white and lemon juice until frothy.
4. On a plate, mix the almonds, bread crumbs, and basil.
5. Separately, dip the fillets into the egg white mixture and then into the almond–breadcrumb mixture to coat. Place the coated fillets on a wire rack to dry while the fries cook.

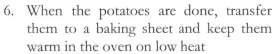

6. When the potatoes are done, transfer them to a baking sheet and keep them warm in the oven on low heat

7. Air-fry the fish in the air fryer basket for 10 to 14 minutes, or until the fish reaches an inner temperature of at least 140°F on a meat thermometer and the coating is browned and crisp. Serve immediately with the potatoes.

Nutrition: Calories: 247, Fats: 5 g, Saturated Fats: 0 g, Protein: 27 g, Carbs: 25 g, Sodium: 131 mg, Fiber: 3 g, Sugar: 3 g

160. Snapper with Fruit

Preparation Time: 15 minutes
Cooking Time: 9–13 minutes
Servings: 2
Ingredients:

- 4 (4-oz.) red snapper fillets
- 2 tsp. olive oil
- 3 nectarines, halved and pitted
- 3 plums, halved and pitted
- 1 cup red grapes
- 1 tbsp. freshly squeezed lemon juice
- 1 tbsp. honey
- ½ tsp. dried thyme

Directions:

1. Put the red snapper in the air fryer basket and drizzle with the olive oil. Air-fry for 4 minutes.
2. Remove the basket and add the nectarines and plums. Scatter the grapes overall.
3. Drizzle with the lemon juice and honey, and sprinkle with the thyme.
4. Put back the basket to the air fryer and air-fry for 5 to 9 minutes more, or till the fish flakes when tested with a fork and the fruit is tender. Serve immediately.

Nutrition: Calories: 245, Fats: 4 g, Saturated Fats: 1 g, Protein: 25 g, Carbs: 28 g, Sodium: 73 mg, Fiber: 3 g, Sugar: 24 g

161. Tuna and Fruit Kebabs

Preparation Time: 15 minutes
Cooking Time: 8–12 minutes
Servings: 2
Ingredients:

- 1 lb. tuna steaks, cut into 1-inch cubes
- ½ cup canned pineapple chunks, drained, juice reserved
- ½ cup large red grapes
- 1 tbsp. honey
- 2 tsp. grated fresh ginger
- 1 tsp. olive oil
- A pinch cayenne pepper

Directions:

1. Thread the tuna, pineapple, and grapes onto 8 bamboos or 4 metal skewers that fit in the air fryer.
2. In a small bowl, whisk the honey, 1 tablespoon of reserved pineapple juice, ginger, olive oil, and cayenne. Brush this mixture over the kebabs. Let them stand for 10 minutes.
3. Grill the kebabs for 8 to 12 minutes, or until the tuna reaches an internal temperature of at least 145°F on a meat thermometer and the fruit is tender and glazed, brushing once with the remaining sauce. Discard any remaining marinade. Serve immediately.

Nutrition: Calories: 181, Fats: 2 g, Saturated Fats: 0 g, Protein: 18 g, Carbs: 13 g, Sodium: 43 mg, Fiber: 1 g, Sugar: 12 g

162. Crab Legs with Butter Sauce

Preparation Time: 3 minutes
Cooking Time: 7 minutes
Servings: 2
Ingredients:

- 2 lb. crab legs, rinsed
- 1 cup water - 4 tbsps. butter
- ½ lemon, juiced
- 4 lemon wedges

Directions:

1. Add water into the instant pot.
2. Place the steamer basket and the crab legs on top.
3. Close the lid and press "Steam."
4. Cook for 7 minutes.
5. Do a quick release, and then remove the crab legs.
6. Mix the butter with the lemon juice.
7. Serve the crab legs with the sauce and lemon wedges.

Nutrition: Calories: 511, Fats: 22.5 g, Carb: 1 g, Protein: 66.7 g

---

163. Shrimp and Crab Stew

Preparation Time: 10 minutes
Cooking Time: 15 minutes
Servings: 2
Ingredients:

- 1 tbsp. coconut oil - ½ onion, diced
- 2 garlic cloves, minced
- 2 celery stalks, chopped
- 1 bay leaf
- 2 tsps. Old Bay® seasoning
- 1 tsp. salt
- 1 lb. shrimp, shelled, deveined, and chopped - 1 lb. lump crab meat
- 4 cups seafood stock
- 2 tbsps. butter
- ¼ cup heavy cream

Directions:

1. Heat the coconut oil on "Sauté" in the instant pot.
2. Add the onions and sauté for 3 minutes.
3. Add the garlic and sauté for 30 seconds.
4. Press "Cancel."
5. Except for the heavy cream, add all remaining ingredients.
6. Close the lid and press "Manual."
7. Cook for 10 minutes on "High."
8. Do a quick release and stir in the heavy cream. Serve.

Nutrition: Calories: 326, Fats: 15.4 g, Carb: 3.2 g, Protein: 28.3 g

164. Shrimp Stir-Fry

Preparation Time: 10 minutes
Cooking Time: 10 minutes
Servings: 2
Ingredients:

- 2 tbsps. coconut oil
- 1 lb. medium shrimp, shelled and deveined
- ½ cup button mushrooms
- ½ cup zucchini, diced
- 2 cups broccoli florets
- ¼ cup liquid aminos
- 2 garlic cloves, minced
- 1/8 tsp. red pepper flakes
- 2 cups cooked cauliflower rice

Directions:

1. Heat the coconut oil on "Sauté" in the instant pot.
2. Add the shrimp and stir-fry until fully cooked, about 5 minutes. Remove and set aside.
3. Add the red pepper flakes, garlic, liquid aminos, broccoli, zucchini, and mushrooms. Stir-fry for 3 to 5 minutes.
4. Add the shrimp back to the pot and press "Cancel."
5. Serve with cauliflower rice.

Nutrition: Calories: 173, Fats: 7.4 g, Carb: 7 g, Protein: 19.3 g

---

165. Buttered Scallops

Preparation Time: 5 minutes
Cooking Time: 5 minutes
Servings: 2
Ingredients:

- 2 tbsp. avocado oil
- 1 lb. large sea scallops, cooked
- 1/8 tsp. salt
- 1/8 tsp. pepper
- 2 tbsp. melted butter

Directions:

1. Press "Sauté" and heat the avocado oil in the instant pot.

2. Season the scallops with salt and pepper.
3. Sear the scallops for 2 to 3 minutes on each side.
4. Pour the butter over scallops and serve hot.

Nutrition: Calories: 190, Fats: 12.4 g, Carb: 3.7 g, Protein: 13.7 g

166. Lemon-Dill Salmon

Preparation Time: 3 minutes
Cooking Time: 5 minutes
Servings: 2
Ingredients:

- 2 (3-oz.) salmon filets
- 1 tsp. chopped fresh dill
- ½ tsp. salt
- ¼ tsp. pepper
- 1 cup water
- 2 tbsps. lemon juice
- ½ lemon, sliced

Directions:

1. Season the salmon with salt, pepper, and dill.
2. Add water to the instant pot and place it on a steam rack.
3. Place the salmon on the steam rack (skin-side down).
4. Drizzle with the lemon juice and put the lemon slices on top.
5. Close the lid and press "Steam."
6. Cook 5 minutes on "High."
7. Do a quick release and serve with the lemon slices and dill.

Nutrition: Calories: 127, Fats: 4.9 g, Carb: 1.5 g, Protein: 17.1 g

167. Lemon-Butter Lobster Tail

Preparation Time: 5 minutes
Cooking Time: 4 minutes
Servings: 2
Ingredients:

- 1 cup chicken broth
- ½ cup water

- 1 tsp. Old Bay® seasoning
- 2 (12-oz.) fresh lobster tails
- ½ lemon, juiced
- 2 tbsp. butter melted
- ¼ tsp. salt
- ¼ tsp. dried parsley
- 1/8 tsp. pepper

Directions:

1. Add the water, broth, and seasoning into the instant pot.
2. Place the lobster tails on the steam rack, shell-side down.
3. Close the lid and press "Manual."
4. Cook 4 minutes on "High."
5. Do a quick release.
6. In a bowl, combine salt, pepper, parsley, butter, and lemon juice.
7. Crack open the tail and dip into the butter sauce.

Nutrition: Calories: 259, Fats: 17.3 g, Carb: 1 g, Protein: 32.9 g

168. Salmon Burger with Avocado

Preparation Time: 10 minutes
Cooking Time: 5 minutes
Servings: 2
Ingredients:

- 2 tbsp. coconut oil
- 1 lb. salmon filets, skin removed and finely minced
- ½ tsp. salt
- ¼ tsp. garlic powder
- ¼ tsp. chili powder
- 2 tbsp. onion, finely diced
- 1 egg
- 2 tbsp. mayo
- 1/3 cup ground pork rinds
- 1 avocado, mashed
- ½ lime, juiced

Directions:

1. Melt the coconut oil on "Sauté" in the instant pot.

2. Place the salmon in a bowl.
3. Add the remaining ingredients except for lime and avocado.
4. Mix and form 4 patties.
5. Place the burgers into the pot, and sear for 3 to 4 minutes per side.
6. Press "Cancel" and set aside.
7. Mix the lime juice and avocado in a bowl.
8. Divide the mash into four sections, and place them on top of the salmon patties.
9. Serve.

Nutrition: Calories: 425, Fats: 27.6 g, Carb: 1.3 g, Protein: 35.6 g

169. Foil Pack Salmon

Preparation Time: 2 minutes
Cooking Time: 7 minutes
Servings: 2
Ingredients:

- 2 (3-oz.) salmon fillets
- 1 tsp. salt
- ¼ tsp. pepper
- ¼ tsp. garlic powder
- ¼ tsp. dried dill
- ½ lemon, sliced
- 1 cup water
- 1 tbsp. Lemon juice, to taste

Directions:

1. Place the salmon on a square of foil, skin-side down.
2. Add the seasoning and drizzle with lemon juice.
3. Place the lemon slices on each filet.
4. Pour the water into the instant pot and place it on a steam rack.
5. Place the foil packets on the steam rack and close the lid.
6. Press "Steam" and cook for 7 minutes.
7. Do a quick release.
8. Serve.

Nutrition: Calories: 125, Fats: 4.6 g, Carb: 0.4 g, Protein: 18.5 g

170. Almond-Pesto Salmon

Preparation Time: 5 minutes
Cooking Time: 7 minutes
Servings: 2
Ingredients:

- ¼ cup sliced almonds
- 1 tbsp. butter
- 4 (3-oz.) salmon fillets
- ½ cup pesto
- ½ tsp. salt
- ¼ tsp. pepper
- 1 cup water

Directions:

1. Press "Sauté" and add butter into the instant pot.
2. Sauté the almonds for 3 to 5 minutes. Remove and set aside.
3. Season the salmon with salt, and pepper. Then brush it with the pesto.
4. Pour the water into the instant pot and position the steam rack.
5. Add the salmon to the rack.
6. Close the lid and press "Steam."
7. Cook for 7 minutes.
8. Serve with the almond slices on top.

Nutrition: Calories: 182, Fats: 20.5 g, Carb: 3 g, Protein: 21.2 g

171. Tomato Cod

Preparation Time: 5 minutes
Cooking Time: 15 minutes
Servings: 2
Ingredients:

- 2 tbsp. butter
- ¼ cup diced onion
- 1 garlic clove, minced
- 1 cup cherry tomatoes, chopped
- ¼ tsp. salt
- 1/8 tsp. pepper
- ¼ tsp. dried thyme
- ¼ cup chicken broth
- 1 tbsp. capers
- 4 (4-oz.) cod filets

- 1 cup water
- ¼ cup chopped parsley

Directions:

1. Melt the butter on "Sauté" in the instant pot.
2. Add the onion and stir-fry until soften.
3. Add the garlic and cook for 30 seconds more.
4. Add the broth, thyme, pepper, salt, and chopped tomatoes.
5. Cook for 5 to 7 minutes, or until tomatoes soften. Press "Cancel."
6. Pour the sauce into a bowl.
7. Add the fish fillets and capers. Cover with foil. Pour water into the instant pot.
8. Place the steam rack on the bottom.
9. Place the bowl on top.
10. Close the lid and press "Manual."
11. Cook for 3 minutes. Do a quick release.
12. Sprinkle with the fresh parsley, and serve.

Nutrition: Calories: 157, Fats: 7.3 g, Carb: 2.2 g, Protein: 21 g

172. Fish Taco Bowls

Preparation Time: 15 minutes
Cooking Time: 5 minutes
Servings: 2
Ingredients:

- 4 cups shredded cabbage

- ¼ cup mayo
- 2 tbsp. sour cream
- 1 lime, halved
- 2 tbsp. pickled jalapeños, chopped
- 3 (4-oz.) tilapia filets
- 2 tsp. chili powder
- 1 tsp. cumin
- 1 tsp. garlic powder
- 1 tsp. salt
- 2 tbsp. coconut oil
- 1 avocado, diced
- 4 tbsp. chopped cilantro

Directions:

1. Mix the jalapeños, lime juice, sour cream, mayo, and cabbage in a bowl.
2. Cover and keep in the refrigerator for 30 minutes.
3. Press "Sauté" and add the coconut oil to the instant pot.
4. Season the filets with the seasonings.
5. Add the filets and sear for 2 to 4 minutes on each side.
6. Press "Cancel."
7. Chop the fish into bite-sized pieces.
8. Divide the slaw into four bowls, and place the fish on top.
9. Add the chopped avocado, and drizzle with the lime juice.
10. Sprinkle with the cilantro, and serve.

Nutrition: Calories: 328, Fats: 23.8 g, Carb: 4.2 g, Protein: 19.4 g

173. Crispy Blackened Salmon

Preparation Time: 5 minutes
Cooking Time: 5 minutes
Servings: 2
Ingredients:

- 2 (3-oz.) salmon filets
- 1 tbsp. avocado oil
- 1 tsp. paprika
- ½ tsp. salt
- ¼ tsp. pepper
- ¼ tsp. onion powder

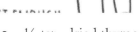

- ¼ tsp. dried thyme
- 1/8 tsp. cayenne pepper

Directions:

1. Drizzle the salmon with avocado oil.
2. In a bowl, mix the remaining ingredients, and rub the mixture over the filets.
3. Press "Sauté" and place salmon into the instant pot.
4. Sear for 2 to 5 minutes, or until the seasoning is blackened.
5. Serve.

Nutrition: Calories: 190, Fats: 11.4 g, Carb: 1 g, Protein: 18.6 g

174. Steamed Clams

Preparation Time: 5 minutes
Cooking Time: 5 minutes
Servings: 2
Ingredients:

- 2 lb. clams
- 1 cup seafood stock
- 4 tbsp. butter

Directions:

1. Place the seafood stock and clams into the instant pot.
2. Close the lid.
3. Press "Steam" and cook for 5 minutes.
4. Do a quick release.
5. Serve with butter.

Nutrition: Calories: 151, Fats: 11 g, Carb: 2.1 g, Protein: 8.7 g

175. Cajun Shrimp, Crab, and Sausage Boil

Preparation Time: 10 minutes
Cooking Time: 5 minutes
Servings: 2
Ingredients:

- ½ lb. smoked sausage
- ½ lb. large shrimp, shelled and deveined
- 2 lb. crab legs
- 2 cups seafood stock
- 1 tbsp. Cajun seasoning

Directions:

1. Place all the ingredients into the instant pot, and close the lid.
2. Press "Steam" and cook for 5 minutes.
3. Do a quick release, and serve.

Nutrition: Calories: 239, Fats: 8 g, Carb: 5.2 g, Protein: 32.2 g

176. Butter Shrimp with Asparagus

Preparation Time: 5 minutes
Cooking Time: 3 minutes
Servings: 2
Ingredients:

- 1 lb. cooked shrimp
- 1 garlic clove, minced
- ½ tsp. salt
- ¼ tsp. pepper
- ¼ tsp. paprika
- 1/8 tsp. red pepper flakes
- ½ lb. asparagus, cut into bite-sized pieces
- ½ lemon, juiced
- 4 tbsp. butter
- 2 tsp. fresh parsley, chopped
- 1 cup water

Directions:

1. Sprinkle the shrimp with red pepper flakes, paprika, pepper, salt, and garlic.
2. Place the shrimp in a bowl and add the asparagus.
3. Drizzle with the lemon juice, and mix.
4. Place the cubed butter around the dish.
5. Sprinkle with the parsley, and cover with foil.
6. Add the water to the instant pot, and position the steam rack.
7. Place the dish on the steam rack and close the lid.
8. Press "Steam" and cook for 3 minutes.
9. Do a quick release. Remove and serve.

Nutrition: Calories: 381, Fats: 23.2 g, Carb: 4.3 g, Protein: 32.7 g

177. Mexican Ceviche

Preparation Time: 30 minutes
Cooking Time: 0 minutes
Servings: 2
Ingredients:

- ½ lb. fresh skinless, white, ocean fish fillet (halibut, mahi mahi, etc.), diced
- 1 cup freshly squeezed lime juice, divided - 2 tbsp. fresh cilantro, chopped and divided - 1 serrano pepper, sliced
- 1 garlic clove, crushed - ¾ tsp. salt, divided - ½ red onion, thinly sliced
- 2 tomatoes, diced
- 1 red bell pepper, seeded and diced
- 1 tbsp. extra-virgin olive oil

Directions:

1. In a large mixing bowl, combine the fish, ¾ cup of lime juice, 1 tablespoon of cilantro, serrano pepper, garlic, and ½ teaspoon of salt. (The fish should be covered or nearly covered in lime juice.) Cover the bowl and refrigerate for 4 hours. Sprinkle the remaining ¼ teaspoon of salt over the onion in a small bowl, and let sit for 10 minutes. Drain and rinse well. In a large bowl, combine the tomatoes, bell pepper, olive oil, remaining ¼ cup of lime juice, and onion. Let rest for at least 10 minutes, or as long as 4 hours, while the fish "cooks."
2. When the fish is ready, it will be completely white and opaque. At this time, strain the juice, reserving it in another bowl. If desired, remove the serrano pepper and garlic.
3. Add the vegetables to the fish, and stir gently. Taste, and add some of the reserved lime juice to the ceviche as desired. Serve topped with the remaining 1 tablespoon of cilantro.

Nutrition: Calories: 122, Fats: 4.1 g, Protein: 11.9 g, Carbs: 11.1 g, Fiber: 2.1 g, Sugar: 4.9 g, Sodium: 404 mg

178. Chard Cod in Paper

Preparation Time: 10 minutes
Cooking Time: 15 minutes
Servings: 2
Ingredients:

- 1 chard bunch, stemmed, leaves and stems cut into thin strips
- 1 red bell pepper, seeded and cut into strips - 1 lb. cod fillets cut into 4 pieces
- 1 tbsp. grated fresh ginger
- 3 garlic cloves, minced
- 2 tbsp. white wine vinegar
- 2 tbsp. low-sodium tamari or gluten-free soy sauce - 1 tbsp. honey

Directions:

1. Preheat the oven to 425°F.
2. Cut 4 pieces of parchment paper, each about 16 inches wide. Lay the four pieces out on a large workspace.
3. On each piece of paper, arrange a small pile of chard leaves and stems, topped by several strips of bell pepper. Top with a piece of cod.
4. In a small bowl, mix the ginger, garlic, vinegar, tamari, and honey. Top each piece of fish with ¼ of the mixture.
5. Fold the parchment paper over so the edges overlap. Fold the edges over several times to secure the fish in the packets. Carefully, place the packets on a large baking sheet. Bake for 12 minutes. Carefully, open the packets, allowing steam to escape, and serve.

Nutrition: Calories: 120, Fats: 1.0 g, Protein: 19.1 g, Carbs: 8.9 g, Fiber: 1.1 g, Sugar: 6.1 g, Sodium: 716 mg

179. Roasted Halibut with Vegetables

Preparation Time: 10 minutes
Cooking Time: 15–20 minutes
Servings: 2
Ingredients:

- 1 lb. green beans, trimmed

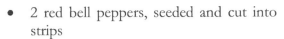

- 2 red bell peppers, seeded and cut into strips
- 1 onion, sliced
- 2 lemons, zest and juiced
- 3 garlic cloves, minced
- 2 tbsp. extra-virgin olive oil
- 1 tsp. dried dill
- 1 tsp. dried oregano
- 4 (4-oz.) halibut fillets
- ½ tsp. salt
- ¼ tsp. freshly ground black pepper

Directions:

1. Preheat the oven to 400°F. Line a baking sheet with parchment paper.
2. In a large bowl, toss the green beans, bell peppers, onion, lemon zest and juice, garlic, olive oil, dill, and oregano.
3. Use a slotted spoon to transfer the vegetables to the prepared baking sheet in a single layer, leaving the juice behind in the bowl.
4. Gently place the halibut fillets in the bowl, and coat in the juice. Transfer the fillets to the baking sheet, nestled between the vegetables. Then drizzle them with any juice left in the bowl. Sprinkle the vegetables and halibut with salt and pepper.
5. Bake for 15 to 20 minutes, or until the vegetables are just tender and the fish flakes apart easily.

Nutrition: Calories: 235, Fats: 9.1 g, Protein: 23.9 g, Carbs: 16.1 g, Fiber: 4.9 g, Sugar: 8.1 g, Sodium: 350 mg

180. Asparagus with Scallops

Preparation Time: 10 minutes
Cooking Time: 15 minutes
Servings: 2
Ingredients:

- 3 tsp. extra-virgin olive oil, divided
- 1 lb. asparagus, trimmed and cut into 2-inch segments
- 1 tbsp. butter

- 1 lb. sea scallops
- ¼ cup dry white wine
- 1 lemon, juiced
- 2 garlic cloves, minced
- ¼ tsp. freshly ground black pepper

Directions:

1. In a large skillet, heat 1 ½ teaspoons of oil over medium heat.
2. Add the asparagus and sauté for 5 to 6 minutes, or until just tender, stirring regularly. Remove them from the skillet and cover them with aluminum foil to keep them warm.
3. Add the remaining 1 ½ teaspoons of oil and the butter to the skillet. When the butter is melted and sizzling, place the scallops in a single layer in the skillet. Cook for about 3 minutes on one side, or until nicely browned. Use tongs to gently loosen and flip the scallops, and cook on the other side for another 3 minutes, or until browned and cooked through. Remove and cover with foil to keep warm.
4. In the same skillet, combine the wine, lemon juice, garlic, and pepper. Bring to a simmer for 1 to 2 minutes, stirring to mix in any browned pieces left in the pan.
5. Return the asparagus and the cooked scallops to the skillet to coat with the sauce. Serve warm.

Nutrition: Calories: 253, Fats: 7.1 g, Protein: 26.1 g, Carbs: 14.9 g, Fiber: 2.1 g, Sugar: 3.1 g, Sodium: 494 mg

181. Shrimp Cocktail

Preparation Time: 15 minutes
Cooking Time: 3 minutes
Servings: 2
Ingredients:

- 1 lb. medium shrimp, peeled and deveined
- 1 cup diced mango

- 2 ripe avocados, diced
- ¼ cup red onion, finely diced
- 2 Roma tomatoes, diced
- ¼ cup fresh cilantro, chopped
- 2 tbsp. low-carb tomato ketchup
- 1 lime, juiced
- 1 orange, juiced
- 1 tbsp. extra-virgin olive oil
- 1 jalapeño pepper, seeded and minced
- Lime wedges, for serving
- Water, as needed

Directions:

1. Fill a large pot about halfway with water and bring to a boil. Meanwhile, fill a large bowl 2/3 of the way with ice and about 1 cup of cold water.
2. Add the shrimp to the boiling water and cook for 3 minutes, or until they are opaque and firm. Drain and quickly transfer to the ice water bath for 3 minutes to stop the cooking and cool them. Drain and pat the shrimp dry with a clean paper towel.
3. In a large bowl, mix together the shrimp, mango, avocado, red onion, tomatoes, and cilantro.
4. In a small bowl, combine the ketchup, lime juice, orange juice, oil, and jalapeño. Mix well and gently fold the sauce into the shrimp mixture.
5. Divide among 4 glasses or small dishes, with a lime wedge on the rim of each.

Nutrition: Calories: 278, Fats: 16.1 g, Protein: 17.9 g, Carbs: 20.1 g, Fiber: 6.1 g, Sugar: 9.9 g, Sodium: 675 mg

182. Crab Cakes with Salsa

Preparation Time: 30 minutes
Cooking Time: 10 minutes
Servings: 2
Ingredients:
For the Salsa:

- 1 cup honeydew melon, finely chopped
- 1 scallion, white and green parts, finely chopped
- 1 red bell pepper, seeded, finely chopped
- 1 tsp. fresh thyme, chopped
- A pinch sea salt
- A pinch of freshly ground black pepper

For the Crab Cakes:

- 1 lb. lump crabmeat, drained and picked over
- ¼ cup red onion, finely chopped
- ¼ cup panko breadcrumbs
- 1 tbsp. fresh parsley, chopped
- 1 tsp. lemon zest
- 1 egg
- ¼ cup whole wheat flour
- Non-stick cooking spray, as needed

Directions:

1. To make the salsa, in a small bowl, stir together the melon, scallion, bell pepper, and thyme.
2. Season the salsa with salt and pepper and set aside.
3. To make the crab cakes, in a medium bowl, mix the crab, onion, breadcrumbs, parsley, lemon zest, and egg until very well combined.
4. Divide the crab mixture into 8 equal portions and form them into patties about ¾ inch thick.
5. Chill the crab cakes in the refrigerator for at least 1 hour to firm them up.
6. Dredge the chilled crab cakes in the flour until lightly coated, shaking off any excess flour.
7. Place a large skillet over medium heat and lightly coat it with cooking spray.
8. Cook the crab cakes until they are golden brown, turning once, about 5 minutes per side.
9. Serve warm with the salsa.

Nutrition: Calories: 233, Fats: 3.1 g, Protein: 31.9 g, Carbs: 18.1 g, Fiber: 2.1 g, Sugar: 6.1 g, Sodium: 770 mg

183. Green Salmon Florentine

Preparation Time: 10 minutes
Cooking Time: 30 minutes
Servings: 2
Ingredients:

- 1 tsp. extra-virgin olive oil
- ½ sweet onion, finely chopped
- 1 tsp. minced garlic
- 3 cups baby spinach
- 1 cup kale, tough stems removed, torn into 3-inch pieces
- Sea salt and freshly ground black pepper, to taste
- 4 (5-oz.) salmon fillets
- Lemon wedges, for serving

Directions:

1. Preheat the oven to 350°F.
2. Place a large skillet over medium-high heat, and add the oil.
3. Sauté the onion and garlic until softened and translucent, about 3 minutes.
4. Add the spinach and kale, and sauté until the greens wilt, about 5 minutes.
5. Remove the skillet from the heat and season the greens with salt and pepper.
6. Place the salmon fillets so they are nestled in the greens and partially covered by them. Bake the salmon until it is opaque, about 20 minutes.
7. Serve immediately with a squeeze of fresh lemon.

Nutrition: Calories: 282, Fats: 15.9 g, Protein: 28.9 g, Carbs: 4.1 g, Fiber: 1.1 g, Sugar: 0.9 g, Sodium: 92 mg

184. Hearty Faux Conch Fritters

Preparation Time: 15 minutes
Cooking Time: 10–14 minutes
Servings: 2
Ingredients:

- 4 medium egg whites
- ½ cup fat-free milk
- 1 cup chickpea crumbs
- ¼ tsp. black pepper, freshly ground
- ½ tsp. ground cumin
- 3 cups frozen scallops, chopped and thawed
- 1 small onion, finely chopped
- 1 small green bell pepper, finely chopped
- 2 celery stalks, finely chopped
- 2 garlic cloves, minced
- 2 limes, juiced

Directions:

1. Preheat the oven to 350°F.
2. In a large bowl, combine the egg whites, milk, and chickpea crumbs.
3. Add the black pepper and cumin, and mix well.
4. Add the scallops, onion, bell pepper, celery, and garlic.
5. Form golf ball–sized patties, and place them on a rimmed baking sheet 1 inch apart.
6. Transfer the baking sheet to the oven and cook for 5 to 7 minutes, or until golden brown.
7. Flip the patties, return them to the oven, and bake for 5 to 7 minutes, or until golden brown.
8. Top with lime juice, and serve.

Nutrition: Calories: 338, Fats: 0 g, Protein: 50.1 g, Carbs: 24.1 g, Fiber: 5.9 g, Sugar: 4.0 g, Sodium: 465 mg

185. Mango Salsa Cod

Preparation Time: 10 minutes
Cooking Time: 5–10 minutes
Servings: 2
Ingredients:

- 1 lb. cod, cut into 4 fillets, pin bones removed
- 2 tbsp. extra-virgin olive oil
- ¾ tsp. sea salt, divided
- 1 mango, pitted, peeled, and cut into cubes
- ¼ cup chopped cilantro

- ½ red onion, finely chopped
- 1 jalapeño, seeded and finely chopped
- 1 garlic clove, minced
- 1 lime, juiced

Directions:

1. Preheat the oven broiler on high.
2. On a rimmed baking sheet, brush the cod with the olive oil and season with ½ teaspoon of salt. Broil until the fish is opaque, about 5 to 10 minutes.
3. Meanwhile, in a small bowl, combine the mango, cilantro, onion, jalapeño, garlic, lime juice, and remaining ¼ teaspoon of salt.
4. Serve the cod with the salsa spooned over the top.

Nutrition: Calories: 200, Fats: 8.0 g, Protein: 21.1 g, Carbs: 12.9 g, Fiber: 1.9 g, Sugar: 7.6 g, Sodium: 355 mg

186. Broiled Cod with Mango Salsa

Preparation Time: 10 minutes
Cooking Time: 5–10 minutes
Servings: 2
Ingredients:
For the Cod:

- 1 lb. cod, cut into 4 fillets, pin bones removed
- 2 tbsp. extra-virgin olive oil
- ¾ tsp. sea salt, divided

For the Mango Salsa:

- 1 mango, pitted, peeled, and cut into cubes
- ¼ cup chopped cilantro
- 1 jalapeño, deseeded and finely chopped
- ½ red onion, finely chopped
- 1 lime, juiced
- 1 garlic clove, minced

Directions:

1. Preheat the broiler on high.
2. Place the cod fillets on a rimmed baking sheet. Brush both sides of the fillets with

olive oil. Sprinkle with ½ teaspoon of the salt.
3. Broil in the preheated broiler for 5 to 10 minutes, or until the flesh flakes easily with a fork.
4. Meanwhile, make the mango salsa by stirring together the mango, cilantro, jalapeño, red onion, lime juice, garlic, and remaining salt in a small bowl.
5. Serve the cod warm and topped with the mango salsa.

Nutrition: Calories: 198, Fats: 8.1 g, Protein: 21.2 g, Carbs: 13.2 g, Fiber: 2.2 g, Saturated Fats: 1 g, Sodium: 355 mg

187. Butter Cod with Asparagus

Preparation Time: 5 minutes
Cooking Time: 10 minutes
Servings: 2
Ingredients:

- 4 (4-oz.) cod fillets
- ¼ tsp. garlic powder
- ¼ tsp. salt
- ¼ tsp. freshly ground black pepper
- 2 tbsp. unsalted butter
- 24 asparagus spears, woody ends trimmed
- ½ cup brown rice, cooked
- 1 tbsp. freshly squeezed lemon juice

Directions:

1. In a large bowl, season the cod fillets with the garlic powder, salt, and pepper. Set aside.
2. Melt the butter in a skillet over medium-low heat.
3. Place the cod fillets and asparagus in the skillet in a single layer. Cook covered for 8 minutes, or until the cod is cooked through.
4. Divide the cooked brown rice, cod fillets, and asparagus among 4 plates. Serve drizzled with the lemon juice.

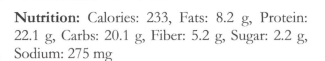 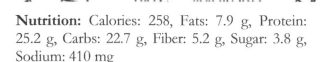

Nutrition: Calories: 233, Fats: 8.2 g, Protein: 22.1 g, Carbs: 20.1 g, Fiber: 5.2 g, Sugar: 2.2 g, Sodium: 275 mg

Nutrition: Calories: 258, Fats: 7.9 g, Protein: 25.2 g, Carbs: 22.7 g, Fiber: 5.2 g, Sugar: 3.8 g, Sodium: 410 mg

188. Creamy Cod Fillet with Quinoa and Asparagus

Preparation Time: 5 minutes
Cooking Time: 10 minutes
Servings: 2
Ingredients:

- ½ cup uncooked quinoa
- 4 (4-oz.) cod fillets
- ½ tsp. garlic powder, divided
- ¼ tsp. salt
- ¼ tsp. freshly ground black pepper
- 24 asparagus spears, cut the bottom 1 ½ inches off
- 1 tbsp. avocado oil
- 1 cup half-and-half
- Water, as needed

Directions:

1. Put the quinoa in a pot of salted water. Bring to a boil. Reduce the heat to low and simmer for 15 minutes, or until the quinoa is soft and has a white "tail." Cover and turn off the heat. Let sit for 5 minutes.
2. On a clean work surface, rub the cod fillets with ¼ teaspoon of garlic powder, salt, and pepper.
3. Heat the avocado oil in a non-stick skillet over medium-low heat.
4. Add the cod fillets and asparagus in the skillet and cook for 8 minutes, or until they are tender. Flip the cod and shake the skillet halfway through the cooking time.
5. Pour the half-and-half in the skillet, and sprinkle with remaining garlic powder. Turn up the heat to high and simmer for 2 minutes, or until creamy.
6. Divide the quinoa, cod fillets, and asparagus into 4 bowls, and serve warm.

189. Creamy Tuna and Zoodle Casserole

Preparation Time: 10 minutes
Cooking Time: 30 minutes
Servings: 2
Ingredients:

- 1 tbsp. avocado oil
- 1 medium yellow onion, diced
- 2 tbsp. whole wheat flour
- 2 cups low-sodium chicken broth
- 1 cup unsweetened almond milk
- 1 (10-oz.) package zucchini noodles
- 1 cup fresh or frozen broccoli, cut into florets
- 2 (5-oz.) cans chunk-light tuna, drained
- 1 cup cheddar cheese, shredded

Directions:

1. Preheat the oven to 375°F.
2. Heat the avocado oil in a non-stick skillet over medium heat until shimmering.
3. Add the onion to the skillet and cook for 3 minutes, or until translucent.
4. Add the flour to the skillet and cook for 2 minutes. Stir constantly.
5. Gently fold in the chicken broth and almond milk, then turn up the heat to high and bring the mixture to a boil.
6. Add the zucchini noodles and broccoli to the skillet. Reduce the heat to medium and cook for 6 minutes, or until the mixture is lightly thickened. Add the tuna to the skillet.
7. Pour the mixture into a casserole dish, and spread the cheese on top. Cover the casserole dish with aluminum foil.
8. Bake in the preheated oven for 20 minutes, or until the tuna is opaque.
9. Remove the aluminum foil and broil for an additional 2 minutes.

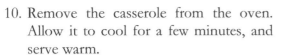

10. Remove the casserole from the oven. Allow it to cool for a few minutes, and serve warm.

Nutrition: Calories: 273, Fats: 11.8 g, Protein: 29.1 g, Carbs: 11.1 g, Fiber: 3.2 g, Sugar: 2.8 g, Sodium: 349 mg

190. Sole Piccata with Capers

Preparation Time: 10 minutes
Cooking Time: 17 minutes
Servings: 2
Ingredients:

- 1 tsp. extra-virgin olive oil
- 4 (5-oz.) sole fillets, patted dry
- 3 tbsp. butter
- 2 tsp. minced garlic
- 2 tbsp. all-purpose flour
- 2 cups low-sodium chicken broth
- ½ lemon, juiced and zested
- 2 tbsp. capers

Directions:

1. Heat the olive oil in a large skillet over medium heat.
2. Add the sole fillets to the skillet and sear each side for about 4 minutes, or until the fish is opaque and flakes easily.
3. Remove from the heat to a plate, and set it aside. Melt the butter in the skillet and sauté the garlic for 3 minutes, or until fragrant. Add the flour and cook for about 2 minutes, stirring frequently, or until the mixture is bubbly and foamy. (It should look like a thick paste.)
4. Stir in the chicken broth, lemon juice and zest. Cook for 4 minutes, whisking constantly, or until the sauce is thickened. Scatter with the capers and spoon the sauce over the fish. Serve immediately.

Nutrition: Calories: 273, Fats: 13.3 g, Protein: 30.3 g, Carbs: 7.1 g, Fiber: 0 g, Sugar: 2.2 g, Sodium: 414 mg

191. Haddock with Cucumber Sauce

Preparation Time: 10 minutes
Cooking Time: 10 minutes
Servings: 2
Ingredients:
For the Cucumber Sauce:

- ½ English cucumber, grated and liquid squeezed out
- ¼ cup plain Greek yogurt
- ½ scallion, white and green parts, finely chopped
- 2 tsp. chopped fresh mint
- 1 tsp. honey - A pinch salt

For the Fish:

- 4 (5-oz.) haddock fillets, patted dry
- Sea salt and freshly ground black pepper, to taste
- Non-stick cooking spray, as needed

Directions:

1. Whisk together all the ingredients for the cucumber sauce in a small bowl, and set it aside.
2. On a clean work surface, lightly season the haddock fillets with salt and pepper.
3. Heat a large skillet over medium-high heat and spritz with non-stick cooking spray.
4. Cook the haddock fillets for 10 minutes, flipping them halfway through, or until the fish is lightly browned and cooked through. Divide the haddock fillets among 4 plates and top them with the cucumber sauce. Serve warm.

Nutrition: Calories: 165, Fats: 2.2 g, Protein: 27.3 g, Carbs: 4.2 g, Fiber: 0 g, Sugar: 3.2 g, Sodium: 105 mg

192. Air-Fried Flounder

Preparation Time: 5 minutes
Cooking Time: 12 minutes
Servings: 2
Ingredients:

- 2 cups low-fat buttermilk

- ½ tsp. onion powder
- ½ tsp. garlic powder
- 4 (4-oz.) flounder fillets
- ½ cup chickpea flour
- ½ cup plain yellow cornmeal
- ¼ tsp. cayenne pepper
- Freshly ground black pepper, to taste

Directions:

1. Whisk together the buttermilk, onion powder, and garlic powder in a large bowl. Add the flounder fillets, coating well on both sides. Let the fish marinate for 20 minutes. Thoroughly combine the chickpea flour, cornmeal, cayenne pepper, and pepper in a shallow bowl.
2. Dredge each fillet in the flour mixture until they are completely coated.
3. Preheat the air fryer to 380°F.
4. Arrange the fish in the air fryer basket and bake for 12 minutes, flipping the fish halfway through, or until the fish is cooked through. Serve warm.

Nutrition: Calories: 231, Fats: 6.2 g, Protein: 28.2 g, Carbs: 16.2 g, Fiber: 2.2 g, Sugar: 7.1 g, Sodium: 240 mg

193. Easy Fish Tacos with Yogurt Sauce

Preparation Time: 5 minutes
Cooking Time: 10 minutes
Servings: 2
Ingredients:
For the Yogurt Sauce:

- ½ cup plain low-fat Greek yogurt
- 1/3 cup low-fat mayonnaise

- ½ tsp. ground cumin
- ½ tsp. garlic powder

For the Tacos:

- 2 tbsp. extra-virgin olive oil
- 4 (6-oz.) cod fillets
- 8 (10-inch) yellow corn tortillas
- 2 cups packaged shredded cabbage
- ¼ cup fresh cilantro, chopped
- 4 lime wedges

Directions:

1. Whisk together all the ingredients for the yogurt sauce in a small bowl. Set aside.
2. To make the tacos, heat the olive oil in a medium skillet over medium-low heat.
3. Add the fish and cook each side for 4 minutes, or until flaky.
4. Arrange the tortillas on a clean work surface. Top each tortilla evenly with the shredded cabbage, cooked fish, cilantro, yogurt sauce, and a squeeze of lime juice.
5. Serve immediately.

Nutrition: Calories: 375, Fats: 13.2 g, Protein: 36.2 g, Carbs: 30.2 g, Fiber: 4.2 g, Sugar: 4.1 g, Sodium: 340 mg

194. Asparagus and Scallop Skillet with Lemony

Preparation Time: 10 minutes
Cooking Time: 15 minutes
Servings: 2
Ingredients:

- 3 tsp. extra-virgin olive oil, divided
- 1 lb. asparagus, trimmed and cut into 2-inch segments
- 1 tbsp. butter
- 1 lb. sea scallops
- ¼ cup dry white wine
- 2 garlic cloves, minced
- 1 lemon, juiced
- ¼ tsp. freshly ground black pepper

Directions:

1. Heat half of olive oil in a non-stick skillet over medium heat until shimmering.
2. Add the asparagus to the skillet and sauté for 6 minutes, or until soft. Transfer the cooked asparagus to a large plate and cover them with aluminum foil.
3. Heat the remaining half of olive oil and butter in the skillet until the butter is melted.
4. Add the scallops to the skillet and cook for 6 minutes, or until opaque and browned. Flip the scallops with tongs halfway through the cooking time. Transfer the scallops to the plate and cover them with aluminum foil.
5. Combine the wine, garlic, lemon juice, and black pepper in the skillet. Simmer over medium-low heat for 2 minutes. Keep stirring during the simmering.
6. Pour the sauce over the asparagus and scallops to coat well, then serve warm.

Nutrition: Calories: 256, Fats: 6.9 g, Protein: 26.1 g, Carbs: 14.9 g, Fiber: 2.1 g, Sugar: 2.9 g, Sodium: 491 mg

195. Seared Scallops with Orange Sauce

Preparation Time: 10 minutes
Cooking Time: 10 minutes
Servings: 2
Ingredients:

- 2 lb. sea scallops, patted dry
- Sea salt and freshly ground black pepper, to taste
- 2 tbsp. extra-virgin olive oil
- 1 tbsp. minced garlic
- ¼ cup freshly squeezed orange juice
- 1 tsp. orange zest
- 2 tsp. fresh thyme, chopped, for garnish

Directions:

1. In a bowl, season the scallops with salt and pepper. Set aside.
2. Heat the olive oil in a large skillet over medium-high heat until shimmering.
3. Add the garlic, and sauté for about 3 minutes, stirring occasionally, or until the garlic is softened.
4. Add the scallops and cook each side for about 4 minutes, or until the scallops are lightly browned and firm.
5. Remove the scallops from the heat to a plate, and cover with foil to keep warm. Set aside.
6. Pour the orange juice and zest into the skillet and stir, scraping up any cooked bits.
7. Drizzle the scallops with the orange sauce and sprinkle the thyme on top for garnish before serving.

Nutrition: Calories: 268, Fats: 8.2 g, Protein: 38.2 g, Carbs: 8.3 g, Fiber: 0 g, Sugar: 1.1 g, Sodium: 360 mg

196. Breaded Scallop Patties

Preparation Time: 15 minutes
Cooking Time: 10–14 minutes
Servings: 2
Ingredients:

- 4 medium egg whites
- 1 cup chickpea crumbs
- ½ cup fat-free milk
- ½ tsp. ground cumin
- ¼ tsp. freshly ground black pepper
- 3 cups frozen scallops, thawed and chopped
- 1 small onion, finely chopped
- 2 garlic cloves, minced
- 2 celery stalks, finely chopped
- 1 small green bell pepper, finely chopped
- 2 limes, juiced

Directions:

1. Preheat the oven to 350°F.
2. Whisk together the egg whites, chickpea crumbs, milk, cumin, and black pepper in a large bowl until well combined.
3. Stir in the scallops, onion, garlic, celery, and bell pepper. Shape the mixture into golf ball-sized balls, and flatten them into patties with your hands.
4. Arrange the patties on a rimmed baking sheet, spacing them 1 inch apart.
5. Bake in the preheated oven for 10 to 14 minutes, or until golden brown. Flip the patties halfway through the cooking time.
6. Serve drizzled with lime juice.

Nutrition: Calories: 338, Fats: 0 g, Protein: 50.2 g, Carbs: 24.2 g, Fiber: 6.2 g, Sugar: 4.2 g, Sodium: 465 mg

197. Shrimp and Vegetable Stir Fry

Preparation Time: 5 minutes
Cooking Time: 15 minutes
Servings: 4
Ingredients:
For the Sauce:

- ½ cup water
- 2 ½ tbsp. low-sodium soy sauce
- 2 tbsp. honey
- 1 tbsp. rice vinegar
- ¼ tsp. garlic powder
- A pinch ground ginger
- 1 tbsp. cornstarch

For the Stir Fry:

- 8 cups frozen vegetable stir fry mix
- 2 tbsp. sesame oil
- 40 medium fresh shrimp, peeled and deveined

Directions:

1. To make the sauce, mix the water, soy sauce, honey, vinegar, garlic powder, and ginger in a small saucepan. Stir to combine. Fold in the cornstarch and whisk constantly until everything is incorporated.
2. Let the sauce boil over medium heat for 1 minute. Remove from the heat and set aside in a bowl.
3. To make the stir fry, heat a large saucepan over medium-high heat until hot. Add the vegetable stir fry mix and cook for 8 to 10 minutes, stirring occasionally, or until the water has evaporated.
4. Reduce the heat, pour in the sesame oil and add the shrimp. Stir well and cook for 3 minutes, stirring occasionally, or until the shrimp are pink and cooked through.
5. Stir in the prepared sauce and cook for another 2 minutes.
6. Remove from the heat and let cool for 5 minutes before serving.

Nutrition: Calories: 299, Fats: 17.3 g Protein: 24.3 g, Carbs: 14.2 g, Fiber: 2.2 g, Sugar: 9.1 g, Sodium: 453 mg

198. Oysters with Artichoke Heats

Preparation Time: 30 minutes
Cooking Time: 20 minutes
Servings: 2
Ingredients:

- 2 cups coarse salt, for holding the oysters
- 1 dozen fresh oysters, scrubbed
- 1 tbsp. butter
- ½ cup artichoke hearts, finely chopped
- ¼ cup red bell pepper, finely chopped
- ¼ cup finely chopped scallions, both white and green parts
- 1 tbsp. fresh parsley, finely chopped
- ½ lemon, zested and juiced
- 1 garlic clove, minced
- Salt and freshly ground black pepper, to taste

Directions:

1. Spread the coarse salt in the bottom of a baking dish.
2. Shuck the oyster with a shucking knife, then discard the empty half, and loosen the oyster with the knife. Arrange the oyster on the shells with juices, then place them on the coarse salt in the baking dish. Set aside.
3. Preheat the oven to 425°F.
4. Put the butter in a non-stick skillet, and melt over medium heat.
5. Add the artichokes hearts, bell pepper, and scallions to the skillet. Sauté for 6 minutes, or until soft.
6. Add the garlic to the skillet and sauté for 1 minute more or until fragrant.
7. Remove them from the skillet into a large bowl, then spread the parsley and lemon zest on top. Drizzle with lemon juice, and then sprinkle with salt and black pepper.
8. Spoon the vegetable mixture in each oyster. Bake in the preheated oven for 12 minutes, or until the vegetables are lightly wilted.
9. Remove them from the oven and serve warm.

Nutrition: Calories: 136, Fats: 6.9 g, Protein: 6.1 g, Carbs: 10.8 g, Fiber: 2.1 g, Sugar: 6.7 g, Sodium: 276 mg

CHAPTER 8:

Snacks

199. Sweet Potato Fries

Preparation Time: 5 minutes
Cooking Time: 13 minutes
Servings: 2
Ingredients:

- 2 medium sweet potatoes, peeled
- 1 tbsp. arrowroot starch
- 2 tbsp. cinnamon
- 1/4 cup coconut sugar
- 2 tsp. unsalted butter, melted
- ½ tbsp. olive oil
- Confectioner's swerve, as needed

Directions:

1. Switch on the air fryer, insert the fryer basket, grease it with olive oil, shut it with its lid, set the fryer to 370°F, and preheat for 5 minutes.
2. Meanwhile, cut the peeled sweet potatoes into ½-inch thick slices, place them in a bowl, add oil and starch, and toss until well coated.
3. Open the fryer, add sweet potatoes to it, close it with its lid, and cook for 8 minutes, or until nicely golden, shaking halfway through the frying.
4. When the air fryer beeps, open its lid, transfer the sweet potato fries into a bowl, add the butter, sprinkle with the sugar and cinnamon, and toss until well mixed. Sprinkle the confectioner swerve on the fries and serve.

Nutrition: Calories: 130, Carbs: 27 g, Fats: 2.3 g, Protein: 1.2 g, Fiber: 3 g

200. Cheese Sticks

Preparation Time: 5–7 minutes
Cooking Time: 10 minutes
Servings: 2
Ingredients:

- 10 spring roll wrappers, separated, quartered
- ¼ lb. sharp cheddar cheese, reduced-fat, sliced into 2x½-inch pieces
- Oil, for spraying
- Water, as needed

Directions:

1. Preheat the air fryer to 400°F.
2. Place the cheese pieces at the widest end of a quartered spring roll wrapper. Moisten the edges and tips of the wrapper with water. Fold the spring roll wrappers over the cheese, and tuck in both ends. Roll the spring roll tightly up to the tip. Place this into a freezer-safe container lined with saran wrap. Repeat the step for all cheese and spring roll wrappers.
3. Freeze for an hour before frying.

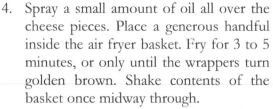

4. Spray a small amount of oil all over the cheese pieces. Place a generous handful inside the air fryer basket. Fry for 3 to 5 minutes, or only until the wrappers turn golden brown. Shake contents of the basket once midway through.

5. Remove from the basket. Set on plates. Repeat the step for the remaining breaded cheese sticks. Serve.

Nutrition: Calories: 229, Carbs: 16 g, Fats: 10 g, Protein: 15 g, Fiber: 1.8 g

201. Zucchini Crisps

Preparation Time: 30 minutes
Cooking Time: 30 minutes
Servings: 2
Ingredients:

- 2 zucchinis, sliced into 1/8-inch-thick disks
- A pinch sea salt
- White pepper, to taste
- Olive oil, for drizzling

Directions:

1. Preheat the air fryer to 330°F.
2. Put the zucchini in a bowl with salt. Let it sit in a colander to drain for 30 minutes.
3. Layer the zucchini in a baking dish. Drizzle in the oil. Season with pepper. Place the baking dish in the air fryer basket. Cook for 30 minutes.
4. Adjust the seasoning. Serve.

Nutrition: Calories: 15.2, Carbs: 3.6 g, Fats: 0.1 g, Protein: 0.6 g, Fiber: 1.3 g

202. Tortillas in Green Mango Salsa

Preparation Time: 30 minutes
Cooking Time: 10 minutes
Servings: 2
Ingredients:
For the Tortillas:

- 4 corn tortillas
- 1 tbsp. olive oil

- 1/16 tsp. sea salt

For the Green Mango Salsa:

- 1 green/unripe mango, minced
- 1 red/ripe Roma tomato, preferably minced
- 1 shallot, peeled and minced
- 1 fresh jalapeño pepper, minced
- ¼ red bell pepper, minced
- 4 tbsp. fresh cilantro, minced
- ¼ cup lime juice, freshly squeezed
- 1/16 tsp. salt

Directions:

1. Preheat the air fryer to 400°F.
2. Mix the lime juice and salt in a bowl. Stir until the solids dissolve. Add in the remaining salsa ingredients. Chill in the fridge for at least 30 minutes. Stir again just before using.
3. Lightly brush the oil on both sides of the tortillas. Cut these into large triangles.
4. Place a generous handful of sliced tortillas in the air fryer basket. Fry these for 10 minutes, or until the bread blisters and turns golden brown. Shake the content of the basket once midway through.
5. Place the cooked pieces on a plate. Repeat the steps for the remaining tortillas. Season with salt.
6. Place equal portions of crispy tortillas on plates. Serve with the green mango and tomato salsa on the side.

Nutrition: Calories: 128, Carbs: 8.6 g, Fats: 3.6 g, Protein: 2.7 g, Fiber: 5.7 g

203. Skinny Pumpkin Chips

Preparation Time: 20 minutes
Cooking Time: 13 minutes
Servings: 2
Ingredients:

- 1 lb. pumpkin, cut into sticks
- 1 tbsp. coconut oil
- 1/2 tsp. rosemary
- 1/2 tsp. basil

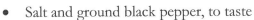

- Salt and ground black pepper, to taste
- Mayonnaise, for serving

Directions:

1. Start by preheating the air fryer to 395°F. Brush the pumpkin sticks with coconut oil; add the spices, and toss to combine.
2. Cook for 13 minutes, shaking the basket halfway through the cooking time.
3. Serve with mayonnaise. Bon appétit!

Nutrition: Calories: 118, Fats: 14.7 g, Carbs, 2.2 g, Protein 6.2 g, Sugars: 2 g

204. Palm Trees Holder

Preparation Time: 5 minutes
Cooking Time: 10 minutes
Servings: 2
Ingredients:

- 1 puff pastry sheet
- 1 cup Sugar

Directions:

1. Stretch the puff pastry sheet.
2. Pour the sugar over and fold the puff pastry sheet in half.
3. Put a thin layer of sugar on top and fold the puff pastry in half again.
4. Roll the puff pastry sheet from both ends towards the center (creating the palm tree's shape).
5. Cut it into sheets 5–8 mm thick.
6. Preheat the air fryer to 356°F and put the palm trees in the basket, and cook for 10 minutes.

Nutrition: Calories: 108, Fats: 12 g, Carbs: 29 g, Protein: 4 g, Sugar: 100 g, Cholesterol: 56 g

205. Air-Fried Ripe Plantains

Preparation Time: 10 minutes
Cooking Time: 10 minutes
Servings: 2
Ingredients:

- 2 large ripe plantains, peeled, sliced into inch thick disks
- 1 tbsp. coconut butter, unsweetened

Directions:

1. Preheat the air fryer to 350°F.
2. Brush a small amount of coconut butter on all sides of the plantain disks.
3. Place one even layer into the air fryer basket, making sure none overlap or touch. Fry the plantains for 10 minutes.
4. Remove the plantains from the basket, and place them on plates. Repeat the steps for all plantains.
5. Serve warm.

Nutrition: Calories: 209, Carbs: 29 g, Fats: 8 g, Protein: 2.9 g, Fiber: 3.5 g

206. Garlic Bread with Cheese Dip

Preparation Time: 10 minutes
Cooking Time: 10 minutes
Servings: 2
Ingredients:
For the Fried Garlic Bread:

- 1 medium baguette, halved lengthwise, cut sides toasted
- 2 garlic cloves, whole
- 4 tbsp. extra-virgin olive oil
- 2 tbsp. fresh parsley, minced

For the Blue Cheese Dip:

- 1 tbsp. fresh parsley, minced
- ¼ cup fresh chives, minced
- ¼ tsp. Tabasco® sauce
- 1 tbsp. lemon juice, freshly squeezed
- ½ cup low-fat Greek yogurt
- ¼ cup reduced-fat blue cheese
- 1/16 tsp. salt
- 1/16 tsp. white pepper

Directions:

1. Preheat the oven to 400°F.
2. Mix the oil and parsley in a small bowl.
3. Vigorously rub the garlic cloves on the cut/toasted sides of the baguette. Dispose of garlic nubs.
4. Using a pastry brush, spread the parsley-infused oil on the cut side of the bread.

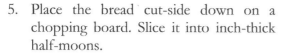

5. Place the bread cut-side down on a chopping board. Slice it into inch-thick half-moons.

6. Place the bread slices in the air fryer basket. Fry for 3 to 5 minutes, or until bread browns a little. Shake the content of the basket once midway through. Place the cooked pieces on a serving platter. Repeat the step for the remaining bread. To prepare the blue cheese dip, mix all the ingredients in a bowl.

7. Place equal portions of fried bread on plates. Serve with the blue cheese dip on the side.

Nutrition: Calories: 209, Carbs: 29 g, Fats: 8 g, Protein: 2.9 g, Fiber: 3.5 g

207. Fried Mixed Veggies with Avocado Dip

Preparation Time: 10 minutes
Cooking Time: 10 minutes
Servings: 2
Ingredients:

- Oil, for spraying

For the Avocado-Feta Dip:

- 1 avocado, pitted, peeled, and flesh scooped out
- 4 oz. reduced-fat feta cheese
- 2 leeks, minced
- 1 lime, freshly squeezed
- ¼ cup fresh parsley, roughly chopped
- 1/16 tsp. black pepper
- 1/16 tsp. salt

For the Vegetables:

- 1 zucchini, sliced into matchsticks
- 1 carrot, sliced into matchsticks
- 1 cup panko breadcrumbs, plus more if needed
- 1 parsnip, sliced into matchsticks
- 1 large egg, whisked, plus more if needed
- 1 cup all-purpose flour, plus more if needed
- 1/8 tsp. flaky sea salt

Directions:

1. Preheat the air fryer to 400°F.
2. Season the carrots, parsnips, and zucchini with salt.
3. Dredge the carrots with flour first, dip them into the whisked egg, and finally into the breadcrumbs. Place the breaded pieces on a baking sheet lined with parchment paper. Repeat the step for all carrots. Then do the same for parsnips and zucchini.
4. Spray vegetables lightly with oil. Place a generous handful of carrots in the air fryer basket. Fry for 10 minutes, or until the breading turns golden brown, shaking contents of the basket once midway. Place the cooked pieces on a plate. Repeat the step for the remaining carrots.
5. Do the previous step for the parsnip and the zucchini.
6. For the dip, except for salt, place the remaining ingredients in a food processor. Pulse a couple of times, and then process to the desired consistency, scraping down the sides of the machine. Taste. Add salt only if needed. Place it in an air-tight container. Chill until needed.
7. Place equal portions of cooked vegetables on plates. Serve with a small amount of the avocado-feta dip on the side.

Nutrition: Calories: 109, Carbs: 4.0 g, Fats: 2.6 g, Protein: 2.9 g, Fiber: 2.5 g

208. Air-Fried Plantains in Coconut Sauce

Preparation Time: 10 minutes
Cooking Time: 10 minutes
Servings: 2
Ingredients:

- 6 ripe plantains, peeled and quartered lengthwise
- 1 can coconut cream
- 2 tbsp. Honey

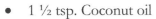

- 1 ½ tsp. Coconut oil

Directions:

1. Preheat the air fryer to 330°F.
2. Pour the coconut cream in a thick-bottomed saucepan set over high heat, then bring it to a boil. Reduce the heat to the lowest setting, and simmer uncovered until the cream is reduced by half and darkens in color. Then turn off the heat.
3. Whisk in the honey until smooth. Cool completely before using. Lightly grease a non-stick skillet with coconut oil.
4. Layer the plantains in the air fryer basket and fry until golden on both sides, then drain on paper towels. Transfer the plantains to plates.
5. Drizzle in a small amount of coconut sauce. Serve.

Nutrition: Calories: 236, Carbs: 0 g, Fats: 1.5 g, Protein: 1 g, Fiber: 1.8 g

209. Beef and Mango Skewers

Preparation Time: 10 minutes
Cooking Time: 4–7 minutes
Servings: 2
Ingredients:

- ¾ lb. beef sirloin tip, cut into 1-inch cubes
- 2 tbsp. balsamic vinegar
- 1 tbsp. olive oil
- 1 tbsp. honey
- ½ tsp. dried marjoram
- A pinch salt
- Freshly ground black pepper, to taste
- 1 mango

Directions:

1. Put the beef cubes in a medium bowl and add the balsamic vinegar, olive oil, honey, marjoram, salt, and pepper. Mix well, then rub the marinade into the beef with your hands. Set aside.
2. To prepare the mango, stand it on end and cut the skin off using a sharp knife.

Then carefully cut around the oval pit to remove the flesh. Cut the mango into 1-inch cubes.

3. Thread metal skewers, alternating with three beef cubes and two mango cubes. Place the skewers in the air fryer basket.
4. Air fry at 390°F for 4 to 7 minutes, or until the beef is browned and at least 145°F.

Nutrition: Calories: 245, Fats: 9 g, Protein: 26 g, Carbs: 15 g, Fiber: 1 g, Sugar: 14 g, Sodium: 96 mg

210. Kale Chips with Lemon Yogurt Sauce

Preparation Time: 10 minutes
Cooking Time: 5 minutes
Servings: 2
Ingredients:

- 1 cup plain Greek yogurt
- 3 tbsp. freshly squeezed lemon juice
- 2 tbsp. honey mustard
- ½ tsp. dried oregano
- 1 bunch curly kale
- 2 tbsp. olive oil
- ½ tsp. salt
- 1/8 tsp. pepper

Directions:

1. In a small bowl, mix the yogurt, lemon juice, honey mustard, and oregano. Set it aside.
2. Remove the stems and ribs from the kale with a sharp knife. Cut the leaves into 2–3-inch pieces.
3. Toss the kale with olive oil, salt, and pepper. Rub the oil into the leaves with your hands.
4. Air-fry the kale in batches at 390°F (199°C) until crisp, about 5 minutes, shaking the basket once during cooking time. Serve with the yogurt sauce.

Nutrition: Calories: 155, Fats: 8 g, Protein: 8 g, Carbs: 13 g, Fiber: 1 g, Sugar: 3 g, Sodium: 378 mg

211. Basil Pesto Bruschetta

Preparation Time: 10 minutes
Cooking Time: 4–8 minutes
Servings: 2
Ingredients:

- 8 French bread slices, ½ inch thick
- 2 tbsp. softened butter
- 1 cup shredded Mozzarella cheese
- ½ cup basil pesto
- 1 cup chopped grape tomatoes
- 2 green onions, thinly sliced

Directions:

1. Spread the bread with the butter and place the butter-side up in the air fryer basket. Bake at 350ºF (177ºC) for 3 to 5 minutes, or until the bread is light golden brown.
2. Remove the bread from the basket and top each piece with some of the cheese. Return to the basket in batches and bake until the cheese melts about 1 to 3 minutes.
3. Meanwhile, combine the pesto, tomatoes, and green onions in a small bowl.
4. When the cheese has melted, remove the bread from the air fryer, and place it on a serving plate. Top each slice with some of the pesto mixture and serve.

Nutrition: Calories: 463, Fats: 25 g, Protein: 19 g, Carbs: 41 g, Fiber: 3 g, Sugar: 2 g, Sodium: 822 mg

212. Cinnamon Pear Chips

Preparation Time: 15 minutes
Cooking Time: 9–13 minutes
Servings: 2
Ingredients:

- 2 firm Bosc pears, cut crosswise into 1/8-inch-thick slices
- 1 tbsp. freshly squeezed lemon juice
- ½ tsp. ground cinnamon
- 1/8 tsp. ground cardamom, or ground nutmeg

Directions:

1. Separate the smaller stem-end pear rounds from the larger rounds with seeds. Remove the core and seeds from the larger slices. Sprinkle all the slices with lemon juice, cinnamon, and cardamom.
2. Put the smaller chips into the air fryer basket. Air-fry at 380ºF (193ºC) for 3 to 5 minutes, or until light golden brown, shaking the basket once during cooking. Remove from the air fryer.
3. Repeat with the larger slices, air-frying for 6 to 8 minutes, or until light golden brown, shaking the basket once during cooking.
4. Remove the chips from the air fryer. Cool and serve or store in an air-tight container at room temperature for up to 2 days.

Nutrition: Calories: 31, Fats: 0 g, Protein: 7 g, Carbs: 8 g, Fiber: 2 g, Sugar: 5 g, Sodium: 0 mg

213. Phyllo Vegetable Triangles

Preparation Time: 15 minutes
Cooking Time: 8–14 minutes
Servings: 2
Ingredients:

- 3 tbsp. minced onion
- 2 garlic cloves, minced
- 2 tbsp. grated carrot
- 1 tsp. olive oil
- 3 tbsp. frozen baby peas, thawed
- 2 tbsp. non-fat cream cheese, at room temperature
- 6 frozen phyllo dough sheets, thawed
- Olive oil spray, for coating the dough

Directions:

1. In a baking pan, combine the onion, garlic, carrot, and olive oil. Air-fry at 390ºF for 2 to 4 minutes, or until the vegetables are crisp-tender. Transfer to a bowl.

2. Stir in the peas and cream cheese to the vegetable mixture. Let it cool while you prepare the dough.

3. Lay one sheet of phyllo on a work surface and lightly spray with olive oil spray. Top with another sheet of phyllo. Repeat with the remaining 4 phyllo sheets; you'll have 3 stacks with 2 layers each. Cut each stack lengthwise into 4 strips (12 strips total).

4. Place 2 teaspoons of the filling near the bottom of each strip. Bring one corner up over the filling to make a triangle, and continue folding the triangles over, as you would fold a flag. Seal the edge with a bit of water. Repeat with the remaining strips and filling.

5. Air-fry the triangles, in 2 batches, for 4 to 7 minutes, or until golden brown. Serve.

Nutrition: Calories: 67, Fats: 2 g, Protein: 2 g, Carbs: 11 g, Fiber: 1 g, Sugar: 1 g, Sodium: 121 mg

214. Red Cabbage and Mushroom Pot Stickers

Preparation Time: 12 minutes
Cooking Time: 12–17 minutes
Servings: 12
Ingredients:

- 1 cup shredded red cabbage
- ¼ cup chopped button mushrooms
- ¼ cup grated carrot
- 2 tbsp. minced onion
- 2 garlic cloves, minced
- 2 tsp. grated fresh ginger
- 12 g yoza/pot sticker wrappers
- 2 ½ tsp. olive oil, divided
- Water, as needed

Directions:

1. In a baking pan, combine the red cabbage, mushrooms, carrot, onion, garlic, and ginger. Add 1 tablespoon of water. Place it in the air fryer and bake at

370°F (188°C) for 3 to 6 minutes, or until the vegetables are crisp-tender. Drain and set aside.

2. Working one at a time, place the pot sticker wrappers on a work surface. Top each wrapper with 1 tablespoon of the filling. Fold half of the wrapper over the other half to form a half circle. Dab one edge with water and press both edges together.

3. For the baking pan, add 1 ¼ teaspoons of olive oil. Put half of the pot stickers seam-side up in the pan. Air-fry for 5 minutes, or until the bottoms are light golden brown. Add 1 tablespoon of water and return the pan to the air fryer.

4. Air-fry for 4 to 6 minutes more, or until hot. Repeat with the remaining pot stickers, the remaining 1 ¼ teaspoons of oil, and another tablespoon of water. Serve immediately.

Nutrition: Calories: 88, Fats: 3 g, Protein: 2 g, Carbs: 14 g, Fiber: 1 g, Sugar: 1 g, Sodium: 58 mg

215. Garlic Roasted Mushrooms

Preparation Time: 3 minutes
Cooking Time: 22–27 minutes
Servings: 2
Ingredients:

- 16 garlic cloves, peeled
- 2 tsp. olive oil, divided
- 16 button mushrooms
- ½ tsp. dried marjoram
- 1/8 tsp. freshly ground black pepper
- 1 tbsp. white wine or low-sodium vegetable broth

Directions:

1. In a baking pan, mix the garlic with 1 teaspoon of olive oil. Roast in the air fryer at 350°F for 12 minutes.

2. Add the mushrooms, marjoram, and pepper. Stir to coat. Drizzle with the

remaining 1 teaspoon of olive oil and white wine. Return to the air fryer and roast for 10 to 15 minutes more, or until the mushrooms and garlic cloves are tender. Serve.

Nutrition: Calories: 128, Fats: 4 g, Protein: 13 g, Carbs: 17 g, Fiber: 4 g, Sugar: 8 g, Sodium: 20 mg

216. Baked Spicy Chicken Meatballs

Preparation Time: 10 minutes
Cooking Time: 11–14 minutes
Servings: 24
Ingredients:

- 1 medium red onion, minced
- 2 garlic cloves, minced
- 1 jalapeño pepper, minced
- 2 tsp. olive oil - 3 tbsp. ground almonds
- 1 egg - 1 tsp. dried thyme
- 1 lb. ground chicken breast

Directions:

1. In a baking pan, combine the red onion, garlic, jalapeño, and olive oil. Bake at 400°F for 3 to 4 minutes, or until the vegetables are crisp-tender. Transfer to a medium bowl.
2. Mix in the almonds, egg, and thyme to the vegetable mixture. Add the chicken and mix until just combined.
3. Form the chicken mixture into about 24 (1-inch) balls. Bake the meatballs, in batches, for 8 to 10 minutes, or until the chicken reaches an internal temperature of 165°F on a meat thermometer.

Nutrition: Calories: 186, Fats: 7 g, Protein: 29 g, Carbs: 5 g, Fiber: 1 g, Sugar: 3 g, Sodium: 55 mg

217. Mini Onion Bites

Preparation Time: 10 minutes
Cooking Time: 18–20 minutes
Servings: 20
Ingredients:

- 20 white boiler onions - 1 cup buttermilk

- 2 eggs - 1 cup flour
- 1 cup whole wheat breadcrumbs
- 1 tbsp. smoked paprika - 1 tsp. salt
- 1 tsp. ground black pepper
- 1 tsp. granulated garlic
- ¾ tsp. chili powder
- Olive oil spray

Directions:

1. Place a parchment liner in the air fryer basket.
2. Slice off the root end of the onions, taking off as little as possible.
3. Peel off the papery skin and make cuts halfway through the tops of the onions. Don't cut too far down; you want the onion to hold together still.
4. In a large bowl, beat the buttermilk and eggs together.
5. In a medium bowl, mix the flour, breadcrumbs, paprika, salt, pepper, garlic, and chili powder.
6. Add the prepared onions to the buttermilk mixture and allow to soak for at least 10 minutes.
7. Working in batches, remove the onions from the batter and dredge them with the breadcrumb mixture.
8. Place the prepared onions in the air fryer basket in a single layer.
9. Spray lightly with olive oil and air fry at 360°F for 8 to 10 minutes, or until golden and crispy. Repeat with any remaining onions, and serve.

Nutrition: Calories: 166, Fats: 2 g, Protein: 6 g, Carbs: 31 g, Fiber: 4 g, Sugar: 7 g, Sodium: 372 mg

218. Crispy Parmesan-Cauliflower Bites

Preparation Time: 12 minutes
Cooking Time: 14–17 minutes
Servings: 20
Ingredients:

- 4 cups cauliflower florets

- 1 cup whole-wheat bread crumbs
- 1 tsp. coarse sea salt or kosher salt
- ¼ cup grated Parmesan cheese
- ¼ cup butter - ¼ cup mild hot sauce
- Olive oil spray, as needed

Directions:

1. Place a parchment liner in the air fryer basket.
2. Cut the cauliflower florets in half and set them aside.
3. In a small bowl, mix the bread crumbs, salt, and Parmesan; set aside.
4. In a small microwave-safe bowl, combine the butter and hot sauce. Heat in the microwave until the butter is melted, about 15 seconds. Whisk.
5. Holding the stems of the cauliflower florets, dip them in the butter mixture to coat. Shake off any excess mixture.
6. Dredge the dipped florets with the breadcrumb mixture, then put them in the air fryer basket. (There's no need for a single layer; just toss them all in there.)
7. Spray the cauliflower lightly with olive oil and air-fry at 350ºF for 14 to 17 minutes, shaking the basket a few times throughout the cooking process. (The florets are done when they are lightly browned and crispy.) Serve warm.

Nutrition: Calories: 106, Fats: 6 g, Protein: 3 g, Carbs: 10 g, Fiber: 1 g, Sugar: 1 g, Sodium: 416 mg

219. Cream Cheese-Stuffed Jalapeños

Preparation Time: 12 minutes
Cooking Time: 6–8 minutes
Servings: 10
Ingredients:

- 8 oz. cream cheese, at room temperature
- 1 cup whole wheat breadcrumbs, divided
- 2 tbsp. fresh parsley, minced
- 1 tsp. chili powder
- 10 jalapeño peppers, halved and seeded

Directions:

1. In a small bowl, combine the cream cheese, ½ cup of breadcrumbs, parsley, and chili powder. Whisk to combine.
2. Stuff the cheese mixture into the jalapeños. Sprinkle the tops of the stuffed jalapeños with the remaining ½ cup of breadcrumbs.
3. Place them in the air fryer basket and air-fry at 360ºF for 6 to 8 minutes, or until the peppers are softened and the cheese is melted. Serve warm.

Nutrition: Calories: 244, Fats: 16 g, Protein: 6 g, Carbs: 19 g, Fiber: 2 g, Sugar: 4 g, Sodium: 341 mg

220. Parmesan French Fries

Preparation Time: 5 minutes
Cooking Time: 20–25 minutes
Servings: 16
Ingredients:

- 2 russet potatoes, washed
- 1 tbsp. olive oil - ¼ tsp. salt
- 1 tbsp. granulated garlic
- ¼ cup grated Parmesan cheese
- ¼ tsp. ground black pepper
- 1 tbsp. fresh parsley, finely chopped (optional)

Directions:

1. Cut the potatoes into thin wedges, and place them in a large bowl.
2. Drizzle the olive oil over the potatoes, and toss to coat. Sprinkle with the garlic, Parmesan cheese, salt, and pepper. Toss again.
3. Place the fries in the air fryer basket and air-fry at 400ºF for 20 to 25 minutes, or until golden and crispy, stirring halfway through to ensure an even cooking.
4. Top with the parsley (if using), and serve warm.

Nutrition: Calories: 209, Fats: 5 g, Protein: 6 g, Carbs: 35 g, Fiber: 2 g, Sugar: 1 g, Sodium: 268 mg

221. Cheesy Ham and Spinach Dip

Preparation Time: 8 minutes
Cooking Time: 7 minutes
Servings: 1 ½
Ingredients:

- 8 oz. cream cheese
- 1 cup shredded Cheddar cheese
- ½ cup mayonnaise - ¼ cup Parmesan cheese - 2 tsp. minced garlic
- 1 tbsp. dried onion, minced
- ½ cup diced ham
- ½ cup fresh baby spinach, chopped

Directions:

1. In a large bowl, mix the cream cheese, Cheddar cheese, mayonnaise, Parmesan cheese, garlic, and onion. Use an electric mixer or a large wooden spoon to blend all the ingredients together.
2. Fold in the ham and spinach.
3. Transfer the mixture to a baking pan, and place it in the air fryer basket.
4. Bake at 400°F for 7 minutes, or until the cheese is melted. Serve.

Nutrition: Calories: 228, Fats: 20 g, Protein: 8 g, Carbs: 4 g, Fiber: 0 g, Sugar: 1 g, Sodium: 398 mg

222. Smoked Salmon Dip

Preparation Time: 10 minutes
Cooking Time: 7 minutes
Servings: 6
Ingredients:

- 1 (6-oz.) can boneless, skinless salmon
- 8 oz. cream cheese, softened
- 1 tbsp. liquid smoke (optional)
- 1/3 cup chopped pecans
- ½ cup chopped green onions
- 1 tsp. kosher salt (or less if the salmon contains salt)
- 1–2 tsp. black pepper
- ¼ tsp. smoked paprika, for garnish
- Cucumber and celery slices, cocktail rye bread, or crackers, for serving

Directions:

1. In a baking pan, mix the salmon, softened cream cheese, liquid smoke (if using), pecans, ¼ cup of green onions, salt, and pepper. Stir until well combined.
2. Place the pan in the air fryer basket. Bake at 400°F for 7 minutes, or until the cheese melts.
3. Sprinkle with the paprika and top with the remaining ¼ cup green onions. Serve with sliced vegetables, cocktail bread, or crackers.

Nutrition: Calories: 235, Fats: 19 g, Protein: 13 g, Carbs: 3 g, Fiber: 0 g, Sugar: 1 g, Sodium: 650 mg

223. Simple Corn Tortilla Chips

Preparation Time: 5 minutes
Cooking Time: 10 minutes
Servings: 2
Ingredients:

- 4 (6-inch) corn tortillas
- 1 tbsp. canola oil - ¼ tsp. kosher salt
- Non-stick cooking spray, as needed

Directions:

1. Stack the corn tortillas, cut them in half, and slice them into thirds.
2. Spray the air fryer basket with non-stick cooking spray, then brush the tortillas with canola oil and place them in the basket. Air-fry at 360°F for 5 minutes. Pause the fryer to shake the basket, then

air-fry for 3 to 5 more minutes, or until golden brown and crispy.

3. Remove the chips from the fryer and place them on a plate lined with a paper towel. Sprinkle with the kosher salt on top before serving warm.

Nutrition: Calories: 72, Fats: 4 g, Protein: 1 g, Carbs: 8 g, Fiber: 1 g, Sugar: 0 g, Sodium: 79 mg

224. Air Fryer Buffalo Cauliflower

Preparation Time: 5 minutes
Cooking Time: 15 minutes
Servings: 4
Ingredients:

- 1/2 cup homemade buffalo sauce
- 1 cauliflower head, cut bite-size pieces
- 1 tbsp. butter melted - Olive oil, as needed - Kosher salt and pepper, to taste
- Non-stick cooking spray, as needed

Directions:

1. Spray the cooking oil on the air fryer basket.
2. In a bowl, add the buffalo sauce, melted butter, pepper, and salt. Mix well.
3. Put the cauliflower bits in the air fryer and spray the olive oil over it. Let it cook at 400°F for 7 minutes.
4. Remove the cauliflower from the air fryer and add it to the sauce. Coat the cauliflower well. Put the sauce-coated cauliflower back into the air fryer. Cook at 400°F for 7–8 minutes, or until crispy. Take out from the air fryer and serve with the dipping sauce.

Nutrition: Calories: 101, Carbs: 4 g, Protein: 3 g, Fats: 7 g

225. Air Fryer Mini Pizza

Preparation Time: 2 minutes
Cooking Time: 5 minutes
Servings: 1
Ingredients:

- 1/4 cup olives, sliced
- 1 pita bread
- 1 tomato
- 1/2 cup shredded cheese

Directions:

1. Let the air fryer preheat to 350°F.
2. Lay the pita flat on a plate. Add the cheese, tomatoes slices, and olives.
3. Cook at 350°F for 5 minutes.
4. Take the pizza out of the air fryer.
5. Slice it and enjoy.

Nutrition: Calories: 344, Carbs: 37 g, Protein: 18 g, Fats: 13 g

226. Air Fryer Egg Rolls

Preparation Time: 10 minutes
Cooking Time: 20 minutes
Servings: 2
Ingredients:

- ½ bag coleslaw mix
- ½ onion
- 1/2 tsp. salt
- ½ cup mushrooms
- 2 cups lean ground pork
- 1 celery stalk
- 4 -6 Wrappers (egg roll)
- Water, as needed
- Oil, as needed

Directions:

1. Put a skillet over medium heat, and then add the onion and lean ground pork. Cook for 5–7 minutes
2. Add the coleslaw mixture, salt, mushrooms, and celery to the skillet and cook for almost 5 minutes.
3. Lay egg roll wrapper flat and add filling (1/3 cup), roll it up, seal with water.
4. Spray with oil the rolls.
5. Put in the air fryer for 6–8 minutes at 400F, flipping once halfway through.
6. Serve hot.

Nutrition: Calories: 245, Fats: 10 g, Net Carbs: 9 g, Protein: 11 g

227. Air Fryer Chicken Nuggets

Preparation Time: 15 minutes
Cooking Time: 15 minutes
Servings: 2
Ingredients:

- Olive oil spray, as needed
- 2 chicken breasts, skinless and boneless, cut into bite pieces
- ½ tsp. kosher salt and freshly ground black pepper, to taste
- 2 tbsp. grated Parmesan cheese
- 6 tbsp. Italian seasoned breadcrumbs (whole wheat)
- 2 tbsp. whole wheat breadcrumbs
- 2 tsp. olive oil
- Kale chips, for serving
- 1 cup Panko

Directions:

1. Let the air fryer preheat to 400ºF for 8 minutes.
2. In a large mixing bowl, add the panko, Parmesan cheese, and breadcrumbs. Mix well.
3. Sprinkle the kosher salt and pepper on the chicken and olive oil; mix well.
4. Take a few pieces of chicken and dip them into the breadcrumbs mixture.
5. Put these pieces in an air fryer and spray them with olive oil.
6. Cook them for 8 minutes, turning halfway through
7. Enjoy with kale chips.

Nutrition: Calories: 188, Carbs: 8 g, Protein: 25 g, Fats: 4.5 g

228. Chicken Tenders

Preparation Time: 10 minutes
Cooking Time: 20 minutes
Servings: 2
Ingredients:

- 4 cups chicken tenderloins
- 1 egg
- ½ cup superfine almond flour
- ½ cup powdered Parmesan cheese
- ½ tsp. kosher sea salt
- 1 tsp. freshly ground black pepper
- 1/2 tsp. Cajun seasoning
- Sauce, for serving
- Oil spray, as needed

Directions:

1. On a small plate, pour the beaten egg.
2. Mix all the ingredients in a Ziploc® bag.
3. Spray the air fryer with oil spray.
4. To avoid clumpy fingers with the breading and the egg, use different hands for the egg and the breading. Dip each tender in egg and then in bread until they are all breaded.
5. Using a fork to place one tender at a time, bring it in the Ziploc® bag and shake the bag forcefully. Make sure all the tenders are covered in almond mixture.
6. Use a fork to take out the tenders and place them in the air fryer basket.
7. Spray oil on the tenders.
8. Cook at 350ºF for 12 minutes, or before they register 160ºF. Raise the temperature to 400ºF to shade the surface for 3 minutes.
9. Serve with sauce.

Nutrition: Calories: 280, Proteins: 20 g, Carbs: 6 g, Fats: 10 g, Fiber 5 g

229. Kale and Celery Crackers

Preparation Time: 10 minutes
Cooking Time: 20 minutes
Servings: 2
Ingredients:

- 1 cup ground flax seed
- 1 cup flax seed, soaked overnight and drained
- 2 bunches kale, chopped
- 1 bunch basil, chopped
- ½ bunch celery, chopped
- 2 garlic cloves, minced
- 1/3 cup olive oil

Directions:

1. Mix the ground flaxseed with celery, kale, basil, and garlic in your food processor. Mix well.
2. Add the oil and soaked flaxseed, then mix again, scatter in the pan of the air fryer, break it into medium crackers, and cook at 380°F for 20 minutes.
3. Serve in cups as an appetizer.
4. Enjoy.

Nutrition: Calories: 143, Fats: 1 g, Fiber: 2 g, Carbs: 8 g, Protein: 4 g

230. Air Fryer Spanakopita Bites

Preparation Time: 10 minutes
Cooking Time: 15 minutes
Servings: 2
Ingredients:

- 4 sheets phyllo dough
- 2 cups baby spinach leaves
- 2 tbsp. grated Parmesan cheese
- 1/4 cup low-fat cottage cheese
- 1 tsp. dried oregano
- 6 tbsp. feta cheese, crumbled
- 2 tbsp. water
- 1 egg white only
- 1 tsp. lemon zest
- 1/8 tsp. cayenne pepper:
- 1 tbsp. olive oil
- 1/4 tsp. kosher salt
- ¼ tsp. freshly ground black pepper

Directions:

1. In a pot over high heat, add water and spinach. Cook until wilted.
2. Drain it and cool for 10 minutes. Squeeze out any excess moisture.
3. In a bowl, mix the cottage cheese, Parmesan cheese, oregano, salt, cayenne pepper, egg white, freshly ground black pepper, feta cheese, spinach, and zest. Mix it well in the food processor.
4. Lay one phyllo sheet on a flat surface. Spray with oil. Add the second sheet of

phyllo on top, and spray more oil. Add a total of 4 oiled sheets.
5. Form 16 strips from these 4 oiled sheets. Add 1 tablespoon of filling in one strip. Roll it around the filling.
6. Spray the air fryer basket with oil. Put 8 bites in the basket, and spray with oil. Cook at 375°F for 12 minutes, or until crispy and golden brown. Flip halfway through.
7. Serve hot.

Nutrition: Calories: 82, Fats: 4 g, Protein: 4 g, Carbs: 7 g

231. Air Fryer Roasted Corn

Preparation Time: 10 minutes
Cooking Time: 10 minutes
Servings: 2
Ingredients:

- 4 corn ears
- 2–3 tsp. olive oil
- Kosher salt and pepper, to taste

Directions:

1. Clean the corn ears, wash them, and pat them dry.
2. Fit them in the basket of air fryer, and cut them if need to.
3. Top with olive oil, kosher salt, and pepper.
4. Cook at 400°F for 10 minutes.
5. Enjoy the crispy, roasted corn.

Nutrition: Calories: 28, Fats: 2 g, Net Carbs: 0 g, Protein: 7 g

232. Crisp Egg Cups

Preparation Time: 10 minutes
Cooking Time: 10–13 minutes
Servings: 2
Ingredients:

- 4 toasted bread slices (whole wheat)
- Non-stick cooking spray, as needed
- 4 large eggs
- 1 ½ tbsp. margarine (trans-fat free)
- 1 ham slice

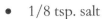

- 1/8 tsp. salt
- 1/8 tsp. black pepper

Directions:

1. Let the air fryer preheat to 375ºF, with the air fryer basket.
2. Take 4 ramekins and spray them with cooking spray.
3. Trim off the crust from the bread, and add margarine to one side.
4. Put the bread down into a ramekin, with the margarine side in.
5. Press it into the cup. Cut the ham in strips, half-inch thick, and add them on top of the bread.
6. Add 1 egg to the ramekins. Add salt and pepper.
7. Put the custard cups in the air fryer. Air-fry at 375ºF for 10–13 minutes.
8. Remove the ramekin from the air fryer, and serve.

Nutrition: Calories: 150, Total Fats: 8 g. Carbs: 6 g, Protein: 12 g

233. Lemon-Garlic Tofu

Preparation Time: 20 minutes
Cooking Time: 15 minutes
Servings: 2
Ingredients:

- 2 cups cooked quinoa
- 2 lemons, zested and juiced
- Sea salt and white pepper, to taste
- 1 block tofu, pressed and sliced into pieces
- 2 garlic cloves, minced

Directions:

1. Add the tofu into a deep dish.
2. In another small bowl, add the garlic, lemon juice, lemon zest, salt, and pepper.
3. Pour this marinade over the tofu in the dish. Let it marinate for at least 15 minutes.
4. Add the tofu to the air fryer basket.

5. Keep the leftover marinade safe. Let it air fry at 370ºF for 15 minutes.
6. Shake the basket after 8 minutes of cooking.
7. In a large deep bowl, add the cooked quinoa with the lemon-garlic Tofu.
8. Enjoy warm or cold.

Nutrition: Calories: 187, Fats: 9 g, Protein: 20 g. Carbs: 8 g

234. Vegan Mashed Potato Bowl

Preparation Time: 10 minutes
Cooking Time: 20 minutes
Servings: 2
Ingredients:

- 3 large red potatoes, cooked with the skin on, cut into one-inch pieces
- 1/4 tsp. salt
- 1/2 cup unsweetened soy milk or vegan milk
- Chopped scallions and roasted cashews, for serving

For the Tofu:

- 1 tsp. garlic powder
- 1 block extra-firm tofu, pressed, and cut into 1-inch pieces
- 2 tbsp. light soy sauce

Directions:

1. To make the mashed potatoes, add the cooked potatoes to a large bowl, mash them with a masher with butter. Mash until pretty lumpy. Then add the soy milk and keep crushing until you mash it till desired the desired consistency.
2. Cover the bowl with plastic wrap so that it keeps warm, and let it rest.
3. Meanwhile, add the tofu in one even layer in the air fryer. Add the garlic powder and soy sauce, and make sure to cover all the tofu. Let it cook in the air fryer at 400ºF for 10 minutes.
4. Cook the corn and kale according to your preference.

5. In 4 bowls, add the mashed potatoes, corn, and kale on top with the tofu.
6. You can add chopped scallions, and roasted cashews. Enjoy.

Nutrition: Calories: 250, Fats: 17 g, Protein: 21 g, Carbs: 13 g

235. Vegan Breakfast Sandwich

Preparation Time: 10 minutes
Cooking Time: 10 minutes
Servings: 2
Ingredients:

- ½ cup Tofu (Egg)
- 1 tsp. garlic powder
- 1/4 cup light soy sauce
- 1/2 tsp. turmeric
- 1 block extra-firm pressed tofu, cut into 4 round slices

For the Breakfast Sandwich:

- 4 vegan English muffins
- 1 avocado, cut into slices
- 1 Tomato slices - 4 vegan cheese slices
- 1 Onions, sliced
- 1 tbsp. Vegan mayonnaise or vegan butter

Directions:

1. Let the tofu marinate overnight.
2. In a deep dish, add the tofu circles with turmeric, soy sauce, and garlic powder. Let it rest for 10 minutes or overnight.
3. Put the tofu (marinated) in an air fryer. Cook at 400°F for 10 minutes. Shake the basket after 5 minutes.
4. Add the vegan butter or vegan mayonnaise to the English muffins. Add the vegan cheese, avocado slices, tomato, onion slices, and tofu. Top with the other half of the English muffin.
5. Serve right away, and enjoy.

Nutrition: Calories: 198, Fats: 10 g, Carbs: 12 g, Protein: 19.9 g

236. Crispy Fat-Free Spanish Potatoes

Preparation Time: 10 minutes
Cooking Time: 35 minutes
Servings: 2
Ingredients:

- 1 1/2 lb. small red potatoes
- 1 tbsp. liquid from cooked chickpeas or Aquafina - 1 tsp. tomato paste
- 1 tsp. sea salt (optional)
- 1/2 tbsp. brown rice flour or any flour (your choice)
- 1 tsp. smoked Spanish paprika
- 1/2 tsp. garlic powder
- 3/4 tsp. sweet smoked paprika
- Dipping sauce, for serving

Directions:

1. Wash and pat dry the potatoes. Cut the potatoes into small quarters, and make sure they are the same size. The maximum thickness of the potatoes should be one and a 1/2-inch thick.
2. Boil the potatoes wedges however you like.
3. Drain the potatoes wedges and add them to a large bowl.
4. In another bowl, add the tomato paste and aquafaba. In the small bowl, mix the remaining ingredients and the flour.
5. Now add the tomato paste mixture to the potatoes, and coat all the potatoes wedges gently with light hands. Add the dry mix to the coated potatoes until every potato is covered.
6. Let the air fryer preheat to 360°F for 3 minutes. Place the potatoes in the air fryer basket and cook for 12 minutes.
7. Shake the basket of the air fryer every 6 minutes. Make sure no potatoes get stuck on the bottom.
8. Let the potatoes be crispy to your liking.
9. Serve hot with a dipping sauce.

Nutrition: Calories: 171, Carbs: 39 g Fiber: 5 g, Protein: 5 g

237. Cheese and Veggie Air Fryer Egg Cups

Preparation Time: 10 minutes
Cooking Time: 14 minutes
Servings: 2
Ingredients:

- 1 cup shredded cheese
- Non-stick cooking spray, as needed
- 1 cup diced vegetables
- 1 tbsp. chopped cilantro
- 4 tbsp. half and a half
- 4 large eggs
- Salt and pepper, to taste

Directions:

1. Take 4 ramekins and grease them with oil.
2. In a bowl, crack the eggs with half the cheese, cilantro, salt, diced vegetables, half and half, and pepper.
3. Pour in the ramekins. Put in the air-fryer basket and cook at 300°F for 12 minutes.
4. Then add the cheese to the cups.
5. Let the air fryer preheat to 400°F for 2 minutes, or until the cheese is lightly browned and melted.
6. Serve hot.

Nutrition: Calories: 195, Carbs: 7 g, Protein: 13 g, Fats: 12 g

238. Low-Carb Air Fryer Baked Eggs

Preparation Time: 10 minutes
Cooking Time: 6–12 minutes
Servings: 2
Ingredients:

- Cooking spray, as needed
- 1–2 tsp. grated cheese
- 1 large egg
- 1 tbsp. frozen or fresh sautéed spinach
- Salt, to taste
- 1 tbsp. milk or half and half
- Black pepper, to taste

Directions:

1. Take the ramekins and spray them with cooking spray. Add the milk, spinach (if using frozen, thaw it before), egg, and cheese.
2. Add the seasoning of salt and pepper according to your taste. Stir everything but do not break the yolk.
3. Let it air fry at 330°F for 6–12 minutes. (1 cup will almost take 5–6 minutes. More than 1 cup will take more time. If you want runny yolks, cook for less time.)

Nutrition: Calories: 115, Carbs: 1 g, Protein: 10 g, Fats: 7 g

239. Easy Air Fryer Omelet

Preparation Time: 10 minutes
Cooking Time: 8–10 minutes
Servings: 2
Ingredients:

- 1 tsp. breakfast seasoning
- 2 eggs - A pinch salt - 1/4 cup milk
- 1/4 cup shredded cheese
- 1 tsp. Green onions
- 1 tbsp. red bell pepper
- 1 tbsp. mushrooms chopped

Directions:

1. In a bowl, mix the milk and eggs, and combine them well. Season with a pinch of salt. Add the chopped vegetables to the egg mixture. Add the egg mixture to a 6x3-inch baking pan. Make sure it is well greased.
2. Put the pan in the air fryer basket.
3. Air-fry at 350°F for 8–10 minutes.
4. After 5 minutes, add the breakfast seasoning into the eggs and top with the shredded cheese. Take it out from the air fryer, and transfer it to the plate.
5. Serve hot with extra green onions, and enjoy.

Nutrition: Calories: 256, Fats: 13 g, Protein: 15 g, Carbs: 8 g

240. Breakfast Bombs

Preparation Time: 10 minutes
Cooking Time: 15 minutes
Servings: 2
Ingredients:

- 3 large eggs, lightly whisked
- 2 tbsp. reduced-fat softened cream cheese
- 1 tbsp. fresh chives, chopped
- 1/4 cup (4-oz.) freshly prepared whole wheat pizza dough
- Cooking spray, as needed
- 3 bacon pieces, center cut
- Water, as needed

Directions:

1. In a skillet, cook the bacon slices for about 10 minutes. Crumble the cooked bacon. Add the eggs to the skillet and cook until loose for almost 1 minute. In another bowl, mix the chives, cheese, and bacon.
2. Cut the dough into 4 pieces. Make it into a 5-inch circle.
3. Add 1/4 of egg mixture in the center of the dough circle pieces.
4. Seal the dough seams with water.
5. Place the dough pockets in one single layer in the air fryer. Spray with cooking oil.
6. Cook at 350°F for 5–6 minutes, or until light golden brown.
7. Serve hot.

Nutrition: Calories: 305, Fats: 15 g, Protein: 19 g, Carbs: 26 g, Fiber: 2 g

241. Air Fryer Breakfast Toad-in-the-Hole Tarts

Preparation Time: 5 minutes
Cooking Time: 20 minutes
Servings: 2
Ingredients:

- 1 tbsp. fresh chives, chopped
- 1 sheet frozen puff pastry, thawed
- 4 large eggs
- 4 tbsp. cooked ham, chopped
- 4 tbsp. cheddar cheese, shredded

Directions:

1. Let the air fryer preheat to 400°F.
2. Lay the puff pastry on a clean surface and slice it into 4 squares.
3. Add 2 squares of puff pastry to the air fryer and cook for 8 minutes.
4. Take them out from the air fryer and make an indentation in the dough's center and add 1 tablespoon of ham and 1 tablespoon of cheddar cheese in every hole. Add the egg into it.
5. Return the basket to the air fryer.
6. Let cook to the desired doneness, about 6 minutes or more.
7. Take them out from the basket of the air fryer.
8. Cool for 5 minutes.
9. Top with the chives and serve hot

Nutrition: Calories: 154, Fats: 7 g, Carbs: 7 g, Protein: 10.1 g

242. Cheesy Chicken Omelet

Preparation Time: 5 minutes
Cooking Time: 14–18 minutes
Servings: 2
Ingredients:

- 1/2 cup cooked chicken breast, diced, divided
- 4 eggs
- 1/4 tsp. onion powder, divided
- 1/2 tsp. salt, divided
- 1/4 tsp. pepper, divided
- 2 tbsp. shredded cheese, divided
- 1/4 tsp. garlic powder, divided
- Olive oil, as needed

Directions:

1. Take 2 ramekins, and grease them with olive oil.
2. Add 2 eggs to each ramekin. Add the cheese and the seasoning.
3. Blend to combine, and add 1/4 cup of the cooked chicken on top.
4. Cook in the air fryer at 330°F for 14–18 minutes, or until fully cooked.

Nutrition: Calories: 185, Protein: 20 g, Carbs: 10 g, Fats: 5 g

CHAPTER 9:

Sides

243. Corn-Crusted Chicken Tenders

Preparation Time: 10 minutes
Cooking Time: 12–14 minutes
Servings: 2
Ingredients:

- 1 lb. Chicken breasts, cut into strips
- Salt and black pepper, to taste
- 2 eggs
- 1 cup ground cornmeal
- Cooking spray, as needed

Directions:

1. Preheat the air fryer to 390°F.
2. In a bowl, mix the ground cornmeal, salt, and black pepper. In another bowl, beat the eggs, and season with salt and pepper. Dip the chicken in the eggs and then coat it in the cornmeal.
3. Spray the prepared sticks with cooking spray and place them in the air fryer basket in a single layer.
4. Air-fry for 6 minutes, slide the basket out and flip the sticks. Cook for 6–8 more minutes, or until golden brown.

Nutrition: Calories: 170, Carbs: 8 g, Fats: 6 g, Protein: 16 g

244. Roasted Bell Pepper

Preparation Time: 5 minutes
Cooking Time: 18–20 minutes
Servings: 2
Ingredients:

- 1 tsp. olive oil

- ½ tsp. thyme
- 4 garlic cloves, minced
- 4 bell peppers, cut into fourths

Directions:

1. Start by putting the peppers in the air fryer basket and drizzling them with olive oil. Make sure they're coated well and then roast them for 15 minutes.
2. Sprinkle with thyme and garlic, roasting for an additional 3 to 5 minutes. (They should be tender.) Serve warm.

Nutrition: Calories: 36, Protein: 1 g, Fats: 1 g, Carbs: 5 g

245. Roasted Parsnips

Preparation Time: 5 minutes
Cooking Time: 40 minutes
Servings: 2
Ingredients:

- 2 lbs. parsnips, peeled and cut into chunks
- 2 tbsp. maple syrup
- 1 tbsp. olive oil
- 1 tbsp. parsley flakes

Directions:

1. Start by heating the air fryer to 360°F, and then add in the ingredients. Make sure that the parsnips are well coated.
2. Cook for 40 minutes, and then serve warm.

Nutrition: Calories: 124, Protein: 4 g, Fats: 3 g, Carbs: 7 g

246. Zucchini Chips

Preparation Time: 5 minutes
Cooking Time: 20 minutes
Servings: 2
Ingredients:

- 2 zucchini
- 1 tsp. olive oil
- 1 tsp. paprika
- Sea salt, to taste

Directions:

1. Preheat your air fryer to 370°F, and then slice the zucchini.
2. Sprinkle the salt and paprika over the zucchini. Sprinkle them down with oil, and then cook for 13 minutes.

Nutrition: Calories: 22, Protein: 1 g, Fats: 1.1 g, Carbs: 1.9 g

247. Pork Rinds

Preparation Time: 5 minutes
Cooking Time: 10 minutes
Servings: 2
Ingredients:

- ½ tsp. black pepper
- 1 tsp. chili flakes
- ½ tsp. fine sea salt
- 1 tsp. olive oil
- 1 lb. pork rinds

Directions:

1. Start by heating the air fryer to 365°F, and then spray it down with olive oil.
2. Place the pork rinds in the air fryer basket, and sprinkle with the seasoning. Mix well, and then cook for 7 minutes.
3. Shake gently, and then serve cooled.

Nutrition: Calories: 329, Protein: 36.5 g, Fats: 20.8 g, Carbs: 0.1 g

248. Bacon Poppers

Preparation Time: 10 minutes
Cooking Time: 18 minutes
Servings: 2
Ingredients:

- 6 crispy bacon strips, cooked

For the Dough:

- 2/3 cup water
- 1 tbsp. butter
- 1 tbsp. bacon Fats:
- 1 tsp. kosher salt
- 2/3 cup all-purpose flour
- 2 eggs
- 2 ½ oz. cheddar cheese, shredded
- ½ cup jalapeño peppers
- A pinch pepper
- A pinch black pepper

Directions:

1. Whisk the butter with water and salt in a skillet over medium heat. Stir in the flour, then stir -cook for about 3 minutes.
2. Transfer this flour to a bowl, then whisk in the eggs and the rest of the ingredients.
3. Fold in the bacon, and mix well. Wrap this dough in a plastic sheet and refrigerate for 30 minutes. Make small balls out of this dough.

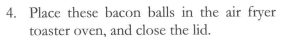

4. Place these bacon balls in the air fryer toaster oven, and close the lid.
5. Select the "Air Fry" mode at 390°F for 15 minutes. Flip the balls after 7 minutes, then resume cooking. Serve warm.

Nutrition: Calories: 240, Protein: 14.9 g, Carbs: 7.1 g, Fats: 22.5 g

249. Panko Tofu with Mayo Sauce

Preparation Time: 10 minutes
Cooking Time: 20 minutes
Servings: 2
Ingredients:

- Tofu cutlets

For the Marinade:

- 1 tbsp. toasted sesame oil
- 1/4 cup soy sauce
- 1 tsp. rice vinegar
- 1/2 tsp. garlic powder
- 1 tsp. ground ginger

Make the Tofu:

- 1/2 cup vegan mayo
- 1 cup panko breadcrumbs
- 1 tsp. sea salt

Directions:

1. Whisk the marinade ingredients in a bowl, and add the tofu cutlets. Mix well to coat the cutlets.
2. Cover and marinate for 1 hour. Meanwhile, whisk the crumbs with salt and mayo in a bowl.
3. Coat the cutlets with the crumb mixture. Place the tofu cutlets in the air fryer basket.
4. Select the "Air Fry" mode at 370°F for 20 minutes. Flip the cutlets after 10 minutes, then resume cooking.
5. Serve warm.

Nutrition: Calories: 151, Protein: 1.9 g, Carbs: 6.9 g, Fats: 8.6 g

250. Pork-Stuffed Dumplings

Preparation Time: 15 minutes
Cooking Time: 12 minutes
Servings: 2
Ingredients:

- 1 cup chopped book choy
- 1 tbsp. chopped fresh ginger
- 1 tbsp. chopped garlic
- 3 ½ oz. ground pork
- 1/4 tsp. crushed red pepper
- 18 dumpling wrappers
- Cooking spray, as needed

Directions:

1. In a greased skillet, sauté the bok choy for 8 minutes, then add the ginger and garlic. Cook for 1 minute.
2. Transfer the bok choy to a plate.
3. Add the pork and red pepper, then mix well. Place the dumpling wraps on the working surface, and divide the pork fillings onto the dumpling wraps.
4. Wet the edges of the wraps and pinch them together to seal the filling.
5. Place the dumpling in the air fryer basket.
6. Set the air fryer basket inside the air fryer toaster oven and close the lid.
7. Select the "Air Fry" mode at 375°F for 12 minutes.
8. Flip the dumplings after 6 minutes, then resume cooking.
9. Serve fresh.

Nutrition: Calories: 172, Protein: 2.1 g, Carbs: 18.6 g, Fats: 10.7 g

251. Stuffed Jalapeno

Preparation Time: 10 minutes
Cooking Time: 10 minutes
Servings: 2
Ingredients:

- 1 lb. ground pork sausage
- 1 (8-oz.) package softened cream cheese
- 1 lb. large fresh jalapeño peppers, halved lengthwise and seeded

- 1 (8-oz.) bottle ranch dressing

Directions:

1. Mix pork the sausage ground with ranch dressing and cream cheese in a bowl.
2. Cut the jalapeno in half and remove their seeds. Divide the cream cheese mixture into the jalapeño halves. Place the jalapeño pepper in a baking tray.
3. Set the baking tray inside the air fryer toaster oven, and close the lid.
4. Select the "Bake" mode at 350°F for 10 minutes. Serve warm.

Nutrition: Calories: 168, Protein: 9.4 g, Carbs: 12.1 g, Fats: 21.2 g

252. Fried Ravioli

Preparation Time: 10 minutes
Cooking Time: 15 minutes
Servings: 2
Ingredients:

- 1 package frozen ravioli
- 1 cup breadcrumbs
- 1/2 cup Parmesan cheese
- 1 tbs. Italian seasoning
- 1 tbs. garlic powder
- 2 eggs, beaten
- Cooking spray, as needed

Directions:

1. Mix the breadcrumbs with the garlic powder, cheese, and Italian seasoning in a bowl. Whisk the eggs in another bowl. Dip each ravioli in the eggs first, then coat them with a crumbs mixture.
2. Place the ravioli in the air fryer basket. Place the air fryer basket inside the oven and close the lid.
3. Select the "Air Fry" mode at 360°F for 15 minutes. Flip the ravioli after 8 minutes, then resume cooking. Serve warm.

Nutrition: Calories: 124, Protein: 4.5 g, Carbs: 27.5 g, Fats: 3.5 g

253. Eggplant Fries

Preparation Time: 10 minutes
Cooking Time: 20 minutes
Servings: 2
Ingredients:

- 1/2 cup panko breadcrumbs
- 1/2 tsp. salt
- 1 eggplant, peeled and sliced
- 1 cup whisked egg

Directions:

1. Toss the breadcrumbs with salt in a tray.
2. Dip the eggplant in the whisked egg, and coat it with the breadcrumb mixture.
3. Place the eggplant slices in the air fryer basket. Put the basket inside the air fryer toaster oven and close the lid.
4. Select the "Air Fry" mode at 400°F for 20 minutes.
5. Flip the slices after 10 minutes, then resume cooking. Serve warm.

Nutrition: Calories: 110, Protein: 5 g, Carbs: 12.8 g, Fats: 11.9 g

254. Garlicky Bok Choy

Preparation Time: 10 minutes
Cooking Time: 6 minutes
Servings: 2
Ingredients:

- 1 bunches baby book choy
- Spray oil, as needed
- 1 tsp. garlic powder

Directions:

1. Toss the bok choy with the garlic powder and spread it in the air fryer basket.
2. Spray them with cooking oil.
3. Place the basket inside the air fryer toaster oven, and close the lid.
4. Select the "Air Fry" mode at 350°F for 6 minutes. Serve fresh.

Nutrition: Calories: 81, Protein: 0.4 g, Carbs: 4.7 g, Fats: 8.3 g

CHAPTER 10:

Desserts

255. Avocado-Chocolate Dessert

Preparation Time: 15 minutes
Cooking Time: 0 minutes
Servings: 2
Ingredients:

- 1 small orange
- 1 ripe avocado
- 1 vanilla pod
- 2 tbsp. cocoa, defatted
- 1 tbsp. cane sugar
- 1 tbsp. almond flakes
- 1/2 cup Cream
- Salt, to taste

Directions:

1. Peel the orange. Remove the white skin from the fruit. Separate the fillets.
2. Cut the avocado open. Take out the core. Peel the pulp with a spoon, and cut it into small pieces.
3. Cut open the vanilla pod and remove the pulp. Purée the avocado meat with the vanilla, a pinch of salt, and the sugar in a mixing bowl. Pour the cream into glasses and garnish with the orange fillets. Let the jars rest in the refrigerator for 2 hours.
4. Toast the almond flakes in a pan without fat. Place the toasted almond flakes on the glasses with the avocado. Sprinkle on the cream.

Nutrition: Calories: 170, Carbs: 13 g, Protein: 5 g, Fats: 9 g

256. Brownies

Preparation Time: 50 minutes
Cooking Time: 0 minutes
Servings: 2 (4 pieces)
Ingredients:

- 150 g Medjool dates
- 75 g almonds, unpeeled
- 90 g walnuts
- 50 g cocoa
- 1/4 tsp. sea salt
- Water, as needed
- Hazelnuts (optional)

Directions:

1. Chop the walnuts and almonds. (You can also use hazelnuts if you like.)
2. Core the dates, cut them into small pieces, and soak them in water for half an hour.
3. Put the nuts in a blender and grind them into fine flour.
4. Put the salt and cocoa in the blender. Drain the dates and add them to the mixture. Add the almonds. Mix everything well.
5. Pour the mixture into a bowl, press firmly, cover it with a kitchen towel and put it in the refrigerator for a day.
6. Take the mixture out of the fridge and cut it into even pieces.

Nutrition: Calories: 439, Carbs: 29 g, Protein: 11 g, Fats: 29 g

257. Baked Apple

Preparation Time: 15 minutes
Cooking Time: 35 minutes - **Servings:** 4
Ingredients:

- 4 large good baking apples, such as Rome Beauty, Golden Delicious, or Jonagold - 1/4 cup brown sugar
- 1 teaspoon cinnamon - 1/4 cup chopped pecans, optional - 1/4 cup currants or chopped raisins - 1 tablespoon butter - 3/4 cup boiling water

Directions:

Preheat your oven:

1. Set your oven to 375°F (190°C).

Cut out holes in apples for stuffing:

2. Rinse and dry the apples. Using a sharp paring knife or an apple corer, cut out the cores, leaving the bottom 1/2 inch of the apples intact. If using a paring knife, first cut out the stem area and then use a small metal spoon to scoop out the seeds. Cut the holes so that they are an inch or so wide.

Stuff with brown sugar, cinnamon, and extras, dot with butter:

3. Place the brown sugar, cinnamon, currants or chopped raisins, and chopped pecans (if using) in a small bowl and stir to combine.
4. Put the apples in a baking dish and stuff each apple with the sugar stuffing mixture. Place a dot of butter (a quarter of the tablespoon called for in the ingredient list) on top of the sugar.

Bake:

5. Pour the boiling water into the bottom of the baking dish. Bake at 375°F (190°C) for 30 to 45 minutes, until the apples are cooked through and tender, but not overcooked and mushy. When done, remove the apples from the oven and baste them with the juices from the pan. Terrific with a side of vanilla ice cream.

Nutrition: Calories 3g Fat 44g Carbs 1g Protein

258. Chickpea Snack

Preparation Time: 25 minutes
Cooking Time: 20 minutes - **Servings:** 2
Ingredients:

- 130 g chickpeas - 1/2 tbsp. rapeseed oil
- 1/4 tsp. turmeric -1/4 tsp. caraway seeds
- 1/4 tsp. smoked salt
- Paprika powder (optional)

Directions:

1. Drain the chickpeas with a sieve and rinse them under the tap. Then dry the peas with a kitchen towel, pour them into a bowl, and mix them with the rapeseed oil, turmeric, caraway seeds, and smoked salt. (You can omit the turmeric and caraway seeds and use paprika powder for them.)
2. Heat a pan without fat and add the mixture to the pan. Fry the peas for about 20 minutes, or until they have turned brown, then put the chickpeas in a suitable bowl and let cool.

Nutrition: Calories: 105, Carbs: 12 g, Protein: 5 g, Fats: 4 g

259. Chocolate Coconut Pudding

Preparation Time: 10 minutes (plus ½ hour to cool)
Cooking Time: 0 minutes
Servings: 2
Ingredients:

- 150 g silken tofu

- 100 g coconut milk
- 25 g cocoa, slightly de-oiled
- 1 tsp. instant coffee powder
- 1/4 tsp. vanilla
- 10 g sugar
- Desiccated coconut or edible flowers, for serving

Directions:

1. Put the coconut milk and the silken tofu in a mixing bowl, and purée with the mixer. Add the cocoa, coffee, vanilla, and sugar. Purée again.
2. Put the pudding in glasses or compote bowl, and chill it in the refrigerator for about ½ hour. Garnish with the desiccated coconut or edible flowers (violets or pansies) to serve.

Nutrition: Calories: 120, Carbs: 10 g, Protein: 8 g, Fats: 5 g

260. Chocolate with Nuts

Preparation Time: 10 minutes (plus 12 hours to cool down)
Cooking Time: 0 minutes
Servings: 2 (1 board)
Ingredients:

- 25 g almonds
- 15 g erythritol
- 40 g coconut oil
- 15 g hazelnut puree
- 1 tbsp. Vanilla powder
- 1 tsp. Ground cinnamon
- 2 cups Cocoa

Directions:

1. Chop the almonds, and caramelize them in a pan with the erythritol.
2. Mix the hazelnut purée with the coconut oil, vanilla powder, cinnamon and cocoa in a bowl. Add the almonds and stir in.
3. Put the warm mass into a chocolate mold and leave it 12 hours in the refrigerator.

Nutrition: Calories: 103, Carbs: 3 g, Protein: 2 g, Fats: 11 g

261. Chicory and Apple Casserole

Preparation Time: 50 minutes
Cooking Time: 30–40 minutes
Servings: 2
Ingredients:

- 2 g chicory
- 8 ham slices
- 1/2 apple
- 1 tbsp. rapeseed oil
- 1 tbsp. pumpkin seeds
- ½ cup Cheese

Directions:

1. Heat up the oven to 170°F. Brush a baking dish with oil.
2. Wash the chicory. Cut the chicory into 4 parts. Wrap the ham around the chicory. Stick a toothpick through so that the ham holds in place.
3. Peel the apple. Remove the core housing. Cut the apple into slices.
4. Place the chicory and apple slices in the baking dish.
5. Scatter the cheese and pumpkin seeds over the contents of the baking dish.
6. Put the baking dish in the oven for 30 to 40 minutes. Serve the chicory warm.

Nutrition: Calories: 343, Carbs: 8 g, Protein: 36 g, Fats: 18 g

262. Apricot Sheet Cake

Preparation Time: 40 minutes
Cooking Time: 30 minutes
Servings: 2
Ingredients:

- 1/4 (720-ml) apricots jar
- 40 g butter
- 15 g fructose
- 1 egg (size M)
- 25 ml milk
- 75 g flour
- 5 g pistachio nuts
- 10 g–20 g baking powder

Directions:

1. Drain the apricots. Put the fat and fructose in a bowl, and stir with a whisk. Stir in the egg and milk. Add the flour and baking powder.
2. Grease a baking sheet. Put the dough on top. Spread the apricots on the batter.
3. Put the cake in the oven and bake at 175ºF for 30 minutes.
4. Let the cake cool down. Sprinkle the pistachio nuts on top.

Nutrition: Calories: 130, Carbs: 13 g, Protein: 3 g, Fats: 7 g

263. Citrus Custard

Preparation Time: 10 minutes
Cooking Time: 5 minutes
Servings: 2
Ingredients:

- ¼ cup sugar
- 2 tbsp. cornstarch
- 2 ½ cups low-fat (1%) milk
- 4 egg yolks, lightly beaten
- ½ tsp. orange zest
- ½ tsp. vanilla
- ¼ cup shortbread cookies, coarsely crushed
- Orange slices, for serving

Directions:

1. Stir together the cornstarch and sugar in a saucepan, and then stir in the milk. Cook until thick and bubbly. Cook and stir for 2 minutes more. Remove from the heat.
2. Bit-by-bit, stir in about 1 cup of the hot mixture into the egg yolks. Return them to the saucepan. Bring them just to boil, and then remove them from the heat.
3. Stir in the orange zest and vanilla. Pour into a serving bowl or 4 dessert dishes, and cover the surface with plastic wrap. Cool slightly.
4. Chill for at least 4 hours before serving. Do not stir.

5. Top the custard with crushed cookies and orange slices.
6. Serve.

Nutrition: Calories: 212, Fats: 7 g, Carb: 28 g, Protein: 8 g

264. Sweet Tapioca Pudding

Preparation Time: 10 minutes
Cooking Time: 8 minutes
Servings: 2
Ingredients:

- 1/2 cup pearl tapioca
- 1 can coconut milk
- 1/2 cup water
- 4 tbsp. maple syrup
- 1 cup almond milk
- A pinch cardamom

Directions:

1. Soak the tapioca in almond milk for 1 hour.
2. Combine all the ingredients, except the water, in a heat-safe bowl, and cover the bowl with foil.
3. Pour 1/2 cup of water into the instant pot, then place trivet into the pot.
4. Place the bowl on top of the trivet.
5. Cover the pot with the lid and cook on manual high pressure for 8 minutes.
6. Once done, allow to release pressure naturally, and then open the lid.
7. Stir well, and place it in the refrigerator for 1 hour.
8. Serve and enjoy.

Nutrition: Calories: 313, Fats: 18.1 g, Carbs: 38.4 g, Sugar: 18.5 g, Protein: 2.4 g, Cholesterol: 1 mg

265. Vanilla Bread Pudding

Preparation Time: 10 minutes
Cooking Time: 15 minutes
Servings: 2
Ingredients:

- 3 eggs, lightly beaten
- 1 tsp. coconut oil

- 1 tsp. vanilla
- 4 cup bread cube
- 1/2 tsp. cinnamon
- 1/4 cup raisins
- 1/4 cup chocolate chips
- 2 cup milk
- 1/4 tsp. salt
- Water, as needed

Directions:

1. Empty the water into the instant pot, then place the trivet into the pot.
2. Add the bread cubes to a baking dish.
3. In a large bowl, mix the remaining ingredients.
4. Pour the bowl mixture into the baking dish on top of the bread cubes, and cover the dish with foil.
5. Place the baking dish on top of the trivet.
6. Seal the pot with its lid and cook on "Steam" mode for 15 minutes.
7. Once done, allow to release pressure naturally, and then open the lid.
8. Carefully, remove the baking dish from the pot.
9. Serve and enjoy.

Nutrition: Calories: 230, Fats: 10.1 g, Carbs: 25 g, Sugar: 16.7 g, Protein: 9.2 g, Cholesterol: 135 mg

266. Blueberry Cupcakes

Preparation Time: 10 minutes
Cooking Time: 25 minutes
Servings: 2
Ingredients:

- 2 eggs, lightly beaten
- 1/4 cup butter, softened
- 1/2 tsp. baking soda
- 1 tsp. baking powder
- 1 tsp. vanilla extract
- 1/2 fresh lemon juice
- 1 lemon zest
- 1/4 cup sour cream

- 1/4 cup milk
- 1 cup sugar
- 3/4 cup fresh blueberries
- 1 cup all-purpose flour
- 1/4 tsp. salt
- Water, as needed

Directions:

1. Add all the ingredients to a large bowl and mix well.
2. Empty 1 cup of water into the instant pot, then place the trivet into the pot.
3. Pour the batter into the silicone cupcake mold, and place it on top of the trivet.
4. Seal the pot with its lid and cook on manual high pressure for 25 minutes.
5. Once done, allow to release pressure naturally, and then open the lid.
6. Serve and enjoy.

Nutrition: Calories: 330, Fats: 11.6 g, Carbs: 53.6 g, Sugar: 36 g, Protein: 4.9 g, Cholesterol: 80 mg

267. Moist Pumpkin Brownie

Preparation Time: 10 minutes
Cooking Time: 35 minutes
Servings: 2
Ingredients:

- 2 eggs, lightly beaten
- 3/4 cup pumpkin puree
- 1/2 tsp. baking powder
- 1/3 cup cocoa powder
- 1/2 cup almond flour
- 1 tbsp. vanilla
- 1/4 cup milk
- 1 cup maple syrup

Directions:

1. Stir all the ingredients into the large bowl and mix until well combined.
2. Spray a spring-form pan with cooking spray.
3. Pour the batter into the pan and cover the pan with foil.
4. Pour 2 cups of water into the instant pot, and place the trivet into the pot.

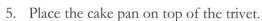

5. Place the cake pan on top of the trivet.
6. Close the pot with its lid, and cook on manual mode for 35 minutes.
7. Once done, release the pressure using the quick-release method, and then open the lid.
8. Slice and serve.

Nutrition: Calories: 306, Fats: 5.5 g, Carbs: 62.9 g, Sugar: 49.9 g, Protein: 5.8 g, Cholesterol: 83 mg

268. Mini Choco Cake

Preparation Time: 10 minutes
Cooking Time: 9 minutes
Servings: 2
Ingredients:

- 2 eggs
- 2 tbsp. Swerve®
- 1/4 cup cocoa powder
- 1/2 tsp. vanilla
- 1/2 tsp. baking powder
- 2 tbsp. heavy cream
- Cooking spray, as needed
- Water, as needed

Directions:

1. In a container, blend all the dry ingredients until combined.
2. Add all the wet ingredients to the dry mixture, and whisk until smooth.
3. Spray 2 ramekins with cooking spray.
4. Empty 1 cup of water into the instant pot, and then place the trivet in the pot.
5. Pour the batter into the ramekins, and place the ramekins on top of the trivet.
6. Close the pot with its lid, and cook on manual high pressure for 9 minutes.
7. Once done, release the pressure using the quick-release method, and then open the lid. Carefully, remove the ramekins from the pot, and let it cool.
8. Serve and enjoy.

Nutrition: Calories: 143, Fats: 11.3 g, Carbs: 22.4 g, Sugar: 15.7 g, Protein: 7.8 g, Cholesterol: 184 mg

269. Cinnamon Pears

Preparation Time: 10 minutes
Cooking Time: 7 minutes
Servings: 2
Ingredients:

- 4 firm pears, peel
- 1/3 cup sugar
- 1 1/2 tsp. cinnamon
- 1 cinnamon stick
- 1 cup orange juice

Directions:

1. Add the orange juice and all the spices into the instant pot.
2. Place the trivet into the pot.
3. Arrange the pears on top of the trivet.
4. Close the pot with its lid, and cook on manual high pressure for 7 minutes.
5. Once done, allow to release pressure naturally, and then open the lid.
6. Carefully, remove the pears from pot, and set them aside.
7. Discard the cinnamon stick and cloves from the pot.
8. Add the sugar to the pot and set the pot on the "Sauté" mode.
9. Cook the sauce until thickened.
10. Pour the sauce over the pears, and serve.

Nutrition: Calories: 221 Fats: 0.6 g, Carbs: 57.5 g, Sugar: 42.4 g, Protein: 1.3 g, Cholesterol: 0 mg

270. Delicious Pumpkin Pudding

Preparation Time: 10 minutes
Cooking Time: 20 minutes
Servings: 2
Ingredients:

- 2 large eggs, lightly beaten
- 1/2 cup milk
- 1/2 tsp. vanilla
- 1 tsp. pumpkin pie spice
- 14 oz. pumpkin purée
- 3/4 cup Swerve®
- Cooking spray, as needed

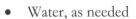

- Water, as needed

Directions:

1. Spray the baking dish with cooking spray, and set it aside.
2. In a large bowl, whisk the eggs with the remaining ingredients.
3. Empty 1 1/2 cups of water into the instant pot, then place a steamer rack in the pot. Pour the mixture into the prepared dish and cover with foil.
4. Place the dish on top of the steamer rack. Close the pot with its lid, and cook on manual high pressure for 20 minutes.
5. As soon as done, discharge the pressure naturally for 10 minutes, and then release it using the quick release method. Open the lid. Carefully, remove the dish from the pot, and let it cool. Place the pudding dish in the refrigerator for 7–8 hours. Serve and enjoy.

Nutrition: Calories. 58, Fats: 2.3 g, Carbs: 36.7 g, Sugar: 33.3 g, Protein: 3.5 g, Cholesterol: 64 mg

271. Saffron Rice Pudding

Preparation Time: 10 minutes
Cooking Time: 13 minutes
Servings: 2
Ingredients:

- 1/2 cup rice
- 1/2 tsp. cardamom powder
- 3 tbsp. almonds, chopped
- 3 tbsp. walnuts, chopped
- 4 cups of milk
- 1/2 cup sugar
- 2 tbsp. shredded coconut
- 1 tsp. saffron
- 3 tbsp. raisins
- 1 tbsp. ghee
- 1/8 tsp. salt
- Water, as needed

Directions:

1. Add the ghee into the pot, and set the pot on the "Sauté" mode.

2. Add the rice and cook for 30 seconds.
3. Add 3 cups of milk and the coconut, raisins, saffron, nuts, cardamom powder, sugar, 1/2 cup water, and salt, blending well.
4. Close the pot with its lid and cook on manual high pressure for 10 minutes.
5. Once done, release pressure naturally for 15 minutes, and then release it using the quick release method. Open the lid.
6. Add the remaining milk and stir well, and cook on the "Sauté" mode for 2 minutes. Serve and enjoy.

Nutrition: Calories: 280, Fats: 9.9 g, Carbs: 42.1 g, Sugar: 27 g, Protein: 8.2 g, Cholesterol: 19 mg

272. Flavorful Carrot Halva

Preparation Time: 10 minutes
Cooking Time: 10 minutes
Servings: 2
Ingredients:

- 2 cups shredded carrots
- 2 tbsp. ghee
- 1/2 tsp. cardamom
- 3 tbsp. ground cashews
- 1/4 cup sugar
- 1 cup milk
- 4 tbsp. raw cashews
- 3 tbsp. raisins

Directions:

1. Add the ghee to the instant pot and set the pot on the "Sauté" mode.
2. Add the raisins and cashews, and cook until lightly golden brown.
3. Add the remaining ingredients, except for cardamom, and blend well.
4. Close the pot with its lid, and cook on manual high pressure for 10 minutes.
5. Once done, allow to release pressure naturally, and then open the lid.
6. Add the cardamom, stir well, and serve.

Nutrition: Calories: 171, Fats: 9.3 g, Carbs: 20.5 g, Sugar: 15.2 g, Protein: 3.3 g, Cholesterol: 14 mg

273. Vermicelli Pudding

Preparation Time: 10 minutes
Cooking Time: 2 minutes
Servings: 2
Ingredients:

- 1/3 cup roasted vermicelli
- 6 dates, pitted and sliced
- 3 tbsp. sliced cashews
- 2 tbsp. sliced pistachios
- 1/4 tsp. vanilla
- 1/2 tsp. saffron
- 1/3 cup sugar
- 5 cups milk
- 3 tbsp. shredded coconut
- 2 tbsp. raisins
- 3 tbsp. almonds
- 2 tbsp. ghee

Directions:

1. Add the ghee to the instant pot, and set the pot on the "Sauté" mode.
2. Add the dates, cashews, pistachios, and almonds into the pot and cook for a minute.
3. Add the raisins, coconut, and vermicelli. Stir well. Add 3 cups of milk, saffron, and sugar. Blend well.
4. Close the pot with its lid, and cook on manual high pressure for 2 minutes.
5. Once done, allow to release pressure naturally, and open the lid.
6. Stir in the remaining milk and vanilla.
7. Serve and enjoy.

Nutrition: Calories: 283, Fats: 13.4 g, Carbs: 34.9 g Sugar: 28.1 g, Protein: 9 g, Cholesterol: 28 mg

274. Yogurt Custard

Preparation Time: 10 minutes
Cooking Time: 20 minutes
Servings: 2
Ingredients:

- 1 cup plain yogurt
- 1 1/2 tsp. ground cardamom
- 1 cup sweetened condensed milk
- 1 cup milk

Directions:

1. Add all the ingredients into a heat-safe bowl, and stir to combine.
2. Cover the bowl with foil.
3. Pour 2 cups of water into the instant pot, and then place the trivet in the pot.
4. Place the bowl on top of the trivet.
5. Close the pot with its lid and cook on manual high pressure for 20 minutes.
6. Once done, release pressure naturally for 20 minutes, and then release it using the quick release method. Open the lid.
7. Once the custard bowl is cool, place it in the refrigerator for 1 hour.
8. Serve and enjoy.

Nutrition: Calories: 215, Fats: 5.8 g, Carbs: 33 g, Sugar: 32.4 g, Protein: 7.7 g, Cholesterol: 23 mg

275. Simple Raspberry Mug Cake

Preparation Time: 10 minutes
Cooking Time: 10 minutes
Servings: 2
Ingredients:

- 3 eggs
- 1 cup almond flour
- 1/2 tsp. vanilla
- 1 tbsp. Swerve®
- 2 tbsp. chocolate chips
- 1/2 cup raspberries
- A pinch salt
- Water, as needed

Directions:

1. Stir all the ingredients into the large bowl, and mix until well combined.
2. Pour 2 cups of water into the instant pot, then place the trivet in the pot.
3. Pour batter into heat-safe mugs. Cover them with foil and place them on top of the trivet.

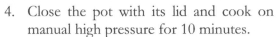

4. Close the pot with its lid and cook on manual high pressure for 10 minutes.
5. Once done, release the pressure using the quick release method, and then open the lid.
6. Serve and enjoy.

Nutrition: Calories: 326, Fats: 25.3 g, Carbs: 20 g, Sugar: 11.3 g, Protein: 11.3 g, Cholesterol: 165 mg

276. Chocolate Mousse

Preparation Time: 10 minutes
Cooking Time: 6 minutes
Servings: 2
Ingredients:

- 4 egg yolks
- 1/4 cup water
- 1/2 cup sugar
- 1 tsp. vanilla
- 1 cup heavy cream
- 1/2 cup cocoa powder
- 1/2 cup milk
- 1/4 tsp. sea salt

Directions:

1. Whisk the egg yolk in a bowl until combined.
2. In a saucepan, add the cocoa, water, and sugar. Whisk over medium heat until the sugar is melted.
3. Add the milk and cream to the saucepan, and whisk to combine. Do not boil.
4. Add the vanilla and salt, and stir well.
5. Empty 1 1/2 cups of water into the instant pot, then place a trivet in the pot.
6. Pour the mixture into the ramekins, and place them on top of the trivet.
7. Close the pot with its lid, and cook on "Manual" mode for 6 minutes.
8. Once done, release pressure using the quick release method, and then open the lid. Serve and enjoy.

Nutrition: Calories: 235, Fats: 14.1 g, Carbs: 27.2 g, Sugar: 21.5 g, Protein: 5 g, Cholesterol: 203 mg

277. Cardamom Zucchini Pudding

Preparation Time: 10 minutes
Cooking Time: 10 minutes
Servings: 2
Ingredients:

- 1 3/4 cups zucchini, shredded
- 5 oz. half and half
- 5 ½ oz. milk
- 1 tsp. cardamom powder
- 1/3 cup sugar

Directions:

1. Add all the ingredients, except the cardamom, into the instant pot, and blend well.
2. Close the pot with its lid, and cook on manual high pressure for 10 minutes.
3. As soon as done, discharge the pressure naturally for 10 minutes, and then release it using the quick release method. Open the lid.
4. Stir in the cardamom, and serve.

Nutrition: Calories: 138, Fats: 5 g, Carbs :22.1 g, Sugar: 19.4 g, Protein: 3 g, Cholesterol: 16 mg

278. Yummy Strawberry Cobbler

Preparation Time: 10 minutes
Cooking Time: 12 minutes
Servings: 2
Ingredients:

- 1 cup sliced strawberries
- 1/2 tsp. vanilla
- 1/3 cup butter
- 1 cup milk
- 1 tsp. baking powder
- 1/2 cup granulated sugar
- 1 1/4 cup all-purpose flour
- Cooking spray, as needed
- Water, as needed

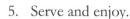

Directions:

1. In a huge container, add all the ingredients, except the strawberries, and stir to combine.
2. Add the sliced strawberries, and fold well.
3. Grease the ramekins with cooking spray, then pour the batter into the ramekins.
4. Discharge 1 1/2 cups of water into the instant pot, and then place the trivet in the pot.
5. Place the ramekins on top of the trivet.
6. Close the pot with its lid and cook on manual high pressure for 12 minutes.
7. As soon as done, discharge the pressure naturally for 10 minutes, and then release it using the quick release method. Open the lid.
8. Serve and enjoy.

Nutrition: Calories: 555, Fats: 22.8 g, Carbs: 81.7 g, Sugar: 39.6 g, Protein: 8.6 g, Cholesterol: 61 mg

279. Peach Cobbler

Preparation Time: 10 minutes
Cooking Time: 10 minutes
Servings: 2
Ingredients:

- 20 oz. can peach pie filling
- 1 1/2 tsp. cinnamon
- 1/4 tsp. nutmeg
- 14 ½ oz. vanilla cake mix
- 1/2 cup melted butter

Directions:

1. Add the peach pie filling into the instant pot.
2. In a bulky container, mix the remaining ingredients, and spread them over the peach pie filling.
3. Close the pot with its lid, and cook on manual high pressure for 10 minutes.
4. As soon as done, discharge the pressure naturally for 10 minutes, and then release it using the quick release method. Open the lid.

5. Serve and enjoy.

Nutrition: Calories: 445, Fats: 15.4 g, Carbs: 76.1 g, Sugar: 47.7 g, Protein: 0.2 g, Cholesterol: 41 mg

280. Hazelnuts Brownies

Preparation Time: 10 minutes
Cooking Time: 25 minutes
Servings: 2
Ingredients:

- 4 eggs
- 1 cup almond flour
- 4 tbsp. hazelnuts, chopped
- 1/4 cup Swerve®
- ¼ cup cocoa powder
- 2 tbsp. butter
- 1/2 tsp. vanilla
- 1/2 cup mascarpone
- 1/2 cup flaxseed meal
- Cooking spray, as needed

Directions:

1. In a huge bowl, stir all the ingredients and beat until well combined.
2. Spray the baking dish with cooking spray.
3. Empty 1 cup of water into the instant pot, then place the trivet in the pot.
4. Discharge the batter into the baking dish, and place dish on top of the trivet.
5. Close the pot with its lid, and cook on manual high pressure for 25 minutes.
6. Once done, release the pressure using the quick release method, and then open the lid. Slice and serve.

Nutrition: Calories: 289, Fats: 23.6 g, Carbs: 18.1 g, Sugar: 11.3 g, Protein: 12.3 g, Cholesterol: 130 mg

281. Apple Pear Crisp

Preparation Time: 10 minutes
Cooking Time: 10 minutes
Servings: 2
Ingredients:

- 4 apples, peel and cut into chunks

- 1 cup steel-cut oats
- 2 pears, cut into chunks
- 1 1/2 cup water - 1/2 tsp. cinnamon
- 1/4 cup maple syrup

Directions:
1. Add all the ingredients into the instant pot, and stir well.
2. Seal the pot with its lid, and cook on manual high for 10 minutes.
3. As soon as done, release the pressure naturally for 10 minutes, and then release it using the quick release method. Open the lid.
4. Serve warm and enjoy.

Nutrition: Calories: 306, Fats: 1.9 g, Carbs: 74 g, Sugar: 45.3 g, Protein: 3.7 g, Cholesterol: 0 mg

282. Mango Bowls

Preparation Time: 10 minutes
Cooking Time: 0 minutes
Servings: 2
Ingredients:

- 2 bananas, peeled and sliced
- 2 mangoes, peeled and cubed
- 1 tbsp. walnuts, chopped
- 1 tbsp. lime juice

Directions:
1. In a bowl, combine the bananas with the mangoes and the other ingredients.
2. Toss and serve.

Nutrition: Calories: 165, Fats: 2 g, Fiber: 4.4 g, Carbs: 38.8 g, Protein: 2.5 g

283. Watermelon Cream

Preparation Time: 2 hours
Cooking Time: 0 minutes
Servings: 2
Ingredients:

- 1 watermelon, peeled and cubed
- 1 tsp. vanilla extract
- ½ tsp. cinnamon powder
- 2 mangoes, peeled and cubed

Directions:
1. In a blender, combine the watermelon with the mango and the other ingredients.
2. Pulse well, divide into bowls and keep in the fridge for 2 hours before serving.

Nutrition: Calories: 75, Fats: 0.5 g, Fiber: 1.9 g, Carbs: 18.4 g, Protein: 1 g

284. Almond-Banana Mix

Preparation Time: 10 minutes
Cooking Time: 0 minutes
Servings: 2
Ingredients:

- 1 cup dates, chopped
- 2 bananas, peeled and sliced
- 1 cup almond milk
- 2 tbsp. cocoa powder - 1 tbsp. honey

Directions:
1. In a bowl, combine the dates with the bananas and the other ingredients. Toss and serve cold.

Nutrition: Calories: 338, Fats: 15 g, Fiber: 7.2 g, Carbs: 56 g, Protein: 3.6 g

285. Coconut Apple Bowls

Preparation Time: 10 minutes
Cooking Time: 0 minutes
Servings: 2
Ingredients:

- 2 large green apples, cored and roughly cubed
- 1 tbsp. honey

- 1 cup coconut cream
- 1 tsp. cinnamon powder

Directions:

1. In a bowl, combine the apples with the cream and the other ingredients.
2. Toss and serve.

Nutrition: Calories: 100, Fat: 1 g, Fiber: 4 g, Carbs: 12 g, Protein: 4 g

286. Pineapple Cream

Preparation Time: 10 minutes
Cooking Time: 20 minutes
Servings: 2
Ingredients:

- 1 cup pineapple, peeled and cubed
- ½ cup walnuts, chopped
- 1 tbsp. honey
- 1 cup coconut cream
- 1 egg, whisked
- ¼ cup coconut oil, melted

Directions:

1. In a blender, combine the pineapple with the walnuts and the other ingredients. Pulse well, divide into 6 ramekins and bake at 370°F for 20 minutes.
2. Serve cold.

Nutrition: Calories: 200, Fats: 3 g, Fiber: 4 g, Carbs: 12 g, Protein: 8 g

287. Coconut-Apple Bars

Preparation Time: 10 minutes
Cooking Time: 25 minutes
Servings: 2
Ingredients:

- ½ cup coconut cream
- 1 cup apples, peeled, cored and chopped
- ½ cup maple syrup
- 1 tsp. vanilla extract
- ½ cup almond flour
- 2 eggs, whisked
- 1 tsp. baking powder

Directions:

1. In a blender, combine the cream with the apples and the other ingredients, and pulse well.
2. Pour this into a baking dish lined with parchment paper, bake in the oven at 370°F for 25 minutes, cool down, cut into bars, and serve.

Nutrition: Calories: 200, Fats: 3 g, Fiber: 4 g, Carbs: 12 g, Protein: 11 g

288. Avocado and Orange Bowl

Preparation Time: 10 minutes
Cooking Time: 0 minutes
Servings: 2
Ingredients:

- 3 oranges, peeled and cut into segments
- 1 avocado, peeled, pitted, and cubed
- 3 tbsp. raw honey - ½ tsp. vanilla extract
- 1 tsp. orange zest, grated

Directions:

1. In a bowl, combine the oranges with the avocado and the other ingredients.
2. Toss and serve.

Nutrition: Calories: 211, Fats: 3 g, Fiber: 4 g, Carbs: 8 g, Protein: 7 g

289. Honey Apples

Preparation Time: 10 minutes
Cooking Time: 30 minutes
Servings: 2
Ingredients:

- 2 apples, cored and halved
- 1 tbsp. grated ginger
- 1 tbsp. turmeric powder
- ¼ cup raw honey - 1 tbsp. grated ginger

Directions:

1. Arrange the apples in a baking dish, add the ginger and the other ingredients, and bake at 390°F for 30 minutes.
2. Divide the apples, mix them between dessert plates, and serve.

Nutrition: Calories: 90, Fats 2 g, Fiber: 1 g, Carbs: 2 g, Protein: 5 g

290. Lemon-Avocado Cream

Preparation Time: 2 hours
Cooking Time: 0 minutes
Servings: 2
Ingredients:

- 2 cups coconut cream
- 1 watermelon, peeled and chopped
- 2 avocados, peeled, pitted and chopped
- 1 tbsp. honey - 2 tsp. lemon juice

Directions:

1. In a blender, combine the watermelon with the cream and the other ingredients, pulse well, divide into bowls, and keep in the fridge for 2 hours before serving.

Nutrition: Calories: 121, Fats: 2 g, Fiber: 2 g, Carbs: 6 g, Protein: 5 g

291. Orange Berry Sorbet

Preparation Time: 2 hours
Cooking Time: 0 minutes
Servings: 2
Ingredients:

- 1 lb. frozen strawberries, halved
- 1 cup orange juice
- 1 tbsp. orange zest, grated
- 1 tbsp. honey

Directions:

1. In a blender, combine the strawberries with the orange zest and the other ingredients.
2. Pulse well, divide into bowls, and keep in the freezer for 2 hours before serving.

Nutrition: Calories: 121, Fats: 1 g, Fiber: 2 g, Carbs: 2 g, Protein: 4 g

292. Vanilla-Pineapple Bowl

Preparation Time: 10 minutes
Cooking Time: 0 minutes
Servings: 2
Ingredients:

- 2 tbsp. almonds, chopped
- 1 tbsp. walnuts, chopped
- 2 cups pineapple, peeled and roughly cubed
- 1 tbsp. lemon juice
- 1 lemon, zested and grated
- ½ tsp. vanilla extract
- A pinch cinnamon powder

Directions:

1. In a bowl, combine the pineapple with the nuts and the other ingredients. Toss and serve.

Nutrition: Calories: 215, Fats: 3 g, Fiber: 4 g, Carbs: 12 g, Protein: 8 g

293. Almond-Chia Pudding

Preparation Time: 30 minutes
Cooking Time: 0 minutes
Servings: 2
Ingredients:

- 2 cups almond milk
- 2 tbsp. honey
- 1 cup chia seeds
- A pinch cardamom powder
- 1 tbsp. lemon zest, grated

Directions:

1. In a bowl, mix the chia seeds with the almond milk and the other ingredients, toss, leave aside for 30 minutes, divide into small bowls, and serve.

Nutrition: Calories: 199, Fats: 2 g, Fiber: 3 g, Carbs: 7 g, Protein: 5 g

294. Orange Mango Smoothie

Preparation Time: 10 minutes
Cooking Time: 0 minutes
Servings: 2
Ingredients:

- 2 cups mango, peeled and chopped
- 1 cup orange juice
- 1 tbsp. grated ginger
- 1 tsp. turmeric powder

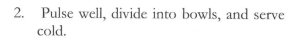

Directions:

1. In your blender, combine the mango with the juice and the other ingredients.
2. Pulse well, divide into 2 glasses and serve cold.

Nutrition: Calories: 100, Fats: 1 g, Fiber: 2 g, Carbs: 4 g, Protein: 5 g

295. Vanilla Chocolate Cream

Preparation Time: 2 hours
Cooking Time: 0 minutes
Servings: 2
Ingredients:

- 2 cups coconut milk
- 2 tbsp. grated ginger
- 2 tbsp. honey
- 1 cup dark chocolate, chopped and melted - ½ tsp. cinnamon powder
- 1 tsp. vanilla extract

Directions:

1. In a blender, combine the coconut milk with the ginger and the other ingredients.
2. Pulse well, divide into bowls, and keep in the fridge for 2 hours before serving.

Nutrition: Calories: 200, Fats: 3 g, Fiber: 5 g, Carbs: 12 g, Protein: 7 g

296. Coconut   Avocado Smoothie Bowl

Preparation Time: 10 minutes
Cooking Time: 0 minutes
Servings: 2
Ingredients:

- 2 avocados, peeled, pitted, and cut into wedges
- 1 tsp. ground cardamom
- ½ cup coconut butter
- 1 cup coconut cream
- 1 tsp. vanilla extract

Directions:

1. In your food processor, combine the avocados with the cream and the other ingredients.

2. Pulse well, divide into bowls, and serve cold.

Nutrition: Calories: 211 g, Fats: 2 g, Fiber: 4 g, Carbs: 11 g, Protein: 7 g

297. Lime-Strawberries Mix

Preparation Time: 10 minutes
Cooking Time: 20 minutes
Servings: 2
Ingredients:

- 1 lb. strawberries, halved
- 2 tbsp. chopped almonds
- 2 tbsp. melted coconut oil
- 2 tbsp. lime juice
- 1 tsp. vanilla extract
- 1 tsp. honey

Directions:

1. Arrange the strawberries on a baking sheet lined with parchment paper. Add the almonds and the other ingredients, toss, and bake at 390°F for 20 minutes.
2. Divide the strawberries mixture into bowls, and serve.

Nutrition: Calories: 220, Fats: 2 g, Fiber: 3 g, Carbs: 8 g, Protein: 2 g

298. Apple Compote

Preparation Time: 10 minutes
Cooking Time: 20 minutes
Servings: 2
Ingredients:

- 1 lime, juiced
- 1 lb. apples, cored and cut into wedges
- 1 tbsp. honey
- 1 ½ cups water

Directions:

1. In a pan, combine the apples with the lime juice and the other ingredients, toss, bring to a simmer, and cook over medium heat for 20 minutes.
2. Divide the mixture into bowls, and serve cold.

Nutrition: Calories: 108 g, Fats: 1 g, Fiber: 2 g, Carbs: 4 g, Protein: 7 g

299. Lime Berries Mix

Preparation Time: 10 minutes
Cooking Time: 0 minutes
Servings: 2
Ingredients:

- 1 cup blackberries - 1 cup blueberries
- 2 tsp. lime zest, grated
- 1 tbsp. raw honey - ½ tsp. vanilla extract
- 1 cup almond milk

Directions:

1. In your blender, combine the berries with the lime zest and the other ingredients.
2. Pulse well, divide into bowls, and serve.

Nutrition: Calories: 217, Fats: 7 g, Fiber: 8 g, Carbs: 10 g, Protein: 8 g

300. Coconut-Berries Mix

Preparation Time: 10 minutes
Cooking Time: 15 minutes
Servings: 2
Ingredients:

- 2 cups coconut milk
- 1 cup strawberries - ¼ tsp. vanilla extract
- 1/3 cup pure maple syrup

Directions:

1. In a small pot, combine the coconut milk with the berries and the other ingredients, toss, cook over medium heat for 15 minutes, divide into bowls, and serve cold.

Nutrition: Calories: 176, Fats: 4 g, Fiber: 2 g, Carbs: 7 g, Protein: 6 g

301. Papaya and Nuts Salad

Preparation Time: 4 minutes
Cooking Time: 0 minutes
Servings: 2
Ingredients:

- 2 apples, cored and cut into wedges
- 1 cup papaya, roughly cubed
- ½ tsp. vanilla extract
- 2 tbsp. almonds, chopped
- 1 tbsp. walnuts, chopped
- 2 tbsp. lemon juice

Directions:

1. In a bowl, combine the papaya with the apples and the other ingredients. Toss, divide into smaller bowls and serve.

Nutrition: Calories: 140, Fats: 1 g, Fiber: 2 g, Carbs: 3 g, Protein: 5 g

302. Orange Coconut Bars

Preparation Time: 2 hours
Cooking Time: 0 minutes
Servings: 2
Ingredients:

- 1/3 cup natural coconut butter, melted
- 1 ½ tbsp. coconut oil
- 2 tbsp. orange juice
- ½ tsp. orange zest, grated
- 1 tbsp. honey

Directions:

1. In a bowl, combine the coconut butter with the oil and the other ingredients. Stir well, scoop into a square pan, spread well, cut into bars, keep in the freezer for 2 hours, and serve.

Nutrition: Calories: 72, Fat: 4 g, Fiber: 2 g, Carbs: 8 g, Protein: 6 g

303. Chia Bowls

Preparation Time: 10 minutes
Cooking Time: 0 minutes
Servings: 2
Ingredients:

- ¼ cup chia seeds
- 1 cup almond milk

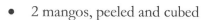

- 2 mangos, peeled and cubed
- 2 tsp. vanilla extract
- ¼ cup shredded coconut
- 1 tbsp. honey

Directions:

1. In a bowl, combine the chia seeds with the mango, the milk, and the other ingredients. Toss, leave aside for 10 minutes, divide into small bowls, and serve.

Nutrition: Calories: 287, Fats: 17.2 g, Fiber: 5.1 g, Carbs: 34.6 g, Protein: 3.2 g

304. Pomegranate Bowls
Preparation Time: 2 hours
Cooking Time: 0 minutes
Servings: 2
Ingredients:

- ½ cup coconut cream
- 1 orange, peeled and cut into wedges
- 1 tsp. vanilla extract
- ½ cup almonds, chopped
- 1 cup pomegranate seeds
- 1 tbsp. orange zest, grated

Directions:

1. In a bowl, combine the orange with the pomegranate seeds and the other ingredients. Toss and keep in the fridge for 2 hours before dividing into smaller bowls and serving.

Nutrition: Calories: 68, Fats: 5.1 g, Fiber: 4 g, Carbs: 6 g, Protein: 1 g

305. Maple-Berries Bowls
Preparation Time: 10 minutes
Cooking Time: 0 minutes
Servings: 2
Ingredients:

- ½ cup dates, pitted
- ½ tsp. vanilla extract
- 1 cup almonds, chopped
- 1 cup blackberries
- 1 tbsp. maple syrup

- 1 tbsp. coconut oil, melted

Directions:

1. In a bowl, combine the berries with the almonds and the other ingredients. Toss, divide into small cups and serve.

Nutrition: Calories: 130, Fats: 5 g, Fiber: 5 g, Carbs: 12 g, Protein: 4 g

306. Mint-Apple Cream
Preparation Time: 10 minutes
Cooking Time: 0 minutes
Servings: 2
Ingredients:

- 1 lb. apples, peeled, cored, and cubed
- 2 cups coconut cream
- 1 tbsp. mint, chopped

Directions:

1. In your blender, combine the apples with the cream and mint. Pulse well, divide into small cups and serve cold.

Nutrition: Calories: 70, Fats: 9 g, Fiber: 3 g, Carbs: 4.4 g, Protein: 3 g

307. Almond-Rhubarb Pudding
Preparation Time: 10 minutes
Cooking Time: 20 minutes
Servings: 2
Ingredients:

- 2 cups rhubarb, sliced
- 2 tbsp. maple syrup
- 3 eggs
- 2 tbsp. coconut oil, melted
- 1 cup almond milk
- ½ tsp. baking powder

Directions:

1. In a blender, combine the rhubarb with the oil and maple syrup, and pulse well.
2. In a bowl, combine the rhubarb purée with the other ingredients. Whisk, divide into 6 ramekins, and bake at 350°F for 20 minutes.
3. Serve the pudding cold.

Nutrition: Calories: 220, Fats: 12 g, Fiber: 3 g, Carbs: 7 g, Protein: 8 g

308. Dates and Pears Cake

Preparation Time: 10 minutes
Cooking Time: 30 minutes
Servings: 2
Ingredients:

- 2 pears, cored, peeled, and chopped
- 2 cups coconut flour
- 1 cup dates, pitted
- 2 eggs, whisked
- 1 tsp. vanilla extract
- 1 tsp. baking soda
- ½ cup coconut oil, melted
- ½ tsp. cinnamon powder

Directions:

1. In a bowl, combine the pears with the flour and the other ingredients. Whisk well, pour into a cake pan, and bake at 360°F for 30 minutes.
2. Cool down, slice, and serve.

Nutrition: Calories: 160, Fats: 7 g, Fiber: 4 g, Carbs: 8 g, Protein: 4 g

309. Pears Cream

Preparation Time: 10 minutes
Cooking Time: 0 minutes
Servings: 2
Ingredients:

- 2 tsp. lime juice
- 1 lb. pears, cored, peeled and chopped
- 1 lb. strawberries, chopped
- 1 cup coconut cream

Directions:

1. In a blender, combine the pears with the strawberries and the other ingredients. Pulse well, divide into bowls, and serve.

Nutrition: Calories. 100, Fats: 2 g, Fiber: 3 g, Carbs: 8 g, Protein: 5 g

310. Orange Bowls

Preparation Time: 10 minutes
Cooking Time: 0 minutes
Servings: 2
Ingredients:

- 2 oranges, peeled and cut into segments
- 1 cantaloupe, peeled and cubed
- 2 tbsp. honey
- 1 cup orange juice
- 1 tsp. vanilla extract

Directions:

1. In a bowl, combine the oranges with the cantaloupe and the other ingredients. Toss and serve.
2. Enjoy!

Nutrition: Calories: 110, Fats: 2 g, Fiber: 3 g, Carbs: 6 g, Protein: 6 g

Meal Plan for 31 Days

Day	Breakfast	Lunch	Snacks	Dinner
1	Zucchini Noodles with Creamy Avocado Pesto	Butternut Fritters	Sweet Potato Fries	Beef Korma Curry
2	Avocado Chicken Salad	Cauliflower In Vegan Alfredo Sauce	Cheese Sticks	Chicken Fried Steak
3	Pancakes with Berries	Creamed Spinach	Zucchini Crisps	Lemon Greek Beef and Vegetables
4	Omelette à la Margherita	Eggplant Parmesan	Tortillas in Green Mango Salsa	Country-Style Pork Ribs
5	Omelet with Tomatoes and Spring Onions	Lime Asparagus with Cashews	Skinny Pumpkin Chips	Lemon and Honey Pork Tenderloin
6	Coconut Chia Pudding with Berries	Cabbage Wedges	Palm Trees Holder	Dijon Pork Tenderloin
7	Eel on Scrambled Eggs and Bread	Broccoli & Bacon Salad	Air Fried Ripe Plantains	Air Fryer Pork Satay
8	Chia Seed Gel with Pomegranate and Nuts	Black Pepper & Garlic Tofu	Garlic Bread with Cheese Dip	Pork Burgers with Red Cabbage Slaw
9	Lavender Blueberry Chia Seed Pudding	Broccoli & Mushroom Salad	Fried Mixed Veggies with Avocado Dip	Greek Lamb Pita Pockets
10	Yogurt with Granola and Persimmon	Homemade Vegetable Chili	Air Fried Plantains in Coconut Sauce	Rosemary Lamb Chops
11	Smoothie Bowl with Spinach, Mango, and Muesli	Collard Greens with Tomato	Beef and Mango Skewers	Delicious Meatballs
12	Fried Egg with Bacon	Okra	Kale Chips with Lemon Yogurt Sauce	Low-fat Steak
13	Smoothie Bowl with Berries, Poppy Seeds, Nuts, and Seeds	Harvest Salad	Basil Pesto Bruschetta	Diet Boiled Ribs
14	Porridge with Walnuts	Spicy Potatoes	Cinnamon Pear Chips	Meatloaf
15	Alkaline Blueberry Spelt Pancakes	Buffalo Cauliflower Wings	Phyllo Vegetable Triangles	Beef with Mushrooms

16	Alkaline Blueberry Muffins	Asian Noodle Salad	Red Cabbage and Mushroom Pot Stickers	Mustard-Crusted Sole
17	Coconut Pancakes	Cheesy Mushroom and Pesto Flatbreads	Garlic Roasted Mushrooms	Almond Crusted Cod with Chips
18	Quinoa Porridge	Honey Roasted Carrots	Baked Spicy Chicken Meatballs	Honey Lemon Snapper with Fruit
19	Amaranth Porridge	Mushrooms Stuffed with Tomato	Mini Onion Bites	Easy Tuna Wraps
20	Banana Barley Porridge	Sweet Potato Salt and Pepper	Crispy Parmesan Cauliflower	Asian-Inspired Swordfish Steaks
21	Healthy Avocado Toast	Sweet Potato Chips	Cream Cheese Stuffed Jalapeños	Salmon with Fennel and Carrot
22	Whole Egg Baked Sweet Potatoes	Cauliflower Rice	Parmesan French Fries	Ranch Tilapia fillets
23	Black Bean Tacos Breakfast	Pizza Stuffed Portobello's	Cheesy Ham and Spinach Dip	Chilean Sea Bass with Green Olive Relish
24	Strawberry Coconut Bake	Cajun Style French Fries	Smoked Salmon Dip	Ginger and Green Onion Fish
25	Paleo Breakfast Hash	Avocado & Citrus Shrimp Salad	Simple Corn Tortilla Chips	Asian Sesame Cod
26	Omelet with Chickpea Flour	Florentine Pizza	Air Fryer Buffalo Cauliflower	Lemon Scallops with Asparagus
27	White Sandwich Bread	Vegetables In Air Fryer	Air Fryer Mini Pizza	Fish Tacos
28	Sprouted Toast with Creamy Avocado and Sprouts	Fried Peppers with Sriracha Mayo	Air Fryer Egg Rolls	Spicy Cajun Shrimp
29	Scrambled Turmeric Tofu	Classic Fried Pickles	Air Fryer Chicken Nuggets	Garlic Parmesan Roasted Shrimp
30	Breakfast Salad	Fried Green Beans with Pecorino Romano	Chicken Tenders	Quick Shrimp Scampi
31	Green Goddess Bowl with Avocado Cumin Dressing	Spicy Glazed Carrots	Kale & Celery Crackers	Mustard-Crusted Fish Fillets

Conclusion

I've found these recipes to be helpful to me and my health. I'm hoping that they will help you too! If you are looking for an easy way to improve your health and try out different foods, this is the perfect cookbook. These recipes are divided into three categories: Breakfast, lunch, and dinner. There are also dessert recipes in the book. It will give you advice on incorporating healthier eating habits into your lifestyle so that they become sustainable habits in your life. It can help anyone who wants to improve their overall health without following a restrictive diet plan with extreme food rules day-by-day or meal-by-meal. It will help you cook nutritious meals that you will continue to make long after the thirty days are over.

The recipes are all healthy and can be made by anyone, regardless of cooking experience level. The recipes are effortless to follow, don't require any fancy ingredients or cooking techniques, and taste great. They can help you eat what you crave without feeling guilty about it; the recipes are low in fat, calories, sugar, carbs, and cholesterol! Some of them also include nutrition facts for each serving. Some of the recipes include foods that have been scientifically proven to reduce the risk of certain diseases, such as Alzheimer's Disease and diabetes.

I recommend this book for anyone trying to improve their health and make healthier eating choices; it's a great resource.

I like this cookbook because it has information on the benefits of eating "real" food rather than processed or packaged foods. It also has some great information on how to make your household chores more accessible and more efficient. I like the recipes in this book because they are easy to follow and relatively quick to make, but they taste great too. This cookbook is full of yummy recipes, easy dinner ideas, excellent tips for saving time in the kitchen, and healthy meals!

If you want to improve your health by eating real food (instead of processed food), this is a good book. I was amazed at how healthy the recipes that I tried were! They were easy to follow and used ingredients that I already had on hand. This book is also useful for anyone who wants to improve their health immediately without dieting or taking supplements every day.

This cookbook will fit your needs if you're searching for an excellent cookbook with easy-to-follow recipes. It's perfect for anyone who doesn't have a lot of cooking experience or time to devote to preparing all their meals from scratch. It also includes some useful hints on how to make cooking easy, quick, and fun. This cookbook will give you creative ideas for making delicious meals that you can use to make your life healthier. It's packed with health-boosting recipes that are very easy to follow.

Made in the USA
Las Vegas, NV
21 January 2022

41998127R00081